First published in Great Britain 1985 by Colour Library Books Ltd.
CLB 1104
© Illustrations and text: Colour Library Books Ltd.,
    Guildford, Surrey, England.
Display and text filmsetting by Acesetters Ltd.,
    Richmond, Surrey, England.
Printed and bound in Barcelona, Spain by Rieusset and Eurobinder.
All rights reserved.
Published 1985 by Crescent Books, distributed by Crown Publishers, Inc.
Printed and bound in Barcelona, Spain by Rieusset and Eurobinder.
ISBN 0 517 463172
h g f e d c b a
D.L.B. 42093-84

# The Story of DIANA

**Text by Trevor Hall**

Designed by
**PHILIP CLUCAS** MSIAD

**Produced by**
**TED SMART and DAVID GIBBON**

## CRESCENT BOOKS
## NEW YORK

JAMES VI and I
*King of England, Scotland,
France and Ireland
1566-1625*

FREDERICK V
*King of Bohemia &
Elector Palatine of the Rhine
1596-1632*

ELIZABETH
*1596-1662*

CHARLES I
*King of Great Britain
1600-1649*

HENRIETTA MARIA
*of France
1609-1669*

ERNST AUGUST
*Elector of Hanover
1629-1698*

SOPHIA
*1630-1714*

CHARLES II
*King of Great Britain
1630-1685*

BARBARA VILLIERS
*Duchess of Cleveland
1641-1709*

GEORGE I
*King of Great Britain,
France and Ireland
1660-1727*

SOPHIA DOROTHEA
*of Brunswick-Luneburg
& Celle
1666-1726*

HENRY (FITZROY)
*1st Duke of Grafton
1663-1690*

Lady ISABELLA BENNETT
*Died 1723*

GEORGE II
*King of Great Britain,
France and Ireland
1683-1760*

CAROLINE
*of Brandenburg-Ansbach
1683-1737*

CHARLES (FITZROY)
*2nd Duke of Grafton
1683-1757*

Lady HENRIETTA
SOMERSET
*Died 1726*

FREDERICK
*Prince of Wales
1707-1751*

AUGUSTA
*of Saxe-Coburg-Altenburg
1719-1772*

FRANCIS (SEYMOUR)
*1st Marquess of Hertford
1718-1794*

ISABELLA
*1726-1782*

GEORGE III
*King of Great Britain,
France and Ireland
1738-1820*

CHARLOTTE
*of Mecklenburg-Strelitz
1744-1818*

Admiral HUGH
SEYMOUR
*1759-1801*

Lady ANNE HORATIA
WALDEGRAVE
*Died 1801*

EDWARD
*Duke of Kent
1767-1820*

VICTORIA MARY
*of Saxe-Coburg-Saalfeld
1786-1861*

Sir HORACE
BEAUCHAMP SEYMOUR
*Knight Commander of
Hanover
1791-1856*

ELIZABETH PALK
*Died 1827*

VICTORIA
*Queen of the United Kingdom
of Great Britain and Ireland,
and Empress of India
1819-1901*

ALBERT
*of Saxe-Coburg-Gotha
Prince Consort
1819-1861*

FREDERICK (SPENCER)
*4th Earl Spencer
1798-1857*

ADELAIDE HORATIA
*Died 1877*

EDWARD VII
*King of the United Kingdom of
Great Britain and Ireland
1841-1910*

ALEXANDRA
*of Denmark
1844-1925*

CHARLES ROBERT
(SPENCER)
*6th Earl Spencer
1857-1922*

Hon. MARGARET BARING
*Died 1906*

GEORGE V
*King of the United Kingdom of
Great Britain and Ireland
1865-1936*

VICTORIA MARY
*of Teck
1867-1953*

ALBERT EDWARD
JOHN (SPENCER)
*7th Earl Spencer
1892-1975*

Lady CYNTHIA ELEANOR
HAMILTON
*Died 1972*

GEORGE VI
*King of the United Kingdom of
Great Britain and Ireland
1895-1952*

Lady ELIZABETH
BOWES-LYON
*Born 1900*

EDWARD JOHN
(SPENCER)
*8th Earl Spencer
Born 1924*

Hon. FRANCES RUTH
ROCHE
*Married 1954*

ELIZABETH II
*Queen of the United Kingdom
of Great Britain and Northern
Ireland
Born 1926*

PHILIP
*Duke of Edinburgh
Born 1921*

Lady DIANA FRANCES
*Born 1961*

CHARLES
PHILIP ARTHUR GEORGE
*Prince of Wales
Born 1948*

WILLIAM
ARTHUR PHILIP LOUIS
*Born 1982*

HENRY
CHARLES ALBERT DAVID
*Born 1984*

Diana Frances Mountbatten-Windsor, Princess of Wales, Countess of Chester, Duchess of Cornwall and Rothesay, Countess of Carrick, Baroness Renfrew, Lady of the Isles and Great Stewardess of Scotland...

Born Diana Frances Spencer, at Park House, Sandringham on 1st July 1961; youngest daughter of Edward John, then Viscount Althorp, by his wife Frances (see below); christened on 30th August 1961 at St Mary Magdalene Church, Sandringham (godparents: Lady Mary Colman, John Floyd, Carol Fox, Alexander Gilmour, and Sarah Pratt); assumed the title of The Lady Diana Spencer on 9th June 1975.

Educated at home until 1968; at Silfield School, King's Lynn, Norfolk, 1968-1969; at Francis Holland School, Kensington and Chelsea, 1969-1970; at Riddlesworth Hall, near Diss, Norfolk, 1970-1973; at West Heath School, near Sevenoaks, Kent, 1973-1977; and at the Institut Alpin Videmanette, Château d'Oex, Rougemont, Switzerland in 1978.

Former residences: Park House, Sandringham, Norfolk, 1961-1975; Althorp, Northamptonshire, 1975-1978; 69 Cadogan Place, London SW1, 1978-1979; 60 Coleherne Court, Knightsbridge, London, 1979-1981; Clarence House, London SW1, 1981.

Engaged on 24th February 1981 to Charles Philip Arthur George Mountbatten-Windsor, KG, KT, GCB, PC, 21st Prince of Wales, born on 14th November 1948, (eldest son of HM Queen Elizabeth II and HRH Prince Philip, Duke of Edinburgh), whom she married at St Paul's Cathedral, London on 29th July 1981, and by him has two children, Prince William Arthur Philip Louis of Wales, born at St Mary's Hospital, Paddington, London W2 on 21st June 1982, christened at Buckingham Palace on 4th August 1982 (godparents: HRH Princess Alexandra, HM King Constantine of the Hellenes, Lady Susan Hussey, Sir Laurens van der Post, Lord Romsey, and Natalia, Duchess of Westminster); and Prince Henry (Harry) Charles Albert David of Wales, born at St Mary's Hospital, Paddington, London W2 on 15th September 1984, christened at Windsor Castle on 21st December 1984 (godparents: HRH Prince Andrew, Lady Sarah Armstrong-Jones, Mrs William Bartholomew, Mr Bryan Organ, Mr Gerald Ward, Lady (Cece) Vestey).

Current residences: Highgrove House, near Doughton, Tetbury, Gloucestershire; Kensington Palace, London W8.

Father: Edward John Spencer, 8th Earl Spencer, born on 24th January 1924, only son and second child of Albert Edward John, 7th Earl Spencer (1892-1975) by his wife Lady Cynthia Elinor Beatrix Hamilton, DCVO, OBE (1897-1972); succeeded as 8th Earl on 9th June 1975; married as his first wife Frances (see below), and as his second wife, on 14th July 1976 at Caxton Hall, London, Raine (born 1929), (only daughter of Alexander George McCorquodale, by his wife Barbara Cartland), former wife of Gerald Humphrey, 8th Earl of Dartmouth, whom she married on 21st July 1948, and by whom she has two children, William, born on 23rd September 1949, and Rupert, born on 1st January 1951.

Mother: The Hon Frances Ruth Burke Shand Kydd (formerly Spencer, formerly Roche), younger daughter and second child of Edmund Maurice Roche (1885-1955), fourth Baron Fermoy, by his wife Ruth Sylvia (nee Gill) DCVO, OBE (now Ruth, Lady Fermoy) (born 1908). Married as her first husband, Edward John (see above) on 1st June 1954 at Westminster Abbey (marriage dissolved April 1969); married as her second husband, Peter Shand Kydd on 2nd May 1969.

Brothers: (1) John, born and died on 12th January 1960.

(2) Charles Edward Maurice, Viscount Althorp, born on 20th May 1964 at the London Clinic; educated at Silfield School, King's Lynn, Norfolk; Maidwell House, near Northampton; Eton and Magdalen College, Oxford.

Sisters: (1) Elizabeth Sarah Louise, born on 19th March 1955 at Barratt Maternity Home, Northampton; married in May 1980 at St Mary's Church, Great Brington, near Althorp, Neil McCorquodale (born 1951), by whom she has one child, Emily Jane, born July 1983. Currently resident at Great Ponton, near Grantham, Lincolnshire.

(2) Cynthia Jane, born on 11th February 1957 at Queen Elizabeth Maternity Home, King's Lynn; married at the Guards' Chapel, London in April 1978, Robert Fellowes (born 1941), assistant private secretary to HM The Queen, and by whom she has two children, Laura, born in June 1980, and Alexander, born in March 1983. Currently resident at 5a Old Barracks, Kensington Palace, London W8.

Official visits abroad: Monaco, September 1982; Australia, March-April 1983; New Zealand, April 1983; Canada, June-July 1983; Norway, February 1984.

Official positions held: President of The Albany Trust, Dr Barnardo's, The Princess of Wales' Charities Trust. Patron of Birthright, the British Deaf Association, the British Red Cross Youth, the Canadian Junior Red Cross, the London City Ballet, the Malcolm Sargent Cancer Fund for Children, the National Children's Orchestra, the National Rubella Council, the New Zealand College of Obstetricians and Gynaecologists, the Pre-School Playgroups Association, The Princess of Wales' Children's Health Camp (New Zealand), the Royal College of Physicians and Surgeons of Glasgow, the Royal School for the Blind, the Swansea Festival of Music and Arts, the Wales Craft Council, and the Welsh National Opera. Freeman of the City of Cardiff; Honorary Freeman of the Grocers' Company; Honorary Fellow of the Royal College of Physicians and Surgeons of Glasgow.

Hobbies, interests and recreations; painting, sketching, music, dancing and swimming.

 t is Sydney, Australia, but for all the attention anyone gives the stylish boldness of the Opera House, or the city skyline glinting gold and glassy against a clear blue sky, it could be almost anywhere. Plastic Union Jacks sell like hot cakes for a dollar apiece; faulty ones – mounted upside-down on their flimsy sticks – change hands at a substantial discount; a sea of people floods the waterside walkways from Farm Cove to the Harbour; a ceiling of colourful umbrellas, some smartly frilled, keep the worst of the sun's assaults off sensitive heads; and a couple of stately old sailing ships, dressed overall, rise majestically above the fretting blue and orange police launches that patrol the water's edge. A 60-strong orchestra, drawn from local schools and massed on the Opera House forecourt, suddenly strikes up with a selection of tunes, imposing and rollicking by turns, to replace the Muzak that has been washing over the growing surge of humanity all morning. Each number is played stirringly, performed with an admirable discipline which disguises nerves and displays a presentational polish as high as the gaudy gleam of the bristling brass section.

It is almost possible, in the thick of such enjoyable activity, to forget why it is all taking place. But then, the first of several

announcements is made, pinpointing, for the benefit of an unseeing public, milestones in a journey that the Prince and Princess of Wales are then making from Sydney Airport to the Opera House. When, ultimately, the news is given that they have transferred to an open car at the Art Gallery, it seems that the entire crowd of ten thousand or more rises a simultaneous half-inch higher, tottering on tip-toe, necks craned and eyes trained in the direction of the point where the Prince and Princess are to arrive. Every minute seems like an age, until the distant but audible sound of cheering, and the first sight of a mass of waving, hand-held flags proclaim their approach. Those with binoculars

are already aware that, standing tall beside her husband in a limousine, Diana Princess of Wales is in the process of another ritual of virtual deification. A forest of hands stretches out in a hopeless attempt to reach her; equally hopeless screams demand that she acknowledge every one of her worshippers

individually; and flowers rain down upon her from all directions – one small bouquet so over-zealously pelted that it strikes her full in the face, and gives an already tense security squad momentary jitters.

Eventually, the sheer force of the swelling crowd brings the motorcade to a halt, and the royal couple dismount for what is supposed to be a formal procession. It quickly evaporates into a walkabout; Diana never could resist them, and the heaving mass of her admirers now encourages her to continue not to resist them. She responds in kind, diving into the crowds, clutching hands by the dozen, half grabbing, half dropping an

endless supply of gifts, from the tiniest bag of sweets to the most gigantic cuddly toy. And all the time she tries to answer the greetings and questions coming from unseen adult lips, while simultaneously ensuring that the three-year-old toddler who has been waiting for hours to hand over his jar of Vegemite is rewarded for his patience by a brief word of appreciation and a solemn promise to try its contents on William's next rusk.

When, at length, some form of order is restored, Neville Wran, the suave Premier of New South Wales, who has been riding high on his instant popularity as Diana's escort, welcomes her officially and hopes that she 'will come to share the interest

in and love for Australia which we all know Prince Charles has held from the days of his youth.' The Prince, answering for her – then as now, she was not renowned for the frequency or profundity of her public statements – speaks highly and appreciatively of the way in which she has been 'enveloped in warmth and affection'. It's as far into the province of

understatement as he dares go. 'Warmth and affection' in this context connotes the terminology of blandness and constraint. When, in an hour's time, Diana leaves the rostrum and makes her way through another vast section of the crowd, they will prove too much for the sweating policemen whose job it is to hold her path open. That 'warmth and affection' will turn into

nothing less than heroine-worship, converting the desire to see her at close quarters into an obsessive fixation that will stop at nothing to touch her. Soon, dozens of people will be vowing that the hand with which they have had the luck to shake the Princess' will not now be washed for the next week; one grown woman will go raging through the crowd in near hysteria, holding her hands aloft, and announcing to everybody, 'She shook hands with me! She spoke to me!' And for every one that can boast some contact of this sort, another hundred will turn away disappointed and even tearful. Meanwhile, the royal Diana roadshow progresses towards the next part of the programme, where an almost identical public response awaits.

Three months later, and a visit to Canada shows that it is not just ordinary members of the public who get carried away by the presence of the Princess among them. Prime Minister Trudeau, noted – sometimes reviled – for his less than traditionally respectful demeanour in the company of royalty, fairly folds before Her Majesty's daughter-in-law at a dinner in Ottawa. Speaking to Prince Charles, he puts forward the frankly preposterous suggestion that 'if by exception the Government of Canada could enlist you into a job, we would like you to become the chief guide of Her Highness. The pay you would not find very high, but I know the company would be very pleasant.' One of his counterparts at provincial level, New Brunswick's Richard Hatfield, goes one better – or one worse? – at a dinner in St. John. 'We have heard and read the lies,' he begins. 'Today it was wonderful to meet and know the truth. It's my turn to propose a toast. In doing so, I say: Let the flame burn, to warm

hope, to cancel cynicism and despair, to heat the soul that remains and remembers. Yes, let the flame burn. For the flame is love. I ask you to join with me in a toast to love – the Prince and Princess of Wales.'

Everyone is acutely embarrassed; Prince Charles' mouth goes into an involuntary spasm; and Diana herself, at whom the compliment is surely directed, giggles with sheer disbelief. Hatfield, a deeply committed monarchist, denies later that he was drunk, except on her charm, and blames his rambling

eulogy on the fact that 'I am not articulate.' Yet his words fly round the world, attracting for him the instant fame – or infamy – of one who, the latest of thousands, has succumbed against all behavioural logic to the magnetism of a girl still only 21 years old. Disraeli once said of flattery that everyone likes it, but that when it comes to royalty you have to lay it on with a trowel. A century later, such behaviour is purely optional, and those born in the purple know it as well as anybody. Yet an age which boasts all manner of liberation from traditional restraints still falls

proud and willing victim to the charms of a young lady who will be our next Queen Consort, but who less than five years ago would have been passed by in the streets of London without a second look.

**M**any years may well elapse before we can bring ourselves to analyse very objectively the forces that make a whole chunk of the world's civilisation hang on every word, hanker after every picture, copy every stitch that has ever had anything to do with Diana, but there is in the meantime no conceivable doubt that she has, perhaps to her own surprise, taken the monarchy by the scruff of the neck in what will probably be the last exercise this century to prepare it for the beginning of the next. It is a sobering thought that, at the time of her birth in July 1961, the Crown had not even made the final push out of the nineteenth century, so uncriticised and uncritically had its unvarying journey through the twentieth been.

The Queen was then in the tenth year of a reign which had seen changes wrought by the impact of television, and in which

the fading of the outward signs of aristocratic influence had been perceived. She was then a 36-year-old mother of three, whose own childhood awareness of her future role in life left her with a natural resistance to change, and many of the rather more unfortunate accomplishments of standard royal behaviour which itself was becoming more famous for its anachronistic courtliness than for its relevance to either present or future. Four years earlier, Lord Altrincham vented a sudden and heavy criticism upon her, describing 'the personality conveyed by the utterances put into her mouth' as 'that of a priggish schoolgirl.' The playwright John Osborne had likened the monarchy to 'the gold filling in the mouth of decay', and had questioned the political value and moral stimulus of 'the royal round of gracious boredom, the protocol of ancient fatuity.' Malcolm Muggeridge complained of the Queen's 'dowdy, frumpish' appearance and 'banal' behaviour, and railed against the cult of kings – 'Aspirins for a sick society,' he once called it disdainfully. 'As a religion, monarchy has always been a failure. A God-King inevitably gets eaten.'

The Palace weathered the storm – as it weathers all storms – by adopting a pained expression, remaining comparatively mute and keeping its head down. Changes continued to be made, fairly imperceptibly, until Prince Charles came of age and was gradually introduced to the royal round in his own right. He was the first heir to the Throne to have enjoyed – if that is the right word – an education other than at the hands of private tutors; the first to mark his entry into public life with a radio interview; and the first to admit openly that, logically, there are inconsistencies in a system which boasts democracy and equality of opportunity, yet which supports the principle of an hereditary and vastly wealthy monarchy. It was difficult to avoid the feeling that he had been well primed with positive thoughts about the relevance of his position, and that in him lay the monarchy's hopes for reconciling the forces of popular appeal and social change with those of traditional dignity and historical continuity. Today, it is tempting to imagine that his choice of wife followed the same inexorable programming, and that the future of the Crown he would eventually represent was as much a factor in his selection as the dictates of the heart.

For, when you consider the impact that Diana has had on

what until her 'arrival' was a very placid royal scene, it seems almost uncannily appropriate that she should have been born at the very beginning of the decade that became known as the Swinging Sixties. The trends that were to characterise that era had barely begun to surface at the time of her birth, but within only a few years they were to force a social pattern which would gently but firmly revolutionise many attitudes that had remained virtually unquestioned for the best part of the century. Not the least significant of those attitudes was the common man's view of the monarchy, in which connection it is worthwhile reminding ourselves that it was not until the year following her birth that the first, mildly irreverent caricature of a member of the Royal Family appeared in any British newspaper or magazine.

The immediate social surroundings into which Diana was born encouraged the reluctance to question attitudes that had become entrenched in favour of the aristocratic Establishment of which she was then unwittingly a part. And within that Establishment, her own family was a supreme example of the combination of sound breeding, wealth, and good social and family connections that made for a world of privilege so strongly based that even decades of intermittent socialism have failed to dislodge, let alone destroy it. For her father was destined to become the eighth in a line of Earls Spencer which has endured for almost three centuries. The family has long been associated with British sovereigns, its august connections stemming as they do from the great Duke of Marlborough for whom Queen Anne ordered the building of Bleinheim Palace in the early years of the eighteenth century.

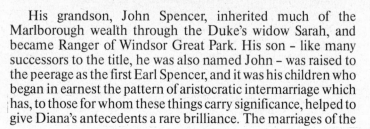

His grandson, John Spencer, inherited much of the Marlborough wealth through the Duke's widow Sarah, and became Ranger of Windsor Great Park. His son – like many successors to the title, he was also named John – was raised to the peerage as the first Earl Spencer, and it was his children who began in earnest the pattern of aristocratic intermarriage which has, to those for whom these things carry significance, helped to give Diana's antecedents a rare brilliance. The marriages of the

first Earl's daughters connected the family with the wealthy Earls of Bessborough and the prestigious Dukes of Devonshire, while his son and heir George married Lavinia, daughter of the first Earl of Lucan – the head of a family that was to achieve notoriety in the Crimea, and further, unsought fame in the twentieth century. George Spencer became the first of the family to receive the Order of the Garter, which King George III accorded him after his spell as First Lord of the Admiralty. His eldest son John, the third Earl, followed him into politics as Chancellor of the Exchequer in Queen Victoria's reign, while the younger son Frederick, who eventually became the fourth Earl, served in the old Queen's household.

Frederick married twice. By his first wife he had a son, John, who inherited as the fifth Earl, and who became Groom of the Stole both to the Prince Consort and to the future King Edward VII, as well as holding three major ministerial posts in government. Frederick's second wife, a daughter of the Marquess of Hertford, bore him two children: a daughter for whom Queen Victoria acted as godmother, and who was appropriately named Victoria Alexandrina; and a son, Charles, who was Groom-in-Waiting to Queen Victoria and Lord Chamberlain in the households of King Edward VII and King George V. Charles became the sixth Earl Spencer; Queen Alexandra was godmother to one of his daughters, while two other daughters became members of the household of Queen

Elizabeth the Queen Mother. Of Charles' three sons one had children to whom Prince George, Duke of Kent and Queen Maud of Norway were godparents. The eldest of Charles' sons, Albert Edward John – later the seventh Earl – married one of the present Queen Mother's Ladies of the Bedchamber, and this couple became the parents of Johnnie Spencer, born to the courtesy title of Viscount Althorp, and since 1975 the eighth Earl Spencer.

The Spencers' royal connections were, in fact, immensely strengthened during the life of the seventh Earl. He possessed that same unconquerable acquisitive urge where art treasures were concerned, for which his great royal contemporary Queen Mary was notorious, and his comprehensive knowledge and appreciation of the arts generally made him one of her most permanent friends and advisors in that sphere. She often visited the Spencers' family home in Northamptonshire, and in September 1939 the Earl invited her to call in for luncheon on

tennis-playing companion of the Duke of York, and through him a late but close friend of his father King George V. It was the King who leased him Park House, a rambling country mansion on the Sandringham estate, in 1935. Lord Fermoy was by then married to the former Ruth Gill, an equally close friend of the Duchess of York, and a lady who, as Ruth Lady Fermoy, is probably now the most famous name in the Queen Mother's household, having during the last two decades become one of her most intimate confidantes.

her way from Sandringham to Badminton House in Gloucestershire, where she would spend the duration of the war. Twenty years earlier, the seventh Earl had married a daughter of the Duke of Abercorn (whose own ancestry was littered with faithful royal retainers) and thus became son-in-law to one godson of Edward VII, brother-in-law to another, and brother-in-law again to one of Queen Mary's Women of the Bedchamber.

Meanwhile, on the other side of Diana's family, the Fermoys were beginning to make their first steps into royal circles. Apart from one great-great-aunt who had married a son of the reigning prince of the Silesian principality of Pless, Diana could have boasted no royal connections on her mother's side before the 1920s. In that decade, the fourth Baron Fermoy became a

That grace and favour tenancy at Sandringham ultimately became a focus for the generation, as yet unborn, of the Spencer clan to which Diana was to belong. Just before midnight on 20th January, 1936, King George V died at Sandringham House. Legend has it – and the sheer romance of it will no doubt keep it alive without any effort from the historians – that among the last words the old King heard on his death-bed was the news that, barely half a mile away, friend Fermoy's wife had just given birth to their second daughter that very day. The daughter was christened Frances, and took her father's surname Roche. Eighteen years later she would marry the heir to the Spencer earldom, and seven years after that would herself give birth to Diana, the daughter who would make her the mother-in-law to a future King. One wonders how many times Diana has passed by a statue of the bearded King George V who befriended her own grandfather, without reflecting how pleased that wise, family-conscious monarch would have been to live to see the day.

That having been said, it is a measure of the changing of the times that neither the King, nor indeed Diana, would recognise the interior of Park House now. Unlived in since she left it at the age of fourteen for Althorp, it has become – in the current economic jargon – unviable for the sort of family existence once enjoyed when food and fuel were plentiful and labour scandalously cheap. Leased rent-free by the Queen to the

Cheshire Homes, it is now being converted for use as a short-term stay centre for severely handicapped people. But for forty years until 1975 it provided the home base, first for the Fermoys, then for the Spencer heirs. The Fermoys continued to occupy the house after the old King's death, and both outlived his son King George VI. In 1955, Lord Fermoy himself died, and his widow Ruth suggested that her daughter Frances, newly married and already a mother herself, should take over the tenancy. She did, and it was there that two further daughters, as well as two sons, were born during ten of the next twenty years that followed. Unfortunately, their upbringing was to prove less idyllic than the circumstances might have suggested.

Diana has been fortunate, in events, in having a doting, good-natured father and a strong-willed, ambitious mother. The mother's determination first showed itself to an almost disbelieving aristocratic public when she was yet a debutante. At her coming-out ball, she had met Viscount Althorp, a 29-year-old bachelor whose undoubted eligibility was about to be

consummated by his imminent engagement to Lady Anne Coke, the eldest daughter of the Earl of Leicester. The Leicesters' country seat in Norfolk was barely equalled by the splendours of the stately Northamptonshire pile which was Althorp's inheritance, and their long, distinguished family history was well complemented by the Spencers' immense wealth. To each family, the Althorp-Coke match seemed a natural step in the progress towards fusing their distinctive qualities and characteristics - but Frances Roche thought otherwise. Somehow - and the circumstances are by no means fully agreed - she prised her Viscount away from his intended and, despite his prolonged absence abroad as Master of the Household during the Queen's six-month-long Commonwealth tour of 1953/4, secured and accepted his

proposal of marriage. The wedding took place at Westminster Abbey in June 1954 - a fairy-tale occasion swathed in silks, satins and tulle, glittering with diamonds and sequins, attended by the Queen, Prince Philip, the Queen Mother and Princess Margaret, and watched, no doubt from afar, by the deprived, sullen Leicester losers. For Frances Roche, it was the culmination of a crusade to win her man against all odds, a spirited warning - ironic in the light of later events - that she would have her way regardless.

By comparison, Viscount Althorp - Johnnie to friends and family - was an easy-going, perhaps easily led young man, and the epitome of the sort of mute, submissive, half-frightened son that is often the product of an authoritarian father. The seventh Earl, well over sixty years of age when Althorp married, was a

short-tempered, sometimes almost apoplectic patriarch, steeped in the traditions of the Victorian age which made a virtual god out of every self-respecting paterfamilias. He was nobody's soft touch, and suffered no fool gladly – or indeed at all. He processed his son through an educational and careers system similar to, though not entirely the same as his own; to Eton rather than Harrow, to agricultural college rather than to

skills among the younger membership of local clubs. His approach displayed the sort of unashamed homeliness that prompted him to welcome the birth of Prince Harry with the almost aggressively-voiced hope that the young prince would eventually play cricket for Gloucestershire, and which led Lord Longford to conclude, after a luncheon with Diana at Windsor Castle in 1981, 'She is obviously much attracted to her father.'

Cambridge, and into the Royal Scots Greys rather than into the Life Guards. Johnnie served in World War II and was mentioned in despatches, paralleling his father's service in World War I during which he came home with wounds. By contrast with the seventh Earl's long succession of public posts in the world of art, Johnnie was launched into diplomatic and royal service, becoming ADC to the Australian Governor-General in 1947, then equerry to both King George VI and subsequently the present Queen, until the year of his marriage.

Unsurprisingly, he emerged as a man not only of conventional reactions, but also of simple tastes and unspectacular pursuits. His early interest was in farming and the shoot, and he shunned the sophisticated prestige of the art world for the more personal satisfaction of encouraging cricketing

iana is his third daughter and fourth child, and he was 37 when, late in June 1961, the mental pacing up and down began as his wife entered the last stages of her pregnancy. It was not just a question of ordinary pre-confinement nerves. Only eighteen months before, the Althorps had awaited the birth of their third child, and had been overjoyed when it turned out to be a boy – a son at last to follow two daughters and provide a direct heir to the earldom. But the jubilation turned to grief when, having survived only a few hours, that son died. A few days afterwards, his body was buried beneath a simple gravestone near to his grandfather Lord Fermoy, in a family plot in the west corner of Sandringham churchyard. (Six years later, the baby's six-day-old cousin, Elizabeth Roche, joined him there, and the body of her father, the fifth Lord Fermoy, was the most recent committal to the same plot, following his suicide from depression in August 1984). The unexpected death of the Althorps' son and heir –

they had, of course, named him John – left them hoping, during those June days of 1961, for a healthy, surviving son to banish the grief of the year before. So, although both confinement and delivery were mercifully free of complications, there may have been a few reservations when yet another baby girl was presented by the midwife to her parents. Nevertheless, her father rejoiced that, at seven pounds twelve ounces, the child was of ample weight, and in rude good health. 'A superb physical specimen,' he pronounced, with the sort of unconfined gratification for which, at later landmarks in that daughter's life, he was to become famous.

With the wealth of royal connections boasted by the family over the centuries, it was perhaps curious, and in the light of events ironic, that Diana should be unable to count a single member of the Royal Family among her godparents when the former Bishop of Norwich – a close friend of the Spencer clan – ventured out of retirement to christen her Diana Frances at Sandringham Church later that summer. The nearest connection was Lady Mary Colman, a sister of the 17th Earl of Strathmore and one of the Queen Mother's fourteen nieces. But Diana was, as it happened, a close contemporary of the Queen's two younger sons, Andrew and Edward, as well as of George and Helen, the elder children of the Duke and Duchess of Kent. Some years later, the Kents came to live at Anmer Hall, one of Sandringham's other grace and favour residences. In later years, Diana was to know the friendship of Princess Margaret's children too: Viscount Linley, who, while at play with Diana's brother Charles, suffered the embarrassment of breaking his pop-gun; and Lady Sarah Armstrong-Jones, who was to become a family bridesmaid. Certain it was that Diana's early childhood did not want for royal contact.

Most aristocrats know how to enjoy their privileges quietly, and it was in that spirit that Diana was brought up. Her father, as with his first two daughters – Sarah, born in 1955, and Jane, born

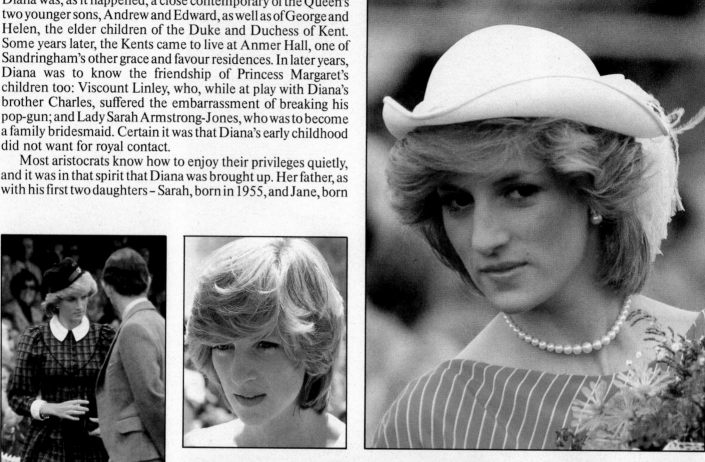

two years later – doted on her: she was, he said, 'a delightful child; as a baby she could have won any beauty competition.' She proved biddable and of equable temperament – a fortunate development for one reared in a family where still reigned much of the patriarchal structure and attitudes normally associated with the days before the lamps went out all over Europe. This almost inevitable legacy of decades of embattled aristocratic conservatism continued barely modified even by the lady of the house, Viscountess Althorp, who was noted as an elegant, socially graceful woman, fun-loving, easy of manner, and with charm as well as determination to spare.

iana was too young to remember much, if any, of the sometimes claustrophobic atmosphere of her formative years, either before or after the birth of her only surviving brother, Charles. Born in 1964, this long-awaited, much hoped-for Spencer heir was accorded the especial favour of counting the Queen among his godparents. But to Diana, then unaware of the royal connection, he was as much her baby as her parents'. She took an amusingly motherly interest in him, and in this respect among others his arrival marked the end of her own days as the baby of the family.

The kindly but strict influence of her governess, Gertrude Allen – a tried and trusted family retainer of many decades' standing – began to bear down upon her and before long she was developing into a model of childlike virtue – 'a conscientious girl... relaxed but somewhat serious... a tidy soul... thoughtful...'

Within the social circle into which she was born, Diana's life was unprepossessing. As a rising five-year-old, she joined the younger of her sisters in the Park House schoolroom, where Miss Allen – 'Ally' to her charges – went about the business of working the three R's into less than receptive heads. For all that Diana tried hard, Ally found her not particularly bright, inclined to daydream as she studied the balloon-patterned wallpaper, far more interested, for example, in the romanticism of kings and

queens than in the causes and effects of history's wars and political turmoils. Outside school hours she looked after a range of domestic pets, climbed trees, went for walks or bicycle rides, or visited the houses of various neighbours, like the Loyds and the Felloweses, who also rented houses on the Sandringham estate from the royal landlords. Holidays were spent with an unimaginative regularity of which George V would have been proud – either at Althorp, on parental visits to her paternal grandparents, or at the homes of various distant cousins, or again at Park House, with the occasional few days spent in the flat, expansive, sandy bays of the North Norfolk coast, especially at Brancaster where the Spencers had a beach hut.

The unchanging certainty of her family's annual round led to that sort of comfortable, secure sensation enjoyed by all children

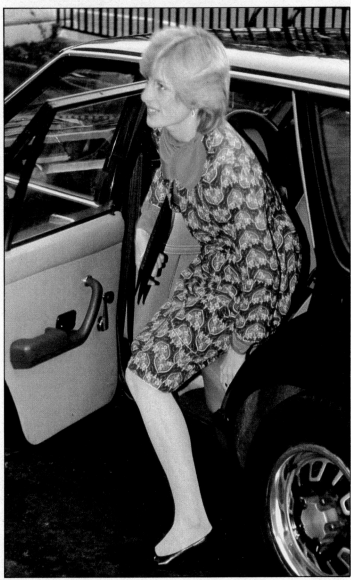

who are well established in loving homes, and to her unquestioning acceptance of her enviable circumstances. It was an attitude which her parents were anxious to foster – an extension of the old family principle which did not encourage too much communication between parents and children – even before their marital relationship began to deteriorate in the mid-1960s. Diana might otherwise have suspected, long before the ultimate trauma, an underlying unhappiness in her parents' marriage. In 1967 her mother left home with a suddenness that, for all that certain more aware members of the household may have suspected and feared the occurrence, confounded her children, perplexed her widowed mother, and devastated her husband. Tired, apparently, of a life of discharging the obligations of a monotonous social and family round, increasingly frustrated by the premature and oppressive conservatism and dullness of her husband, and having at last fulfilled her dynastic mission to provide the Spencers with an heir, Viscountess Althorp had decided to quit both home and family for good. By the time her husband discovered her new whereabouts, he had already acknowledged the hopelessness of his situation. She had, in fact, gone off to live with Mr Peter Shand Kydd, on the strength of which liaison his own wife was later to sue successfully for divorce. For a long time, Diana's father was too disorientated, almost too disbelieving to do anything, but he was eventually stung into action when his estranged wife sued for divorce on grounds of cruelty. He had no alternative but to contest, and at the cost of a prolonged and unhealthy public battle in the courts, for which he had felt obliged to engage some of the best legal brains in the country, he won both the case and – unusually for those days – custody of his four children.

It is a brave man who would attempt to estimate the psychological effect of this domestic upheaval on the six-year-old Diana. Her maternal grandmother, Ruth Fermoy, stepped in to try to fill the breach, mothering the children and feeding the inconsolable Johnnie Spencer with advice and encouragement. The household underwent a major overhaul and many of the staff found their services no longer required. The schoolroom was disbanded and Diana was sent – somewhat earlier, comparatively speaking, than her sisters – to Silfield, a primary

day-school near King's Lynn. It seemed a rational move at the time, but two years later it proved hard for Diana to bear the stares and mockery of schoolchildren who learned second-hand of the acrimonious divorce proceedings between her parents. Although she could count on the support of her sister Jane, who was still at the school, and a few close friends, including

Alexandra Loyd, the daughter of the Queen's Sandringham land agent, she was transferred to Francis Holland School, a private day-school in Sloane Square, which her future cousin Lady Sarah Armstrong-Jones would attend three years later. During her short time there, her mother married Peter Shand Kydd and went to live at Itchenor in Sussex. Meanwhile Lord

Althorp, though desperately short of company, agreed that Diana should go to prep school, and back at Park House he watched her leave to begin her three years at Riddlesworth School, near Diss on the Norfolk/Suffolk border. It was 'a dreadful day' for him, and his sense of loss must have rubbed off on Diana as, in her cherry-red and grey school uniform, she watched her trunks and cases – marked simply D.F. Spencer (though she could have added 'The Hon' as a prefix) being loaded into the brake.

Diana's own sense of emptiness did not last long. True to her new school's motto, 'Facing Forward', she distinguished herself in the eyes of her headmistress by her cheerfulness, and in the eyes of her schoolfriends by her high spirits. She took an active, if middling part in the social life of the school, delighting in any opportunity the tuck-shop offered to indulge her now

celebrated sweet tooth, and making full use of the mini-complex of hutches which the school provided for the pupils to keep their pets in. She made many friends, though she can hardly be said to have stood out academically or socially among them. The most controversial comment that her headmistress, Miss Elizabeth Ridsdale, could find to relate was that 'she was a perfectly ordinary, nice little girl, good at swimming, awfully sweet with the little ones'. She might have thought differently had she discovered, as someone did a decade later, the initials DS scrawled on a dormitory wall. The graffito, pretty ordinary for its time, now enjoys the status, virtually, of an historic document. 'We'll probably decorate round it,' said a spokesman, after it had been spotted, 'or just have a square patch so the writing shows through.'

In the spring of 1973, Diana sat the Common Entrance exam for a place at West Heath, an exclusive girls' boarding school near Sevenoaks in Kent, which both her sisters had joined some years earlier, and which Sarah, the elder, had just left. Diana passed her exam 'quite well', and that September, accompanied by her Riddlesworth chum Carolyn Harbord-Hammond, attended her first and, in events, only secondary school. Under its headmistress, Miss Ruth Rudge, its twelve-hour-a-day

uring her four years at West Heath, new family developments began to reshape her home life. In 1972 her mother and stepfather moved to Scotland where they had bought a 1,000-acre hillside farmstead on the island of Seil in Argyllshire. Although Diana had several times visited her mother both at her London flat in Cadogan Square and at the Shand Kydds' Sussex house, 1973 saw the beginnings of a long line of regular, happier and more fulfilling holidays on the north-west Scottish coast, where Diana's real love of the great outdoors was nourished. Then, two years later her paternal grandfather, the octogenarian 7th Earl Spencer, died and Diana's father succeeded as the eighth Earl. He and his four children – the eldest now 20 and the youngest 11 – moved into the palatial mansion that is Althorp, little suspecting the massive financial problems which claims for Estate Duty and Capital Transfer Tax would for the next eight years involve. Park House was thus abandoned, never more to be used for family purposes.

Though Diana was already well acquainted with Althorp when the family moved in, the change of surroundings was immense. In place of the ten-bedroomed house she had been

curriculum was designed to encourage people to develop their own minds and tastes, and to realise their duties as citizens. Diana certainly didn't find the academic side of life to her particular liking, but she threw herself wholeheartedly into hockey, in which she eventually captained the school side; into swimming, in which she won cups; and into social work, at which she was amazed to find she had won the school's 'special award for service'. She began to learn to play the piano, but abandoned it for the ballet class – she had taken up ballet in a desultory way at the age of three-and-a-half – and tap-dancing sessions. And it was here that she met two girls who were to feature prominently in her later life: Carolyn Pride, ultimately one of the famous three flatmates, and Kay Seth-Smith, whom Diana was to join in running the Young England Kindergarten.

brought up in, she felt almost lost in an aristocratic vastness comprising over a hundred rooms, and set in 15,000 acres of parkland which once contained a private racecourse. Developed from a late 15th-century moated courtyard house – the two massive wings were added in 1575 – it was originally the second home of a Spencer family whose roots lay in Warwickshire where, in Tudor times, they had farmed sheep. When their principal manor house there was razed to the ground by Cromwell's troops in the Civil War, they moved to Althorp, which they developed, decorated and furnished with a vision of

such grandeur that a contemporary visitor deemed it worthy of any great prince. Renovated by the architect Holland in the late eighteenth century, it soon reached the zenith of its reputation, famed for its grand staircase, converted in the mid seventeenth century from an internal courtyard; its long picture gallery, thick with portraits by Lely and Van Dyck; its superb collection of Marlborough plate, given to the family by Sarah, Duchess of Marlborough; the portraits of three generations of Spencers which Sir Joshua Reynolds painted; the Marlborough and Rubens rooms whose walls were lined with the work not just of

Reynolds, but of Gainsborough, Titian, Holbein and Kneller; and the King William room, where William of Orange slept in the elegant four-poster bed. The collection of art treasures was enhanced by the 7th Earl Spencer in the first half of this century – perhaps his most cherished piece was the Derby vase bearing the picture of Spencer House, the family's former London home, which Queen Mary – who was more widely celebrated for her ability to wrest objects of artistic elegance or importance from other collectors – actually gave to him in the 1920s. By the time of his death in 1975, Althorp contained one of the finest private art collections in Europe – 'a testament to all those

Spencers who managed to add their own special contribution to the house.'

Those words were written by Raine, the former Lady Dartmouth who, a year after the present Lord Spencer succeeded to the Earldom, came into his life of lonely splendour and took him as her new husband. It would be wrong to invert the phrase, and say that he took a new wife: on her own admission, Raine was by nature not one who waited to be asked for anything, and she was well used to being the driving force behind any project, including marriage, that took her fancy. She

had dominated the London social scene both before and after her first marriage, to the Hon. Gerald Legge, Viscount Lewisham, later Earl of Dartmouth, primarily because she showed the early promise of emulating the eccentricities of her mother, Barbara Cartland. Her early married life had been much publicised in the gossip columns for its panache and controversies, particularly when she headed crusades against issues as diverse as dirty restaurant crockery, and some even dirtier films then being shown in London.

As an outspoken Conservative Greater London Councillor, representing Richmond and Twickenham, she soon began to weave her own web, and by the mid-1970s was in the process of asserting her independence by divorcing her husband. Her marriage to Lord Spencer in 1976 presented a most delightful new challenge – the regeneration, against all odds, of the Spencer family fortunes. Faced with her husband's colossal problems of raising £2¼ million to pay off the Inland Revenue's bill for death duties, not to mention the recurrent difficulty of finding £80,000 a year to maintain the house, she cast off her

obsession with London, and began to rationalise the entire set-up at Althorp. Economies of staffing, resources and outgoings provided one obvious way out, but her main thrust was directed towards the development of the mansion's touristic attractions – even before Diana's marriage had rendered it obligatory sightseeing material.

'We got the show on the road right away,' Raine said when it was all over. 'No hanging about.' It was no understatement. For a woman then close on fifty, she showed a remarkable vitality, a clear and unwavering sense of purpose, and a business-like disdain for sentimentality as she set about her task. To raise money, she had over £2 million worth of the Spencer art treasures sold off. Of the 720 paintings then at Althorp, three Van Dycks went in 1976. A batch of about a dozen Gainsborough drawings followed, along with a Reynolds portrait. Selling began in earnest in 1979 – a giltwood table alone fetching £10,000 – and by the end of 1981 the sale, for no less than £1 million, of more old masters had been negotiated. Early the next year, a pair of solid gold wine coolers, made for the Duke of Marlborough three centuries earlier, were sold to the British Museum for £274,000, and that July a 220-year-old painting by the Scottish artist Gavin Hamilton was acquired by the Tate Gallery. In March 1984, a painting by Salvator Rossa, dated 1646, and acquired by the Spencer family in 1761, was sold to the National Gallery for £350,000. In addition, many works of art were turned over to the State in satisfaction of the Treasury's financial claims consequent upon the 7th Earl's death.

At first sight, it seemed a perverse and savage line for Raine to adopt; she who had turned her hand to the pen only once – with a book called *What Is Our Heritage?* – who was also a noted campaigner for keeping the nation's art treasures within the confines of the United Kingdom, and who, like Princess Michael of Kent, was soon to become one of the trustees of the Victoria and Albert Museum. But Lord Spencer was quick to point out in her defence that not more than 25 paintings had actually been sold, while Raine herself insisted that 'nothing mportance has left the collection', and that many prospective sales out of the country had proved abortive because of the Government's refusal to grant export licences.

The flip side of the operation was also its main purpose. As soon as the first returns came in, the Spencers – 'Everything has been done together,' said the Earl – set about renovating and refurbishing Althorp from top to bottom. Every one of the five hundred pictures now in the house was cleaned and restored, every room was redecorated, most items of furniture and drapery were repaired and bought back to their original colour and condition, fire surrounds were re-brassed, chandeliers

replaced, and new gold leaf shone everywhere. It was, not surprisingly, a very expensive business. Some chairs cost as much as £2,000 each to restore and re-gild; the expense of cleaning ancient carpets, particularly that in the State Dining Room – 'A hundred years of gravy has come off,' mused the Earl afterwards – was astronomical. Tatty old Victorian drapes, cushion-covers and silk patchwork quilts, all beyond repair, were unceremoniously despatched to the National Trust, who found the cost of restoration more affordable. Conscious of the price of today's fuel, the new, forward-looking Lady Spencer had double-glazing installed – a move which provoked considerable

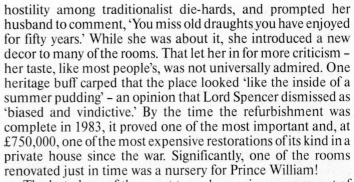

hostility among traditionalist die-hards, and prompted her husband to comment, 'You miss old draughts you have enjoyed for fifty years.' While she was about it, she introduced a new decor to many of the rooms. That let her in for more criticism – her taste, like most people's, was not universally admired. One heritage buff carped that the place looked 'like the inside of a summer pudding' – an opinion that Lord Spencer dismissed as 'biased and vindictive.' By the time the refurbishment was complete in 1983, it proved one of the most important and, at £750,000, one of the most expensive restorations of its kind in a private house since the war. Significantly, one of the rooms renovated just in time was a nursery for Prince William!

The last phase of the quest to make a going concern out of Althorp began in the early 1980s, with a renewed push to make the house one of the major British tourist attractions. Parts of the mansion had been open to the public since 1854, and over 130

years later trade is thriving. Diana's wedding helped of course – takings quadrupled in the fifteen months immediately after it – but Raine Spencer was bent on new exploitations. In 1982, she opened a wine bar, with Saturday night sing-songs, and introduced the idea of musical dinner evenings, at which up to a hundred guests at a time paid £30 per head for the privilege of dining by candlelight, in the glittering new Sunderland Room, on game terrine, sirloin of beef, and Grand Marnier chocolate

secured in the first week alone. Raine Spencer was justly flushed with her success as mistress of Althorp. In its wake, she tellingly explained to a lunch-time audience at the Café Royal in October 1982 that times had changed since the nineteenth century, when only four occupations were open to females – those of nun, housewife, prostitute and witch. She even urged today's women to get on and do what was necessary, even at the cost of their marriages!

mousse – before transferring to the Great Room for Gilbert and Sullivan recitals by the London Operetta Ensemble. Althorp was also made available for wedding receptions, champagne business lunches and the like, and one of its outlying cottages was first rented out to holiday-makers in April 1982 for £85 a week. In that same year, the Spencers tried their hand in the world of fashion jewellery, selling by mail order replicas of Spencer heirlooms, under the distinctive title *The Althorp Jewels Collection*. With pieces priced at between £60 and £230, the collection proved popular, and orders worth £2,000 were

Her efforts certainly put no strain on her own second marriage, except in the early days when the Spencer children found her clean-sweep attitudes far too radical and insensitive. Diana's two elder sisters jibbed mightily at her new approach – Sarah giving orders over and above Raine's head, and Jane hardly able to bring herself to speak to her for almost two years. Diana does not seem to have taken too readily to her mother-in-law either, but unlike her sisters she tactfully concealed any reservations she may have harboured. 'Diana was sweet,' Raine later admitted. 'She did her own thing.'

he truth was that Diana was still extremely vulnerable. It was, after all, a confusing time for her. The wrench from Park House, though she must have suspected its happening sooner or later, involved not just a farewell to the only house she ever knew, but also the loss of neighbours who had become close friends. The need to reconcile her attitude to her much loved father, her far-away mother, and a stepmother who prided herself on her backbone of steel, was not the best aid to a stress-free adolescence. Having reached their majorities, Diana's sisters were more able to cope with new demands, and less dependent on the goodwill of their new stepmother, but at only 15 – and a somewhat immature 15 at that – Diana was in no position to air her feelings, even if she had untangled them in her own mind. So she came quickly and quietly to terms with the new *status quo* as she proceeded towards her last full year at West Heath. It proved not to be an encouraging time for her. She failed her 'O' levels in the summer of 1977, and left the school for good that Christmas after her second attempt again produced not a single pass. Bookish she would clearly never be, and though faced with a secure, if somewhat colourless existence on a huge Northamptonshire estate, it was difficult to see how she might be prompted into something a little more purposeful than sitting back to enjoy the privileges ready-made for the daughter of a wealthy Earl.

It was her mother who suggested that Diana should follow her sister Sarah to the Swiss finishing school, the Institut Alpin Videmanette at the Château d'Oex at Rougemont near the fashionable skiing resort of Gstaad, and for want, it seems, of anything better to do, Diana went. But the venture was a mistake. She missed the wide and open camaraderie of school,

baulked at the rules forbidding conversations in any language but French, and looked disapprovingly towards the prospect of spending a regulation summer 'picking Alpine flowers'. The school's aim of producing 'healthy and happy pupils by ensuring that they work hard and play hard in a relaxed family atmosphere' failed to cut any ice with her. Bored, disorientated and possibly a little homesick, she returned to England within six weeks, and the school never received any explanation of her failure to report again for the rest of the term.

That year proved an eventful one, with the 21st birthday celebrations, and then the wedding, of Diana's sister Jane – both events happening within a few weeks of each other that spring. For Diana, it was an intensely happy time too. She saw that the coolness between Jane and Raine Spencer had dissolved, and sensed a refreshingly gracious, tolerant wind of change blowing through family attitudes. This was especially gratifying to Diana because Jane was closer to her both in age and in temperament than her other sister Sarah. Born in 1957 at the Queen Elizabeth Maternity Home in King's Lynn, and a goddaughter of the then bachelor Duke of Kent, Jane had always got on well with Diana at home, despite the elder girl's far superior intellectual abilities

which had earned her no fewer than eleven 'O' levels at West Heath School. She had been a prefect there, played tennis for the school, and captained its First XII at lacrosse. A purposeful artistic career seemed on the cards when, in 1976, she left West Heath with 'A' levels of sufficient grades to spend six months studying art and the history of art in Florence, but she came back to begin a secretarial course in London, eventually joining the staff of the fashion magazine *Vogue* as an editorial assistant. That

job gave her connections which were to be useful to Diana in later years: in 1980 Diana's first portrait by Lord Snowdon appeared in the magazine, and after her engagement, she was able to use *Vogue's* immense resources to try out new designs with a view to choosing her first 'royal' outfits and, indeed, selecting her first designers.

Jane's marriage in April 1978 perpetuated the Spencers' royal links into a new generation. The family of her husband, Robert Fellowes, had not only been well-known as neighbours of the Althorps when both lived on the Sandringham estate, but Robert himself had also recently given up his job as a discount broker on the Stock Exchange to become an assistant Private Secretary to the Queen. He is highly tipped to succeed her present Private Secretary, Sir Philip Moore, and has since his marriage lived with his wife and two children – Laura, born in June 1980 and Alexander, born in March 1983.

Diana was chief bridesmaid at Jane's wedding, her gracefully tall figure aptly set off in a long, Regency-style dress with a modest floral-print pattern. And there was to be a welcome spin-off for Diana after the wedding. The flat at Warwick Square, Pimlico, which Jane had taken before her marriage, was now no longer needed, and she arranged that her mother should have the future use of it. Mrs Shand Kydd duly quit her own flat in Cadogan Square, which in turn she gave over to Diana, who was thus for the first time – though not yet seventeen – able to set herself up for a life of relative independence. Her first companions in this venture were Laura Greig, a West Heath schoolfriend, and Sophie, the daughter of Conservative MP Marcus Kimball. They have remained two of Diana's closest friends ever since, and she attended each of their weddings – in July 1984 and November 1982 respectively. Back in those early bachelor-girl days, Diana was no budding socialite, and certainly not one for the deb scene. A non-smoker, non-drinker, and preferring the quiet life, she pursued a comparatively modest and private lifestyle in the company of her new companions. Eventually, she took a succession of jobs as a family nanny and child-minder before approaching her old friend Kay Seth-Smith for more permanent employment caring for young children.

The Young England Kindergarten is now, thanks to Diana, probably the most famous of its kind in the world. It had been established in a run-down church hall in Pimlico by Mrs Victoria Wilson, assisted in time by Kay Seth-Smith, to cater for about four dozen under-fives. Its informal curriculum and the absence of restrictions immediately appealed to Diana, who had already convinced herself that she had a way with children. Her mother had described her as 'a positive Pied Piper with children', and she had no hesitation in joining the staff of the kindergarten, relishing the unstuffy go-as-you-please approach as much as the endearing dependence of the youngsters upon her. 'Miss Diana', as she was addressed by them all, found that her lack of formal training was no great bar to fulfilment, and the fact that, after her long, gypsy-feet existence, she remained in post for eighteen months, illustrates how satisfying the experience was for her. She was to miss her charges greatly on becoming engaged, and made several visits to the kindergarten in the months after she quit the job.

The arrival of her eighteenth birthday in July 1979 only served to increase her sense of independence and adventure, not least because, like both her sisters before her, she became entitled to a share of the capital of a family trust fund which enabled her to buy her own flat. She chose a suite of rooms at Coleherne Court, off the Brompton Road in up-market Knightsbridge, and with her went her Cadogan Square flatmates. Here was a place they could really call their own, and the girls, who all shared the running costs, set to work painting, decorating and furnishing as if their lives depended on stamping the flat with their own identities. There was nothing rebellious about this: as with her own rooms at Kensington Palace and Highgrove now, Diana restricted herself to soft colours and gentle, almost traditional designs, pleasing without being over-imaginative, unassuming without being dull.

In due course, her two original flatmates left and, after a

succession of changes, were ultimately replaced by the three girls – Carolyn Pride, Anne Bolton and Virginia Pitman – who later became household names throughout the length and breadth of the country, envied for their closeness to Diana in her hour of triumph, and applauded for their discretion and loyalty to her in her hour of need. Carolyn Pride, slim, blonde and chatty, was a West Heath contemporary, though she enjoyed only a nodding acquaintance there with Diana, whose indifferent academic performance she bettered with a clutch of 'O' levels, and progress at 'A' level that took her eventually to the Royal College of Music for a three-year course of study. She saw a great deal of Diana even after her marriage to Prince Charles, and when she herself married in September 1982 – to the 25-year-old William Bartholomew, son and heir of a Wiltshire brewer – both Diana and Charles left their three-month-old son William at Balmoral to attend the wedding at Chelsea Old Church. Eventually, Carolyn took a teaching job in Kensington, filling in her spare time by helping her husband run Juliana's, a mobile discotheque for very fashionable disco parties, whilst looking for the opportunity to follow the singing career for which her three years at music college had prepared her. She was very

much the organising force behind the consortium at Coleherne Court, and even now Diana pays a special tribute to the friendship by frequently attending concerts given by the Royal College of Music.

Anne Bolton, a smaller, sharp-featured and slightly older girl, had known Diana during a comparatively lengthy secretarial career at the Mayfair branch of Savill's, a reputable and well-connected firm of estate agents for whom Diana's elder sister Sarah also worked. In addition, Anne had been a friend of Diana's Sandringham companion Alexandra Loyd, and had met Diana herself during a skiing holiday in 1979. In the months of relentless press interest in Diana, Anne was to prove an invaluable help as a spokesman who knew how to parry intrusive journalistic questions with courtesy, tricky ones with equal cunning, and impossible ones with decisive refusals to comment. A year after Diana's wedding, Anne left Britain for a new life in Australia where, after some months working as a waitress, cook, and almost anything else to pay her way, she met Noel Hill. A well-heeled New South Wales farmer, he is the son of Sinclair Hill, who was for several years Prince Charles' polo coach and a person of such forthright outspokenness that he has

achieved the considerable distinction of being the only man able to get away with swearing at the Queen's eldest son. In March 1983, shortly before her engagement to Noel, Anne was guest in the royal box at Warwick Farm, near Sydney, where Diana watched Prince Charles play polo one weekend during the Australian tour. The following October, Diana attended the Hills' grand wedding in the City of London, before they left for New South Wales to farm in the vastness of 300,000 acres, which leaves them not less than seventy miles from their nearest neighbours.

Virginia Pitman remains the only unmarried member of Diana's faithful trio, despite her cheerful, busy – some say motherly – appearance. It says much for the triviality of the press at the time of Diana's engagement that her most celebrated contribution to the Coleherne Court household was thought to have been a goldfish called Battersea, but in fact she introduced a useful touch of domesticity to the group. With her Cordon

Bleu training, she probably taught Diana all she knows about cookery, and as she was just about to start on a diploma course in design at the Chelsea College of Art, she had a significant say on the subject of changes to the flat's decor. When, immediately after her engagement, Diana quit the flat and gave notice that eventually her friends would have to leave, it was to Virginia's new home in Fulham that they all went. Now, with her diploma firmly under her belt, Virginia has set up a business in interior

design, in partnership with designer Louise Ashton.

The flat-sharing interlude was comparatively brief, but incredibly successful. 'Four girls in a flat can be fatal,' said Virginia three years later, 'but it never was with us.' Carolyn thought it 'simply extrordinary that we never fell out.' It was all the more so because the three girls knew almost nothing of each other before Diana brought them together: 'Diana was the link between us,' one of them said later. And long after the momentous events of 1981, they were grateful that the relationship had worked so well that 'the whole experience of sharing a flat with Diana could have changed our lives, but it didn't. Everything that has happened to us since then would have happened anyway, whatever Diana had done. We are still seeing the same friends, being the same people.' Certain it was in those early days of 1980, that this unsuspecting trio, pushing out the boat on their first adventure in life, little realised how much they were going to mean to Diana. One wonders how difficult it was for her to balance her loyalty to these friends and the need to keep them reasonably well informed, with her growing awareness that her association with the heir to the Throne required particularly delicate handling where all others were concerned.

s the Spencers and the Mountbatten-Windsors had always seen a lot of each other, pin-pointing the first meaningful meeting between Diana and Prince Charles is a hazardous, purely academic, and indeed futile exercise. If any familial matrimonial hope burgeoned, it was probably directed at a union between Diana and Prince Andrew, who were pretty well coevals, or between Prince Charles and Diana's elder sister Sarah. Sarah was seven years younger than Charles, but she had in the mid-1970s been one of many strongly-tipped favourites for his hand. Much more extrovert and strikingly different, with her blushed complexion and auburn hair, from most of his previous companions, she was seen with him constantly during 1977 and 1978 at polo matches and hunts, and was a frequent guest at Sandringham and Balmoral. In the wake of the disproved Jubilee Year news that Charles was to marry Princess Marie Astrid of Luxembourg, Lady Sarah's royal links put her at the top of that year's speculative ratings.

She had been born in 1955, at Barratt's Maternity Home, Northampton – this was shortly before her parents moved from Orchard Manor on the Althorp estate to Park House, Sandringham – but the unprepossessing surroundings of her birth were soon compensated for at her christening. This took place at Westminster Abbey and, being the first child of the new Spencer generation, she had a royal godparent – this time in the

The couple now live at Little Ponton, near Grantham in Lincolnshire, where they farm and hunt on the McCorquodale family estate. Their only child, a daughter named Emily Jane, was born in July 1983.

Prince Charles' association with Lady Sarah Spencer is commonly thought to have been brought to an abrupt and unexpected halt when, in 1978, she denied, in an interview for a woman's magazine, that she had any intention of marrying him.

shape of the Queen Mother. Until Diana emerged from early childhood, Sarah's constant companion was, naturally, her sister Jane, her junior by two years. At Park House, the two sisters shared a pony called Romany; they both went to West Heath School together in that autumn of 1967 when their parents split up; and they both took joint responsibility for keeping their two younger siblings amused and cared for during holiday times.

But the similarities between Sarah and Jane ended there. At school, Sarah became bored almost in direct proportion to Jane's increasing studiousness. Despite a varied school career – she had been in several school plays, had ridden in the school team at the Hickstead Horse Trials, and had complemented her creditable 'O' level success of six passes with a Grade V piano certificate at the age of 15 – she sensed disillusion and aimlessness. She behaved accordingly, and to the mutual relief of her teachers and herself, did not return for 'A' levels in 1972. Instead, she was packed off to the finishing school in Switzerland that Diana was later to attend, and returned to take up a secretarial course in London – a move which Jane later copied. Her career as a single girl took her to the Berkeley Square branch of Savills, within easy commuting distance of her Chelsea flat. But hers was an indecisive, slightly rebellious approach to womanhood. She made no secret of her smoking and drinking habits, though neither was excessive, and her decline into anorexia nervosa back in 1977 has made headline news ever since it was feared that Diana would follow suit five years later. Her relationship with her eventual husband was a long, cautious, hot-and-cold business, until in May 1980 they were married at St Mary's Church, Great Brington, near Althorp. The bridegroom, Neil McCorquodale, was a kinsman of Raine Spencer and his impeccable credentials include a school career at Harrow and service in the Coldstream Guards.

WELCOME TO CANTERBURY PRINCESS DIANA

PRE-SCHOOL PLAYGROUPS ASSOCIATION

'I think of him as the big brother I never had,' she said. 'If he asked me to marry him, I would turn him down.' But in fact, Sarah lost nothing – save, temporarily, the Prince's goodwill – by these revelations. She was already aware of the almost unbelievable fact that Charles was beginning to turn his well-schooled eye towards her younger sister Diana. It was in November 1977 that, spending a weekend at Althorp as Sarah's guest, Charles may have felt his romance with Diana spark off. The Prince later identified the place at which the spark was struck as 'a ploughed field', but for how long he and Diana had gazed into each other's eyes during that autumn shoot at Althorp is unrecorded. He came away thinking her 'a jolly and attractive 16-year-old'; she found him 'pretty amazing'. Lady Sarah merely looked on, feeling not a little helpless. 'They just

clicked' she said later. 'I just played Cupid'. If things were as serious as that, no wonder Diana dipped her 'O' levels, for the second time, a month later.

She seemed to betray her feelings in the new year, when Charles took Sarah on a skiing holiday to Klosters. As it happened, they were not very far from Diana's finishing school at Rougemont, and Mme. Yersin, her headmistress, suspected that she was in love with the Prince. Her suspicions, voiced only after Diana's engagement, were so perspicacious as to impute the benefit of hindsight, but if the sentiment really existed, Diana showed remarkable patience, not to say determination, for it was to be a year before she saw Charles again. A Sandringham weekend in January 1979 proved to be the first of several more meetings, though even by August of that year, when Diana was invited to Balmoral to join Prince Andrew and Prince Edward, Charles was still showing only a platonic interest in her. Aware of the need to be circumspect, he has rarely if ever

been particularly forward with girls, and the evidence on this occasion is that, as with most family guests at Balmoral, Diana merely accompanied the royal princes on shoots and salmon-fishing expeditions. Six months later she was at Wood Farm, one of the houses on the Sandringham estate used by individual members of the Royal Family when the Queen and Prince Philip have moved back to London. On this occasion, Diana had travelled from London with fellow guest Amanda Knatchbull who, a 22-year-old granddaughter of the recently assassinated Lord Mountbatten, was herself once considered a possible candidate for the Prince's hand. Charles betrayed no hint of romantic intentions towards either of the young ladies.

That was not entirely surprising, since he was throughout much of this time clocking up a sizeable tally of other girlfriends – much to the joy of gossip-columnists everywhere. It was not until the summer of 1980, and after some very public disappointments in this pursuit, that meetings between Charles and Diana at Balmoral, where Diana was despatched to help her sister Jane with her first baby, made Charles 'realise what was going on in my mind and hers in particular'. Their excursions for walks on the estate began to increase in number, and Charles – the Royal Family's second most successful salmon-fisher – was delighted to discover that Diana was no mere beginner with a fishing rod. This newly found common interest proved, in events, a distinct disadvantage. In mid-September, the couple were fishing for salmon in the River Dee when a stray photographer – one of remarkably few lurking in the hills and

woods of Balmoral that summer – caught the picture of the year: Prince Charles and his very latest girlfriend. At the age of nineteen years and two months, Lady Diana Spencer's private life came irreversibly to an abrupt end.

The sequence of events from that point is by now well ·known. Diana returned to her job at the Young England Kindergarten to find herself a celebrity, pursued by newspaper reporters and photographers in ever growing numbers. The route from her flat to Pimlico became the most heavily trodden in the whole of London; her flatmates were harassed, her kindergarten besieged, and she – followed on foot, by car, and even on and off buses – became the butt of questions and the whirring of motor-driven cameras, as if no-one had any conceivable doubt that she would in fact be the next Princess of Wales. Incredibly in those circumstances, the victims kept level heads. Flatmates said nothing, acted as willing decoys for Diana,

and organised a few successful escapes from the attentions of the press. 'It's like protecting your sister,' said one of them. 'We would simply never let Diana down.' Her fellow teachers laudably combined non-committal responses with endless patience. Diana herself, though she found her life a daily ordeal in which, quite unable to dodge public attention, she had to draw upon reserves of diplomacy, tact and tolerance almost unthinkable in a 19-year-old, answered pertinent questions with good humour and impertinent ones with charm, but never once did she give anything away. Except, that is, the shape of her legs. Early on in the battle, and in the swift but vain hope of peace, she agreed to pose for photographs in the garden of her playschool. Enticed into a position with her back to the light, she stood for just a few moments while a strong autumn sun streamed through her thin skirt, projecting the silhouette of her legs into alarming and unmistakable relief. It was a well-organised trick for which those involved have never been forgiven. The satirist Clive James compounded the mischief later by referring to her as Lady Diana Seethrough-Spiffing in his latter-day epic poem *Charles Charming's Challenges on the Pathway to the Throne.*

In between whiles there were clandestine meetings at Birkhall, the Queen Mother's Scottish retreat, which afforded ample privacy, and outings together to the Beaufort Hunt and Ludlow Races, where Charles competed in his first National Hunt event. Diana was invited to a belated fiftieth birthday party for Princess Margaret, held at the Ritz in London early in November, and went up to Sandringham to help Charles celebrate his own birthday – his 32nd – ten days later. It was this meeting, amid and despite all the rumour and denial, which above all seemed to justify the continued speculation. The press, convinced that this express compromising of Diana's privacy

was a sign that the Prince had made up his mind, bayed for confirmation. When Charles refused to give it, one Sunday paper ran a story that the couple had been involved in two late-night 'love trysts' on the royal train as it stood in sidings in Wiltshire. The Queen demanded, but failed to obtain, a retraction. Two weeks later, the Press Association published an interview in which Diana had allegedly said she wanted to marry soon. This too was denied. While the Palace stood helplessly by,

it was Diana's mother who took up the cudgels in the form of a strongly-worded letter to *The Times*, condemning the intrusion and harassment suffered by her daughter, and begging an end to it all.

Needless to say, it didn't happen. By then, Prince Charles was on a three-week tour of India and Nepal, and the press contingent split into two in order to cover the supposed romance from both ends. In Delhi, Charles bemoaned the difficulty he

faced in choosing a wife: 'It's all right for you chaps', he told reporters at a press reception. 'You can live with a girl before you marry her. I've got to get it right from the word go.' One of his party noticed that, after a three-day private sojourn in the Himalayas, Charles came back to civilisation looking 'as if some huge burden had been lifted from his shoulders.' Speculation again increased, and the word spread: back home, Diana read a report in the *The Guardian*, of all papers, that her engagement to Charles would be announced that day. It was 15th December, and it passed uneventfully. Diana's rumoured invitation to spend Christmas at Windsor Castle proved similarly inaccurate, and the only New Year meeting – a two-day stay at Sandringham – was accomplished in complete secrecy, despite saturation coverage of the entire estate by the press. It was on that holiday that Prince Charles cast his fierce and unusually malevolent blast of execration at a jostling mass of reporters, wishing them 'a happy New Year, and your editors a particularly nasty one.' It

didn't stop them. Although a weekend at Althorp had already been successfully arranged and privately spent, a dawn rendezvous at the Lambourn home of Charles' National Hunt trainer, Nick Gaselee, was rumbled in time for the photographers to be on the doorstep as the couple left.

So the cat-and-mouse game went on, until even the Queen was said to be impatient of the continuing uncertainty and to have blamed Charles for it as much as anything or anyone else. One journalist in particular was later to claim, on Fleet Street's behalf, the credit for having forced the couple into marriage under an implied threat that, if the friendship were broken off, the papers would have made Prince Charles out to be the biggest blackguard of the century. But it was Diana's impending trip to

visit her mother in Australia that prompted Charles to act. On 4th February he invited Diana to dine with him at Buckingham Palace. Then and there he popped the question, pointed out the disadvantages of saying 'Yes', and asked her to give him her answer when she and her family had had a chance to think it over. 'I wanted to give her time,' he explained later, 'to consider whether it was all going to be too awful.'

But Diana *had* already thought it over, and she accepted him on the spot. Next day, she told her flatmates of her decision before leaving for Australia – where, of course, the press were again waiting for her. Evidently Mrs Shand Kydd had no qualms about Diana's intentions. She was convinced that Diana loved Charles and, as she was later to say, 'I greatly approve of my daughters marrying men they love'. So when Diana returned to Britain – almost unnoticed while the press concentrated on Prince Andrew's 21st birthday – she was able to confirm her decision, and the engagement was effectively concluded. The settlement was not attended by the best of omens. The following day, Diana was again at Lambourn watching Charles taking the

gave a dinner party at Windsor Castle in honour of their engagement, and two days later Lady Fermoy held another one at her Eaton Square residence, at which Diana was joined by her brother Charles, and Jane and Robert Fellowes.

The man in the street had grown rather indifferent to the six-month-long orchestration of rumour, and the speculation had in any event become patchy and stale. Even a small report in *The Times* on 24th February that the Prince's engagement to Lady Diana was expected that day raised few eyebrows, and far fewer serious hopes. But at eleven o'clock that morning, the Lord Chamberlain, Lord Maclean – the man eventually detailed to mastermined the wedding – announced the betrothal in the

Queen Mother's horse Allibar for a training gallop. On their way back to the stables, the horse collapsed and died, and Diana shared with Charles his sudden, uncomprehending grief at a seemingly unjust and certainly frustrating tragedy. But there was no time for prolonged sadness. That weekend the Queen

presence, and on the instructions, of the Queen, to an audience of over three hundred people gathered to witness or take part in an Investiture at Buckingham Palace. The news was released simultaneously on radio and television and through the press, and the Palace immediately became the focal point for crowds

diamonds surrounding a single, large sapphire, which had cost Charles the equivalent of almost a tenth of that year's Duchy of Cornwall revenue – £28,500.

It was illustrative of the growing media interest, and indeed its influence, in matters of this kind that the Queen considered it necessary, if not desirable, to allow her son and future daughter-in-law to be interviewed, once for the papers and once for television and radio, as well as being filmed and photographed that afternoon in the grounds of the Palace. The wisdom of filmed interviews was called into question after the unfortunate example of Princess Anne and Captain Mark Phillips shortly before their wedding eight years earlier, and indeed Charles and Diana fared little better, their nerves and the privately intimate, and publicly banal, nature of the subject-matter making it difficult for them not to feel inhibited. 'Of course we are in love,' said Diana in answer to one superfluous question. 'Whatever "in love" means,' checked Charles, rather self-consciously, and looking immediately as if he wished he hadn't. Diana revealed that she had never thought about the twelve-year age gap between them; a confession which, if it was true, almost defies comment. But Charles defended her, and himself: 'You are only as young as you think you are,' he said. 'Diana will certainly keep me young.'

from all over London. Among them was Lord Spencer, snapping and filming away to record the event for his family archive, and his wife Raine, who surely voiced more than her own feelings when she said she was 'very pleased that it's all been resolved.'

Diana was already at the Palace when the news broke. She had had her hair done for the occasion at 8.30 that morning, though her hairdresser, the soon-to-be-famous Kevin Shanley, said that he had never suspected the reason for such an unusually early appointment. Prince Andrew, on special leave from helicopter training at RAF Culdrose, was also there, and joined the family for a special lunch. It was here that Diana wore for the first time her white-gold engagement ring of fourteen

o ended the demanding and difficult saga of how a Prince of Wales woos and wins his lady in modern times. It compares appallingly, from the participants' point of view, with the discreet and respectful manner in which such procedures were accomplished even as recently as the immediate post-war period. But the British monarchy has since then learned to live and indeed cope with the potential intrusions into the private lives of its members, inevitable consequences of the publicity machine which records relentless details of its public activities as a matter of course. It must be said that both Prince Charles, who had

stages of preparing a book about royal gardens, he was reputedly to have taken Diana out on the night her engagement became public, but it is in truth doubtful that he was anything but a sporting red herring during that delicate time. In 1984, he himself married into quasi-royalty: his wife was Alexandra, daughter of the White Russian Prince Michael Cantacuzene.) Meanwhile, deprived of real grounds for complaint or scandal on Diana's engagement, most of Fleet Street did the decent thing and rejoiced with the royal couple, and indeed the nation. The *Morning Star*, however, turned predictably to spite and criticised her decision to marry 'a domineering layabout, for the sake of a few lousy foreign holidays'. And almost alone among

tolerated over a decade of speculation about his possible marriage partner, and Diana who, twelve years his junior, endured her baptism of fire with consummate good grace, had both proved themselves equal to some of the worst excesses of public exposure at a time of most intense personal pressure.

Without doubt, the following months gave Prince Charles a new lease of life. Haunted for years by the need to choose a wife who was also acceptable to his future subjects, he was overwhelmed by the way the British public took Diana immediately and unreservedly to their hearts. The newspapers were saturated with facts and figures about her, from the eminence of her ancestry to the endearing details about her propensity to bite her nails and giggle. Any attempts to discover skeletons in the cupboard of Virtue proved bootless, a couple of papers having only her brief, platonic relationship with a Guards officer to show for their unceasing efforts to besmirch her reputation. (He was George Plumptre, a son of the 21st Baron Fitzwalter, whose family has been undistinguished by royal connections since the time of Mary Tudor. Then in the final

over six hundred Members of Parliament, Willie Hamilton added another chapter to his long history of Crown-baiting, anticipating 'a winter of phoney romance' and 'six months of mush'.

For Diana personally, it was six months of change, hard work, and not a little mental strain. The most fundamental changes were obvious – the farewell to the little ones at the Young England Kindergarten, the move from her very own flat to the immensity of Clarence House, the inescapable presence of personal detectives, the substitution of her nippy little red Mini Metro for the suave, gracious dimensions of gleaming black royal limousines, the bowing and scraping from all and sundry, and above all the immediate inability to move around London without being trailed and anticipated by huge crowds of curious people, or filmed and photographed by hordes of pressmen now released from any remaining constraints by the

new-found legitimacy of their purpose. She faced up to the prospect and the eventual reality with incredible confidence and a dash of courage. On her first official night out she wore a dress which has since become famous – the strapless black taffeta number with a neckline which threatened to draw style into conflict with modesty – and she bore the gasps of amazement and popping of flashbulbs with the cheekiest of grins, royal or otherwise. It was the first in a long line of examples of her ability to combine youth, novelty and chic in her choice of wardrobe.

It was also her way of giving notice that she was not one to be frightened off easily. She took part in very few official engagements before her wedding, but when she did appear before the public she showed instant charm, a modicum of native wit, and a naturalness which took many people by surprise. At first, having your hands kissed by schoolboys, or stooping down to show children your teeth, were not considered ways for aspiring royalty to behave, but the common touch struck chords where it mattered, and before long the walkabout befitted Diana's style as if it had been invented specifically for her. In fact it seemed almost inappropriate that she should on these occasions be included in the stilted, perfectionist jargon of the Court Circular, but there she was – 'the Lady Diana Spencer' – recorded in black and white alongside the Prince of Wales in the most up-market daily diary in the world.

The Palace were even busy struggling to explain to a bemused public the protocol surrounding her title on her forthcoming marriage. It caused some surprise when they announced that 'the Princess of Wales' and 'Diana, Princess of

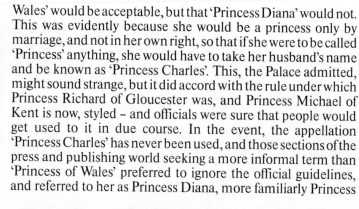

Wales' would be acceptable, but that 'Princess Diana' would not. This was evidently because she would be a princess only by marriage, and not in her own right, so that if she were to be called 'Princess' anything, she would have to take her husband's name and be known as 'Princess Charles'. This, the Palace admitted, might sound strange, but it did accord with the rule under which Princess Richard of Gloucester was, and Princess Michael of Kent is now, styled – and officials were sure that people would get used to it in due course. In the event, the appellation 'Princess Charles' has never been used, and those sections of the press and publishing world seeking a more informal term than 'Princess of Wales' preferred to ignore the official guidelines, and referred to her as Princess Diana, more familiarly Princess

Di, and even more simply, and affectionately, Di.

Behind the scenes, she was being coached in protocol and practice by Lady Susan Hussey, the Queen's senior lady-in-waiting, whose work with Diana was to be rewarded by a place among Prince William's six godparents, and eventually a DCVO from the Queen. With Lady Susan only a step or two behind her on the grand ceremonial occasions – lunch with the President of Ghana, dinner with the King of Saudi-Arabia, the Garter ceremony, Royal Ascot and the Trooping – Diana quickly learned that it was possible never to put a foot wrong. And from the day of her engagement to this, only a pedant would claim that she ever has. Indeed, so well did she respond that plans were early set afoot for a couple of major royal tours, to Australasia and Canada, to be completed within a year of her wedding.

eanwhile, Diana learned how to endure some of those disadvantages of which Prince Charles had warned her. Had she, like him, been historically minded, she might have recalled the plaintive words of Queen Mary, shortly after she became Queen Consort in 1910. 'The position,' she had written to a favourite aunt, 'is no bed of roses.' The present Queen Mother no doubt experienced the same feeling in the early weeks of her husband's reign, coming as it did hard on the heels of the traumas of King Edward VIII's abdication; and perhaps the Queen herself found the first few months of her reign fraught with difficulties she had never had cause to envisage. Certainly Diana who, in the television interview on the day of her engagement had proclaimed – with a confidence which, in a nineteen-year-old girl, had possibly been equalled only by Queen Victoria on her accession – that she never had any doubts about what she was doing, must have been

Airport, tears streaming down her cheeks, as she watched her fiancé leave for five long weeks in New Zealand and Australia. Despite the pre-wedding activity that was to keep her busy during his absence, her sense of isolation could not have been alleviated by growing reports of disaffection, as one left-wing local councillor after another protested stridently against the extravagance of the forthcoming wedding, nor by the appearance of a weekly series in the satirical magazine *Private Eye*, called *Born to be Queen*, which presented some pretty unlikely interpretations of life behind Palace doors, and depicted Diana as an ingenuous girl who realised too late that she had lost rather more than she had gained.

In real life, she might have believed that when, shortly after Prince Charles returned to Britain from his tour of Australasia, a rather more squalid matter came to their notice. During his visit, Prince Charles had stayed at the private residence of Sinclair Hill in New South Wales. Mr Hill was, and still is, a close friend of the

seriously assailed by misgivings within a matter of weeks.

The disadvantages were quickly encountered. Though we regard the Royal Family as a close-knit entity, it leads one of the most disruptive existences in the Western world. Diana discovered this to her cost, only a month after her engagement. At the end of March, she sat in the VIP lounge at Heathrow

Prince's and, as we have seen, was his polo coach for several years. He had gone to the trouble of installing in his house a private telephone for the sole use of the Prince, who needed to keep in touch with his family and fiancée back home. Despite the precaution of bypassing the national telecommunications network, it was claimed that some of the Prince's conversations with the Queen, and with Diana, had been surreptitiously recorded on tape. In addition to the obviously very personal nature of the calls, the revelation of which would understandably cause dismay, Charles was alleged to have passed on some embarrassingly unflattering references about Mr Malcolm Fraser, the then Prime Minister of Australia, whom he had necessarily met several times during his visit.

Tapes had been acquired by a freelance journalist, Simon Regan, the author some years previously of the book *Charles, the Clown Prince*, and he eventually sold the rights to his article based on the transcripts of the tapes to the German weekly magazine *Die Aktuelle*. The news caused great distress to the young couple, who were then trying to enjoy a short break together at Balmoral before resuming their duties, as well as immediate and feverish activity between the Palace and its lawyers, Farrer and Co. Believing then that the tapes might be genuine, and on the failure of diplomatic moves to discourage the imminent publication of the article, Charles and Diana obtained an injunction in Nuremberg on the very eve of publication. The editor of the German magazine had, however,

anticipated the prohibition. Printing was deliberately commenced earlier than usual, and by the time the injunction was legally served, several thousand copies had been printed and were in the course of distribution – thus effectively nullifying the injunction.

Almost a million copies were produced by the end of that week – about half as many again as normal – and although the British government prohibited the entry of copies of the magazine into the United Kingdom, a few versions of the article did appear in Northern Ireland, Scotland and Northern England by way of an Irish newspaper which had secured the right to reproduce parts of it in Eire. By then, however, the Palace had been able to study the entire contents of the tapes, and to establish that they were not genuine. A week later it was revealed, after a three-week investigation by Australian police and Federal Intercom officials, that none of the telephone

conversations could have been bugged, and that it would have been totally impossible to monitor the Prince's calls.

Diana had also to cope, in those early days, with what at one time seemed a press campaign to encourage popular antipathy towards members of her own family. Much of the effort was expended against her 'step-grandmother', Barbara Cartland, the author of some three hundred novels full of young, aristocratic and pure virgin love, which some found romantic and readable, and others found gushing and unrealistic. It was imagined that she might use the forthcoming royal wedding to plug or justify some of her past utterances on the sanctity of marriage, and the sheer exquisite romance of a pure young couple falling in love. In effect, she hardly had the chance. An ill-concealed contempt, particularly from the gossip columns of the tabloid press, burst into frenzied criticism after disclosures that Miss Cartland had helped to arrange for British Airways to bring over parties of wealthy Americans to visit the newly-famous Spencers at Althorp, and take tea with them for an all-in sum of £900 a head.

Although the fury at this supposed 'cashing in' on the royal wedding died down when it was discovered that the tour had been arranged many months before the engagement was announced, the affair soured those early weeks – as indeed did the lesser matter of the allegations, the full veracity of which they denied, that the Spencers were now charging preposterous sums for photographers to take pictures of their Northamptonshire home and its contents. Though the Spencers remained

place which might otherwise go to a younger member of the family. Later, something nearer the real truth came out when she complained that she was 'sick to death' of the royal wedding, which she described as 'a frightful bore' which everyone had spoiled by being 'so horrid and bitchy'.

These were trying times for a 19-year-old girl, but hardly as alarming as the incident in the Mall when the Queen was fired at as she rode to that June's Trooping ceremony, nor as tumultuous as the almost uncontrollable press interest in Diana as the day of her wedding approached. On her final weekend as a single woman, she attended a polo match at Tidworth in which Prince Charles took part. A huge contingent of photographers descended upon the enclosure, though not with any thought of polo. While Diana was a spectator, it was *her* every movement that interested them as, no doubt with hopeless optimism, she tried to enjoy the afternoon's entertainment. After several attempts to move away from a writhing mass of inhumanity jockeying in ugly fashion for position, she burst into tears and, head in hands, was led away to a waiting car by her companion Lady Romsey. Prince Charles kept his patience with the press – a gesture as surprisingly tolerant as it was futile, for the following day almost exactly the same thing happened at an international polo match at Windsor.

In the three days between then and the wedding, Diana was mercifully out of the public eye, except for her visit to St Paul's

untroubled, by the time the wedding invitations were out, Barbara Cartland had decided to quit. She declined an invitation sent to her from Lord Spencer's batch of fifty, on the ostensible grounds that the occasion was essentially one for young people, and she in her eightieth year did not think it right to take up a

Cathedral for a last-minute rehearsal. It went well, gave no cause for concern, and was carried out without leaking a single detail to an avidly curious public – although the use of a very long length of makeshift train might have given away some clue as to the design of the bridal dress. Meanwhile half the country, it

seemed, was converging on London, establishing territorial claims on pavements from Palace to Cathedral in preparation for the great day. For Diana, it was a time for the nervousness that comes with long, enforced waiting. On the very eve of the wedding, when London celebrated with the most monumental firework display for over 230 years, duly attended by almost all the Royal Family, she stayed at Clarence House and settled for an early night. With the certain prospect of being woken up at six the next morning, that wasn't a bad idea.

The couple's decision to hold the wedding at St Paul's Cathedral caused some surprise at first, and not a little hurt pride among the Dean and Chapter of Westminster Abbey, where almost every royal wedding had been staged since the marriage in 1922 of Princess Mary, the only daughter of King George V and Queen Mary, to the 6th Earl of Harewood. Although the possibility of a variation of venue in 1981 had not been totally discarded, the almost sanctified tradition which bought three generations of royal brides to Westminster had seemed immutable.

For Prince Charles, there were thought to be other considerations. With his close family ties, he doubtless bore in mind that in recent years two particularly enjoyable occasions – his mother's Silver Jubilee and his grandmother's eightieth birthday – had been celebrated by thanksgiving services at St

Paul's. He was as inevitably mindful too that, less than two years previously, it was to Westminster Abbey that he had gone to mourn, with the bitter grief of an admiring great-nephew for an admirable great-uncle, the death of Earl Mountbatten of Burma, assassinated in August 1979 by the IRA. That sombre ceremony in the beautiful but severely Gothic Abbey may well have proved too memorable for the Prince to have chosen it for his own nuptials.

St Paul's had the additional advantages of light, architectural warmth and, most significantly of all, space. It was reckoned that the building was capable of seating at least five hundred more people than Westminster Abbey, and although the wedding was essentially a private occasion, it was clear that the distinction between the Royal Family's private and official connections could not be drawn sufficiently sharply to exclude large numbers of people from the necessity of being invited. 'It is not

every day', said Queen Victoria in 1858, 'that one marries the eldest daughter of the Queen of England.' Given that that was said in a different context, a large seating capacity could be justified now on the the grounds that the marriage of the Prince of Wales was a similarly rare occurrence.

That wedding has since become almost legendary. The combination of grandeur, nobility, emotion, enormous tension, popular enthusiasm, exquisite timing, a feast of mind-boggling statistics, and the fundamental human simplicity festooned in its fairy-tale trappings, gripped just about the whole of the United Kingdom and much of the civilised world. Despite the outward ecclesiastical form, the religious content, and indeed purpose of the occasion was swamped by the blaze of colour and light, the gorgeous music and the eminence of the invited guests – royal,

political, diplomatic, family and friends. The buzz and pop of photographic apparatus punctuated every word spoken by the Archbishop of Canterbury, while his intoned lines signifying each stage in the service, though greeted by a respectful silence within, brought forth almost heretical bursts of cheers and applause from the thousands round the Cathedral, and their sound washed through the seventeenth-century

stonework into the building itself. There was plenty to disturb the holy thoughts of everyone. Both Diana and Charles misspoke their lines, some of the younger bridesmaids yawned and fidgeted, the Queen Mother pressed a small hankie to her eyes every now and then, and the Queen grinned delightedly as a rather over-enthusiastic choir-master sent a choir-stall lampshade flying while conducting one of the anthems.

Above all, heads persistently bobbed and necks were craned to see how Diana coped with her appalling ordeal. Most were frankly staggered that she did so with what seemed consummate ease. She managed that great, enveloping dress of hers with supreme elegance and poise, and even supported her father as he supposedly led her up the aisle. He, the victim of a massive cerebral haemorrhage in 1978, was still unsteady on his pins, and wandered at times dangerously far from the centre of that unending red carpet. Diana's one verbal mistake was soon put into perspective by an affectionate glance and, later, a furtive squeeze of the hand from Prince Charles. The firm confidence of her demeanour reflected her decision *not* to promise to obey, and when the kissing, handshaking and congratulations over the signing of the registers were done, she reappeared triumphantly on the arm of her husband. Suddenly, it seemed, her head was held unusually high, her eyes looking fully ahead: gone was the childish, rather embarrassed lowering of face and eyelids which had characterised many of her public appearances to date. Her emergence from St Paul's itself to receive and acknowledge a thunder of cheering was the high point of the morning. She smiled, laughed and waved in her own right, a heroine – almost, for a brief moment, a goddess. She had indeed arrived.

Surely Prince Charles could not have believed his luck. After all his searching, questioning and waiting, he had done what he always said was so difficult for a man in his position – to get it right from the word go. The fantastic, unstoppable reception he and his wife received as they travelled back to Buckingham Palace and later appeared no fewer than four times on its draped and tasselled balcony, left him in no doubt as to Diana's storming popularity. Part of it was due to what without close inspection appeared to be an almost childish naivety of the sort

relax, and wallow in the unaccustomed peace of it all. The only known lasting record of the three-day stay reposes in a few photographs taken just before they left, and now on display in that part of the house still open to the public.

The touring part of the honeymoon – a twelve-day cruise in *Britannia* from Gibraltar to Port Said – was equally private, much of it spent socialising with the Royal Yacht's crew both in

that led to that celebrated kiss on the balcony. She had shrugged her shoulders before giving it, as if to cock a snook at stuffy royal traditions, and immediately afterwards she cast a look of helpless apology towards Prince Philip, which suggested that she had, rather too late, had second thoughts. But the incident delighted everyone; it provoked calls for more of the same, and made headlines and front-page pictures all the way round the world the next day. Diana was already international property.

'For the first few months, perhaps years, of her new life,' wrote Prince Charles' biographer shortly before the wedding, 'the Princess will be able to enjoy a good measure of the privacy so unfamiliar to her husband.' In fact, any privacy she enjoyed did not last longer than three months, and even then it was a fragile luxury. Broadlands, the Mountbatten home where she and Charles spent the first part of their honeymoon, was kept from the inquisitive only by a massive police presence both on the ground and in the air. Diana ventured out only rarely, leaving Prince Charles to go out salmon-fishing in the river Test, or tramping the 6,000-acre estate. She was content to unwind,

the bars and in private suites. On one occasion Diana turned up, uninvited, at a party the crew were having, and reportedly played the piano and sang with them. On another, she invited them to a private video showing of the wedding ceremony. When the couple did venture onto land, during the journey through the Greek Islands, it was only after an advance party of Household staff and security men had cleared the proposed areas for safety and privacy. The stone-wall secrecy maintained by the Palace both before and during the honeymoon did not prevent newspapers from endeavouring to track and discover *Britannia's* whereabouts, and considerable sums of money changed hands in the attempt. Only in Egypt did the press catch up with the Yacht, as Charles and Diana exchanged courtesies with President Sadat and his wife.

The royal couple's two days in Egypt began what could have

been a lifetime's friendship with the ill-fated President. He was charmed by Diana's spontaneous, outgoing confidence, expressed in public by the kiss she gave him just before leaving Hurghada Airport for Scotland. The news, barely two months later, that he had been assassinated during a military parade in Cairo brought home to Diana – as if the Trooping the Colour incident the previous June had failed to do so – the horrifying dangers of being the wife of a future monarch, with its sometimes unbearable necessity of being in full public view. But the meeting with the Sadats had already forged an important

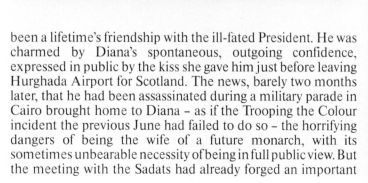

friendship for Diana. Though Prince Charles attended the President's funeral in Egypt alone, Diana was to play hostess to his widow a year later when she came to London for a three-day private visit.

Anticipating the further and unwelcome attentions of the press during the remainder of their summer holiday at Balmoral, Charles and Diana invited them up for a photocall just a few days after their own arrival from Egypt. There is a nice story, probably apocryphal, that Prince Charles and his Private Secretary had fixed the date for this facility for 18th August, without consulting Diana, and that she was furious when she discovered that she had been left out of the discussions. She

refused to give her consent until only shortly before the press-call was due, and then, as if to emphasise her right to have her say, put the date of the appointment back by one day, to 19th August.

However that may be, it brought the press of Britain and Europe to their doorstep in droves. Over seventy photographers made the 600-mile journey from London: one of them who ran out of petrol at five in the morning cheerfully persuaded a Scottish garage-owner out of bed with the promise of a crisp fiver in addition to the price of a full tank. The photo session, on the banks of the River Dee, was a great success: one photographer presented Diana with a bouquet of flowers, a gesture of appreciation which also added interest to his pictures; another decided to play dirty and ran towards the royal couple, camera poised for a unique close-up, before being hauled back by

bodyguards. Charles twitted them all, making great play of their unsuccessful attempts to find the Royal Yacht in the Mediterranean, while Diana, echoing the thoughts of Queen Victoria, said that Balmoral was the best place in the world.

She was certainly in the right place to be reminded of the events that had bought her here as Princess of Wales, and Balmoral holds many romantic associations for her. Tales of her boredom with the Highlands of Scotland, a hardy perennial form of press entertainment, lack credibility in the face of the evidence that she and Charles willingly spend several weekends

a year herein addition to the main royal summer vacation. When the Queen is not in residence, the Castle itself is shut and they set up home at Craigowan Lodge, one of the many smaller residences on the huge estate.

But equally important in Diana's affections is the eighteenth-century mansion to which Charles first took her in October 1980 – Highgrove House, said to have cost the Prince almost £1 million when he bought it earlier that year from the late Viscount Macmillan of Ovenden. For, while Craigowan Lodge and, for that matter, the Wales' official residence at Kensington

Palace are the property of the Queen, it is Highgrove that Diana can stamp with her own identity – and has. Shortly after her engagement, she was supervising its redecoration and renovation, co-opting the services of David Hicks, an interior designer who also happens to be married to Charles' cousin, the former Lady Pamela Mountbatten. An enormous amount of restructuring had to be done to make the huge and rather rambling house the homely weekend retreat it now is, though Diana has retained many of its distinctive features, including the huge tapestries and the massive marble fireplace in the drawing room, complete with dolphin embellishments.

 s Princess of Wales, Diana's first official public duty was to visit her principality. Almost exactly three months after her wedding, she accompanied Prince Charles on a three-day whistle-stop tour of Wales, which turned out to be arguably the most stupendous of all royal visits there. It was not a very sophisticated trip, consisting as it did mainly of stopping at towns large and small, spending half an hour walking through crowds in the streets, or passing displays at leisure centres, or visiting castles, churches, hospitals and theatres. But it was a visit of immense goodwill,

especially in the face of new threats from Welsh Nationalists who, after a lengthy quietus following the investiture of Prince Charles in 1969, were back in the news with schemes to upset plans for the tour. Huge security operations became indispensible as the first day of the visit approached: the whereabouts of known extremists were checked, buildings bordering the royal routes were scrutinised, and last-minute thorough searches took place after an incendiary device was found at Pontypridd. The tour itself was not without its ration of protest incidents – anti-royalist or anti-English banners, hostile shouting and chanting *en masse*, stink bombs and the spraying of the royal car with aerosol paint – but overall the whirlwind programme incorporating over a dozen towns and every county was a resounding success.

Diana was of course the person everyone came to see, and on the first day she tactfully wore an outift of very Welsh design and

in the equally Welsh colours of red and green. In spite of the bitterly cold weather, thousands of people waited long hours to greet her and they were well rewarded as she spent much of her time on walkabouts talking to children and shaking hands with their mothers. On one occasion, she stopped to embrace a child suffering from spina bifida who had been drawn up to the front of the crowd in a wheelchair. Later on at Rhyl, she was asked by a seven-year-old boy if he could give her a kiss too – she said yes, so he did. Also in line for a kiss was Lord Snowdon who, as Constable of Caernarvon Castle, greeted his nephew and new niece as they arrived to visit the site of Prince Charles' investiture. With these three much-reported gestures, Diana made it plain that she would concede little of her natural, innovative approach to the rather more staid traditions of royalty's contact with its subjects.

On the second day, it was the turn of south-west Wales to welcome the royal couple. This time the weather was thoroughly unwelcoming, with heavy and persistent rain to accompany the dismal cold. But again, spirits remained high.

The tone of indifference to the weather was set by Diana herself, whose dashing ostrich-feather hat became bedraggled and cloying as she continued her walkabout in the rain, regardless of personal discomfort. It was with some difficulty that Prince Charles, who was a noticeably solicitous husband throughout the tour, eventually persuaded her to use an umbrella. Much to the cynicism of Welsh Nationalists, the Princess had learned to say a few words of Welsh – *Diolch yn fawr* (Thank you very much) – as she received numerous gifts of flowers, Welsh dolls and chocolates from people in the crowds.

At St David's, they both attended a service of thanksgiving to commemorate the 800th anniversary of the Cathedral, with Prince Charles reading the lesson in English and Welsh. There was, however, an embarrassing moment when Diana's Welsh utterly failed her. At one point in the service, *Land of My Fathers* was sung in Welsh, and while the Prince sang lustily, Diana

bowed her head apologetically and almost in shame. But embarrassment was soon forgotten as, ten minutes behind schedule, the couple visited Haverfordwest, where they mingled freely with the crowds, paying special attention to a group of mentally handicapped people. Then on to Carmarthen, where crowds six deep waved and cheered in the appalling weather: the rain sheeted down, flowing through the streets and slopping over the shoes of the royal visitors, who were almost standing in the gutters to reach their admirers.

It was clear by now that both Prince Charles, and Diana in particular, had taken the principality by storm. On the third day, though there was more rain at Pontypridd, the demonstrations of public affection for them were greater than ever, as if its citizens were striving to outdo the welcomes they received in previous towns. At Builth Wells, they visited an agricultural showground and were given a Welsh Black heifer and a Welsh Mountain ewe for their farm at Highgrove. Eventually, the couple arrived at Cardiff, where an ecstatic crowd gathered to see them open a huge recreation and community complex.

They completed their tour with the ceremony at Cardiff's City Hall in which Diana received the freedom of the city to a heartwarming standing ovation. The ceremony was as impressive and charged with fervour as Diana's own words of thanks were simple, hurried, and rather unconvincing: 'I realise it is a great honour. I am glad to be Princess of such a wonderful place.' She hoped that she would be able to pay future visits to Wales, and that she would be able to speak more Welsh by then. At that point, it seemed as if a second visit could not be far away; the goodwill engendered by the huge, uniformly affectionate crowds and by the visitors they had all come to cheer, was

testimony to the fact that, even in this hard-pressed principality, the magic of the monarchy had been successfully worked again.

Part of that final day in Wales had been spent at the maternity unit of Llwynpia Hospital, where Diana indulged in baby talk with expectant and nursing mothers. Prince Charles was no less interested, and during a conversation with one mother, let slip his approval of the idea that husbands should be present at the

birth of their children. 'I am sure that' a very good thing,' he said – then seeing the television cameras and eyeing the reporters, wryly added, 'I expect I shall get a lot of letters about that.' Little did anyone suspect the news the following week would bring! For, less than a fortnight after her first round of official engagements had started, Diana announced that she was pregnant. The then Lord Mayor of London, Sir Ronald Gardner-Thorpe, was given the first opportunity to encapsulate the rapturous public response. Only two hours after the official announcement was made, he was hosting the new parents-to-be at a Guildhall luncheon, held to mark the City of London's appreciation of what it rightly regarded as a sign of sublime royal favour – that the Prince and Princess had held their wedding ceremony at St Paul's Cathedral, within the City's bounds. The cold light of history has already cast a disdainful sneer on the

Mayor's indulgent reference to babies as 'bits of stardust blown from the hand of God', and to the memory of the Waleses' marriage as 'a gold ingot that has now been supremely hallmarked by this morning's announcement that Your Royal Highnesses are to be blessed with a child, for which we all rejoice.' At the time, however, the sentiment and its expression seemed hardly overdone. The country made little secret of the fact that it was positively thrilled with the news that this paragon of all that was good and sensible, wifely, golden and glittering

was to provide the Crown of a thousand years with its next monarch but one.

Indeed, it is doubtful if even Diana, with her own recent experience of the intensity of public curiosity in and admiration for her, anticipated the enormity of the reaction which her news attracted. Anybody who for a moment considered that the Wedding of the Century, so excellently orchestrated to its timely and colourful climax, had exhausted popular interest in the nation's first family, found himself in a hopeless minority.

Crowds, already accustomed to assembling in their thousands to jostle for a glimpse of Diana on every occasion, seemed to double and treble with each succeeding appearance. The newspapers, when they had got over the initial shock of having their speculative thunder stolen, filled their columns with medical advice, royal baby anecdotes, projected horoscopes, and the everyday minutiae of impending motherhood, as if the seven months remaining until the expected birth would simply not be enough. (It is, in fact, worth remembering that in those seven months, hardly a day passed without some new or rehashed angle on the forthcoming event finding its way into Fleet Street's daily offerings). Some columnists remembered that, back in September, Diana had made the occasional day trip

from Balmoral to London, and concluded that the official reason for her visits – to see an exhibition of her wedding gifts at St James's Palace, or to revisit her old kindergarten – were merely intended to put the press off the scent while she also saw her gynaecologist George Pinker. Others recalled the cosy remarks both she and Prince Charles had made when they toured that maternity ward in South Wales at the end of October, and kicked themselves for having been decent enough not to put two and two together. Even Harry Arnold, ace royal-watcher for

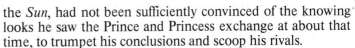

the *Sun*, had not been sufficiently convinced of the knowing looks he saw the Prince and Princess exchange at about that time, to trumpet his conclusions and scoop his rivals.

It was a fact – and it caused great satisfaction at the Palace – that the news, and the speed of its telling, caught everyone on the hop. Quite apart from the fact that few had got over the vivid memory of the royal wedding and had not therefore begun to think of the Prince and Princess in the context of parenthood, there was every justification for not expecting them to start a family quite as early as they had obviously intended. Diana's youth had something to do with it: despite her mature bearing, she was still only twenty – an age which many young women regard as too young to be giving up the pleasures of comparative freedom for the demands and responsibilities of motherhood. In addition, her high-speed introduction to the specialised world of the Royal Family had thus far been at best basic, and although many types of duties were covered, many others were left unexplored. Among these were the royal visits abroad, and it was indeed a series of forthcoming tours – of Australia, New

Zealand and Canada – promised for 1982, which caused the early announcement of Diana's pregnancy. It was clear that they would have to be put off, and to have done this without explanation would have invited unhealthy speculation.

In the light of events, however, we may now reflect that other considerations might have been stronger in persuading the royal couple to start a family early. Diana's abiding love of children is now almost taken for granted, and the prospect of having her own was probably one she was unwilling to wait for. It is instructive that, after the announcement, Diana's former flatmates insisted that they were not surprised by the news. For his part, Prince Charles, then almost thirty-three, would equally understandably not want to submit to the experience of public (and possibly family) pressure on him to produce children, particularly with the memory fresh in his mind of the prolonged and sometimes onerous advice he had for so many years had to tolerate from those who thought he ought to be married. In addition, there was a more general, if emotionally nebulous concern to ensure the line of succession by producing a further direct heir to the Throne – a materialistic rather than spiritual desire, but inevitable given the strong dynastic nature of the institution of which he, and now his wife, was part.

The news brought the Spencers and the House of Windsor together once again in mutual delight and self-congratulation. The official announcement said that the Queen's immediate family was pleased, and that the Queen had been personally informed of the news some days before. She gave one of her luncheon parties that day, and the guests noticed how very relaxed and contented she seemed, looking, as one described it, 'definitely at peace with the world as everyone offered their congratulations.' Diana's father could not sufficiently express

his pleasure, but intimated how much his daughter had wanted a baby, and said what a marvellous mother she would make. Her own mother, Mrs Shand Kydd, said it was 'wonderful news', and hinted that she might just bend her own tee-total rules to celebrate it. Meanwhile, Barbara Cartland, soothed by the mollifying influence of the wedding and its aftermath, cooed contentedly and mused over the success of the love match. She looked forward to the beautiful baby which, she said, was always the result of a pregnancy conceived between two people truly in love. This sentiment was echoed by Harold Brooks-Baker of Debrett who anticipated 'the emergence of new royal genes of excellence.'

B y comparison with most royal pregnancies, Diana's was revolutionary. Princess Anne had broken the mould of concealment and secrecy in 1977 when, on occasion, she ventured out in mid-term wearing jeans and jumpers which did nothing to hide her condition, as a spectator at various equestrian events. Diana was the first to acknowledge not only that royalty did not have to be kept under wraps or cocooned within palace walls for the duration of pregnancy, but also that a balance between fulfilling official duties and avoiding physical stress could easily be achieved without conceding dignity. The old alibi – that a Princess 'will

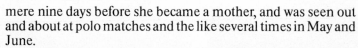

mere nine days before she became a mother, and was seen out and about at polo matches and the like several times in May and June.

This openness was not only typical of Diana's unforced quest for natural behaviour; it also added point to her official engagements and her style of carrying them out. Walkabouts, which she had already rescued from growing formality, became rewarding for visitor and spectator alike. Clusters of housewives and long lines of school-children rejoicing on their day off, found Diana's prospective motherhood something they could all chat about freely, inquisitively and with good grace and humour. She was bombarded with questions about it. Did she

not carry out any public engagements until further notice' – was not for her. Her diary was already booked up several months in advance, and other engagements were being considered. There was no virtue, Diana thought, in disappointing people for the sake of hiding a pregnancy with everybody knew existed and which, in a much more liberated society, could fairly effortlessly be accommodated. Indeed, she maintained her official book up to within five weeks of her confinement, attended the Trooping a

want a boy or a girl? When was it due? Had the names been chosen? Was she going in for any special diets? Was she making her own baby clothes? By and large, she was willing to answer them all. She thought that the baby's soundness was a more important consideration than its sex; she was delighted with the thousands of small gifts already flooding into Buckingham and Kensington Palaces; names had not yet been short-listed; and, yes, Prince Charles *was* taking a hearty interest in the proceedings, reading books about pre-natal exercises and baby-care and 'always telling me what to do'. In these impromptu conversations, those who were already mothers were treated very much as equals, and the inevitable comparisons were much mulled over and enjoyed. Surprisingly few feople – even the avowed enemies of the Crown and all it stands for – sought to trivialise these rather unspectacular revelations, or their constant retailing by newspaper and television. However commonplace the content, the basic approach was not to be mocked. The institution must keep in touch – and be seen to keep in touch – with its ultimate supporters. Diana may have done more to ensure this than many of her more restricted in-laws.

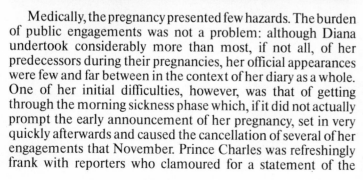

Medically, the pregnancy presented few hazards. The burden of public engagements was not a problem: although Diana undertook considerably more than most, if not all, of her predecessors during their pregnancies, her official appearances were few and far between in the context of her diary as a whole. One of her initial difficulties, however, was that of getting through the morning sickness phase which, if it did not actually prompt the early announcement of her pregnancy, set in very quickly afterwards and caused the cancellation of several of her engagements that November. Prince Charles was refreshingly frank with reporters who clamoured for a statement of the obvious: he told them that they all had wives and must therefore know the problems. On one occasion at Bristol, he apologised to his audience for not having been able to bring his wife, and cheerfully accepted all responsibility for her condition! But, despite an attempt to fulfil some later engagements, the indisposition seemed to go on and on. 'Nobody ever told me it would be as bad as this,' complained Diana at Chesterfield – and as less and less was seen of her right up to Christmas, it did seem as if she was suffering more prolonged and severe bouts of sickness than normal, and was powerless to shake them off.

There was a nasty incident the following month, when she

fell downstairs at Sandringham – an accident which was swiftly reported by Buckingham Palace, presumably as a precaution lest the worst should happen and require an explanation. But, generally speaking, the official bulletins confirmed that she was now 'perfectly well, except for the odd indisposition caused by her pregnancy', and the promise was that she would undertake a programme of engagements until early in April, and probably beyond. 'The Princess,' came the assurance, 'wants to carry out engagements for as long as she feels able and well enough.' For a short time the threat existed that she might not be well enough for much longer. Princess Michael of Kent let slip a remark that Diana was going through a phase of obsessively strict dieting, as an antidote to the inevitable process of weight gaining which accompanies advancing pregnancy and involves an addition to normal body weight of up to 24 pounds. Overwhelming advice flooded in from all quarters in a well-meant attempt to save Diana from imminent extinction. Eating for two was loudly praised, though the more cautious specified that little and often

was the watch-word, with lean meat, fish, cereal and dairy products predominating over sugar and carbohydrates.

But then, contrary as she has often been thought to be, Diana was spotted nipping out of her car into a sweet shop in the King's Road, and emerging again with a fistful of sweets and chocolates – an incident gaily passed off as a forgivable concession to her celebrated sweet tooth. There was little to support the theory that it represented a surrender to the attentions to which she was supposed to have been subjected in recent weeks – over-much publicity, a few spats with Prince Charles, the first movements of the baby – but some sections of the press milked the story for all it was worth. She was said to be looking decidedly peeky by mid-February, but Buckingham Palace insisted that she was 'perfectly fit and well' and would extend her programme of official engagements to take in the opening of a South London community centre barely a month before the expected birth.

Diana's early indifferent health was never forgotten by the press, who looked persistently for signs of subsequent

difficulties as the pregnancy progressed. In March, Diana accompanied Prince Charles to Cheltenham for an afternoon's racing on Gold Cup Day. Here she seemed to experience one of those unexplained black moods of which she had long been suspected, and which had contributed to the image of a woman with her own uncompromising set of likes and dislikes. Either she had not wanted to go to the races that day, or the weather was too cold for her, or there were deeper problems that onlookers could only speculate upon, but she certainly made no secret of having a pretty miserable time. She was noticeably distant with her husband, rarely smiling at him and visibly ignoring his attempts to engage her in conversation. Much of her time seemed to be spent brooding aimlessly, and dejectedly watching the crowds below. The newspapers made dramatic capital of it all, as they did a week later when, leaving London for Balmoral, Diana looked in no better humour, and resolutely failed to acknowledge the crowds which came to greet her and Prince Charles as they arrived that Sunday at Crathie Church for morning service.

It came as no surprise, therefore, to hear that her doctors had ordered her to have a complete rest – an announcement coupled with, and no doubt justifying, the revelation that the couple would spend part of April holidaying at the Prince's cottage 'Tamarisk' in the Isles of Scilly. The prospect thrilled the

Scillonians, and seemed to improve Diana's temperament immediately. It also left everyone wondering about her supposed deterioration in the first place, and commentators were kept busy piecing together a jigsaw of possibilities which included the pressures of moving house, the difficulty of adjusting to her new role, the preoccupation with security, and the intrusions into her privacy. It might have been as well simply to pass it all off as the sort of temporary depression or mild nervous fatigue invariably connected with pregnancy from time to time – an explanation which, in the light of the unremitting

good health and cheerful spirits in which Diana enjoyed the last two months before her confinement, is probably as good and sufficient as any. As her public engagements tailed off, sightings of her were confined to the polo fields of Ham, Windsor and the New Forest, where she was seen in the full bloom of approaching motherhood, and where there was no mistaking her evident enjoyment of life.

Despite minute scrutiny by the press, those seven months – which to Diana must have seemed like an age – passed off without undue controversy. The only unresolved question was

the choice of birthplace. Many people took it for granted in the early days that the baby – a possible future sovereign – would be born at Buckingham Palace. Others thought it might be Kensington Palace, birthplace of Queen Victoria and many other latter-day royals, or even Highgrove. Few people thought it remotely possible that Diana would choose to be confined in a hospital bed, and when the possibility was floated, the rumour immediately sprung to life that the Queen and her daughter-in-law had been locked in an insoluble argument on the matter. The Queen, ran the stories, insisted that the birth should take place within the Palace; Diana meanwhile stuck firm to her idea, much favoured by all royal mothers since the Duchess of Kent gave birth to her third and last child in 1970, of a hospital confinement. In fact, there was no material difference of opinion, far less pressure from the Queen. Whatever the preferences, it was cheaper, safer and less of an upheaval for all concerned to use hospital services. And again it was difficult to avoid the impression that the idea of breaking new ground appealed to Diana. It certainly did nothing to lessen her popularity.

Nevertheless, the decision was kept secret until the end. With perfect timing, Diana was installed in the Lindo Wing of St Mary's Hospital, Paddington on 21st June 1982, and before most other Britons were awake – thus, at the end of a very public pregnancy, not a single photographer recorded her arrival on this day of all days. She spent it in one of the hospital's standard rooms for private patients – one hundred and fifty square feet of it, costing around £1 per square foot per day. After a long, though not difficult labour lasting sixteen hours, the birth was accomplished; Diana was delivered of a 'beautiful' (to quote Prince Charles) baby, and Britain was presented with its next king but one. Both the lady and the nation expressed relief and joy, though Prince Charles hinted that his wife may have had a bit of a hard time. 'Give us a chance', he retorted to someone in the crowd who suggested a second baby ere long. 'You ask my wife. I don't think she will be too pleased just yet'.

But Diana looked pleased enough the next day when, almost thirty hours after her admission to hospital, she left again with her day-old son in her arms. There was no ritual or ceremony: she was wearing a shapeless, green, polka-dot dress which she had worn to a polo match three weeks earlier, and a pair of simple, flat, red shoes. She took her son from Prince Charles, who had carried him outside, and without more ado manoeuvred herself gently into her car and was immediately whisked off. Barring the crowd of spectators, photographers and policemen, it was no more or less of an occasion than befalls most newly-delivered mothers – the common touch again.

ccording to Diana's official pen-picture, 'Her Royal Highness' interests include dancing, music and painting. She is particularly concerned with anything to do with children.' It didn't provide much in the way of ideas for carving out her own public life, but it was a start.

Shortly after her marriage, she selected five charities for royal patronage, all of which in some way reflected those interests – the Malcolm Sargent Cancer Fund for Children, the Pre-School Playgroups Association, the Welsh National Opera, the Royal School for the Blind, and the Albany Trust – an East London organisation which assists the unemployed to secure decent social facilities. To these five she has since added three Commonwealth patronages – of the Canadian Junior Red Cross, the New Zealand College of Obstetricians and Gynaecologists, and The Princess of Wales's Children's Health Camp – and ten more British patronages and presidencies – those of the British Deaf Association, the Wales Craft Council, the Swansea Festival of Music and Arts, the Royal College of Physicians and Surgeons of Glasgow, the

National Children's Orchestra, the National Rubella Council, the British Red Cross Society's junior division, The Princess of Wales's Charities Trust, Birthright, Dr Barnardo's, and the London City Ballet.

Her patronage of this last is a commitment which reflects her one-time ambition to be a ballet dancer, which was frustrated by the fact that she grew too tall: she stands barely an inch shorter than Prince Charles. It is also a commitment which warms the cockles of the heart of the Ballet's founder, Harold King, as it was only after his persistent applications that he secured her services as Patron. In his efforts to do so, he persuaded her initially to attend some rehearsals, and eventually won her round. 'She was really interested in what makes dancers tick – what motivates them,' he said. 'That showed how keen she was. She wants to help as much as possible.' And she did. She saw more rehearsals – then in February 1984 went off on a much publicised visit to Norway by herself, to watch them give a performance of *Carmen* in Oslo. Meanwhile, the Princess of Wales's Charities Trust, which she launched late in 1982, began to pay off when the Royal Marsden Hospital received a body scanner, paid for from Trust funds, for the detection of cancer.

When, in November 1983, she became Patron of the National Rubella Council, she did so as the Council launched a

£2 million campaign to warn mothers-to-be of the dangers of German measles to the unborn child. 'Immunisation is quick, easy and painless,' Diana told an audience at Lancaster House during the inauguration ceremony, 'and the side effects are trivial.' She did, however, regret that there was no alternative to injections, and revealed that she would prefer to see immunisation by means of sugar-lump treatment because 'needles terrify me.' For some people, the royal boost to the continuing attempts to lessen embryo and infant mortality came none too soon. Diana was clearly a godsend to one woman who had encountered an alarming degree of medical indifference and even ignorance when she herself had asked to have tests for this purpose. 'One hopes,' she said, 'that this will have the effect of making doctors' practices and family planning clinics more aware of women's fears.'

Diana's officially stated interest in music seems to be a rather one-sided affair. Her grandmother, Ruth Lady Fermoy, has for many years been a leading light in the King's Lynn Music Festival; Prince Charles is, of course, a dedicated classical music lover; and Diana's friend Caroline Pride, as we have seen, has a talent for classical music that might, one would not unreasonably expect, have rubbed off onto her. But she does not seem to have maintained a natural interest in what we rather too readily called serious music. From the very first, the impression was given to the public that she was more at home listening to the cassette offerings of the latest pop groups, and for a time the story did the rounds that she could often be seen jinking down the corridors of Buckingham Palace, carrying a pocket tape

recorder, and sporting earphones planted firmly over her head, blissfully unaware of the presence or approach of the Queen, or indeed of any of her royal relations. She has certainly been a great fan of Duran Duran. When she told them that they were her favourite band, they offered her free membership of their fan club – though Diana politely refused. She also likes the music of Dire Straits, who presented her with a compact disc collection of their albums – which, incidentally, she was unable to play until the Japanese firm Sony stepped in and lent her a disc record player. Meanwhile, Diana has attended concerts given by Neil Diamond and Barry Manilow, and is even reported to have expressed an interest in meeting Boy George.

She has for a long time been an avid listener to Capital Radio, who, just before her wedding, invited both her and Prince Charles to submit ten of their favourite items of music which the radio's disc jockeys offered to play on the air as a wedding

present. Diana's preferences consisted almost entirely of pop and golden oldies, whereas Prince Charles put in a formidable list of heavy classics. Unfortunately, and for reasons unexplained, Buckingham Palace prevented the station from broadcasting the music. It would have been an instructive exercise in demonstrating what has often been described as a fairly wide cultural difference between the Princess and her husband. Indeed, Diana has been heard to say that she is bored by classical music and opera, despite Prince Charles' maturing interest in these art forms. She goes with him to classical concerts both officially and privately, but says that she extracts 'a promise each time that he will take me dancing in return.'

Diana is in fact a fairly accomplished ballroom dancer – an unusual quality for someone of her years in an age which has

seen ballroom dancing decline almost to the point of ridicule. She has taken the floor with Prince Charles in public a few times, and is no slouch when it comes to opening the evening's dancing with a whirling quickstep or foxtrot. But, as if to justify that official commitment she has to the London City Ballet, she still attends dance sessions on her own account. At the end of 1983, for instance, she booked herself in for a series of six lessons at the Chiswick studio of Merle Park, the director of the Royal Ballet, amid speculation that she was combining her old interest with a course of aerobics.

The official revelation that Diana had an interest in painting came as something of a surprise, and its truth has never been particularly obvious to the public. One can hardly claim that she has been seen dodging into art galleries in her spare time, and the rare occasions on which she has visited one as part of her public engagements have not been attended by overt evidence of her fascination. From that point of view, Prince Philip and Princess Michael of Kent, and even Prince Charles and Prince Andrew, seem to be streets ahead of her, yet it is already clear that Diana is not without artistic ability. Just after Prince William's first birthday, she lent a drawing she had done of him

to an exhibition to raise funds for Mencap, the charity which assists mentally handicapped children and adults. It shows the toddler Prince in short-sleeved shirt and dungarees, standing against a table, perhaps, with his hands set flat against its surface for support. The pencil sketch, which had been done on Royal Yacht *Britannia* notepaper, drew praise from all quarters. The artist Ruskin Spear thought it had been done 'with great vigour and conviction – a sheer love of just drawing', and commended Diana for tackling such a difficult subject as a baby. 'She's had a jolly good stab at his mouth! The hand has form, and there's a nice sense of anatomy in that fat little wrist and the forearm,' he said. Fellow artist John Bratby thought it interesting that 'she's seeing him as he really is, which isn't very flattering. She doesn't pretend that he's beautiful.' Sir Hugh Casson, a close friend of Diana's, thought she had decided the battle between love and truth in favour of truth. When the picture was published, there was certainly a measure of agreeable wonder at Diana's obvious ability. Her old school-teacher, Elizabeth Ridsdale, was 'thrilled that she had been able to do it', while Ruskin Spear thought that 'either she's a remarkable sort of person or she's had some training in drawing somewhere. If she were a student of mine, I'd be very interested. This shows a talent worth pursuing. If she devoted a lot of time to drawing, she could easily end up with a show in a West End gallery.' Estimates of the drawing's value reached £50,000; unofficial bids went to £1,500; but all to no avail. The drawing now forms part of the Windsor archives – perhaps the first of Diana's personal contributions to this historic and fascinating royal collection.

There is one more interest which Diana is said to have, and that is Wales – but there has been very little real evidence of this in her public or private utterances. Her official schedule has included a total of a dozen days spent in the principality, including the three-day tour of October 1981, and a two-day tour a year later – but she shows no signs of having increased her capacity for speaking Welsh, nor her concern for or knowledge

of the economic, social and cultural problems of Wales and the Welsh since she became their Princess. It is tempting to conclude that, in asserting her preoccupation for the principality, Buckingham Palace felt it imperative that Wales should not be excluded from her list of interests on the grounds that, as Princess of Wales, it could hardly be admitted that she did *not* have such an interest! Perhaps she hoped that the future would take care of itself in this respect.

Nevertheless, she is, by royal standards at least, an indefatigable campaigner for bringing a ray of sunshine into the lives of the disadvantaged. Many of her engagements look dull and bland on paper, an impression not leavened by the choice of venue in the more unloved areas of the capital and major cities in the United Kingdom. The reality is altogether different. As the authorised version quoted above implies, she is at her best in the company of the young, never more solicitous than when perched on the edge of a child's hospital bed, nor more patient than when listening to the long explanations which accompany home-made gifts, nor more tolerant that when acceding to endless requests for kisses. In her short time, she has completely bridged the age gap, and won over the admiration of the old. From them, she has accepted all kinds of well-meant advice – tips about the need to put on weight, or not to bite her nails – which, coming from the lips of others, would seem impertinent. Even for the adults who wait, spick and span, in presentation lines, there is scarcely time to bow or curtsey before being engaged in conversation, and the obligatory 'Your Royal Highness' becomes suddenly out of place, a mumbled embarrassment, before someone who may be Royal but doesn't, thank God, act the Highness. When due to tour a Glasgow hospital in 1983, she begged for the place to be left exactly as normal, and for no expensive or time-consuming preparations to be made for her visit. Usually such a plea falls on deaf ears. On this occasion it didn't, and everyone was happy.

It is quite a feat of diplomacy to keep public company with the ordinary man, woman and child, as Diana does and clearly enjoys doing, without giving away too much in the way of personal secrets. Chatty conversations can wander dangerously, and familiarity, if it does not breed contempt, certainly invites its share of uncomfortable moments if the subject matter is not kept within bounds. Fortunately, the birth and upbringing of Prince William was the first really private matter to afford Diana not only a topic of easy conversation with individuals in the crowd that avoids most of the dangers, but also a subject very close to her own heart.

**D**uring the whole of his first two years, Prince William Arthur Philip Louis, like his father before him, became the most famous baby in the world, and Diana found herself on the receiving end of public adulation, curiosity and congratulation. She and Prince Charles chose his four very family-orientated names, and Buckingham Palace told the press that abbreviations of William were not to be adopted for public use. Like the previous 'Princess Charles' directive, this proved a forlorn hope. Everything from 'Wee Wilie Windsor' to 'Billy the Kid' was immediately seized upon, while a variety of nicknames – 'Prince of Wails', 'Prince of Wheels', 'Prince of Whales' and 'Prince of Wellies' – have reflected his behaviour, his transport, favourite toys and footwear respectively. His parents call him Wills.

His birth and full names were registered a month after he was born, when the local registrar called at Kensington Palace. 'The ceremony was lovely', she said, 'and Prince Charles and the Princess of Wales were proud and happy'. Two weeks later he was christened. Prince Charles – well brought up to respect royal continuity – chose his grandmother Queen Elizabeth's 82nd birthday for the occasion, and that magnificent Victorian joined the other members of the immediate family at Buckingham Palace that day. Prince Andrew was prevented by exigencies in the Falklands, Princess Margaret by an Italian holiday, from being present. But it seemed the whole nation was there, spurred into involvement by the publication six days earlier – on

spell of British weather than that which saw his birth assured him of several hours spent *al fresco* in the spanking new pram delivered by its South Wales manufacturers early that July. A low-slung, collapsible model, with its cot removable from the base, it was perfect for popping it into and out of the back of the car which took him, and now takes his brother Harry, regularly to local parks and gardens for afternoon outings.

William spent the first part of the following three months at Balmoral with his parents, and public sightings of him were necessarily rare. Prince Charles carried him in his carrycot off the plane that landed at Aberdeen early in August, and the growing baby was seen being wheeled in one of the Royal Family's older, coach-built, stand-by prams on the estate in mid-October. It was not till late that month that Diana finally

Diana's first wedding anniversary – of the first official photographs. Taken by Lord Snowdon, they showed an informal and relaxed couple fairly cocooning their pride and joy; Prince William looks quietly surprised at it all.

He was less silent as the Archbishop of Canterbury brought him into the Christian fold in the Palace's bow-windowed Music Room. William's repeated whimpers were welcomed as a token that the Devil had left his body, though all too soon were more correctly interpreted as the first signs of hunger. He yelled so loudly at the subsequent photo-call that the Queen Mother could only praise him for his healthy lungs, and the Queen for his early attempts at speechmaking. It was Diana who, by putting the tip of her finger into his mouth, fooled him into silence until the session was over; and eventually he was driven back to Kensington Palace and the relative calm of his nursery. Most of his first six weeks had been spent there: a more pleasant

returned to London to resume her public engagements. Buckingham Palace agreed that one of the reasons for such a long stay was that she wanted to be near Prince William, though a full ten or twelve-week Balmoral break is par for the royal course. Prince William subsequently joined his parents at Kensington Palace during each week, with weekend breaks at Highgrove, where the accommodation is much more expansive. In addition to a night nursery and a bathroom, Prince William has a special day nursery decorated, on Diana's instructions, with murals of fourteen Disney cartoon characters – a specially commissioned fantasy which took almost a month to complete.

By that time, William was beginning to creep into the news in his own right. When Diana toured the London headquarters of Capital Radio, she received a book called *Tales for a Princess*, which contained stories written by children for children – in this

case everyone thought they would do well for Prince William. Diana responded by thanking the young contributors on his behalf, and by assuring the Capital Radio's disc-jockey that she always listened to his programme while bathing her son. Only two days later, the issue of the colour of William's hair blazed into the headlines. Princess Michael of Kent had just divulged that he had 'little tufts of red hair all over his head, and absolutely

gorgeous blue eyes.' Buckingham Palace confirmed the information about the red hair, but Diana herself stepped in to contradict both of them the following day. 'William is blond,' she said during a trip to Wales. 'He has masses of blond hair.' The confusion was ultimately put down to a trick of the light and, as official photographs the following month showed, blond was – if

not conclusively accurate – the nearer of the two.

That tour of Wales – in November 1982 – was one in which Diana was irresistibly drawn into more baby talk with excited and enquiring housewives. 'We all know about that, don't we?' she joked as one baby's persistent cries interrupted one of her conversations. But it was Prince William they all wanted to

know about, and Diana was unable to stop herself repeating details of his bright blue eyes, his rate of growth – 'He's getting very heavy' – and the fact that he was so active that she could not stop playing with him. One person even asked her whether she was experiencing any sleepless nights because of Prince William. She said not, and that he was being very good. He was not being allowed a dummy, though he had acquired the habit of sucking his fingers. Meanwhile, in another conversation, Prince Charles praised his son as 'wonderful fun: he really makes you laugh. He's not at all shy: he is a great grinner, but he does dribble a lot.' Diana couldn't resist chipping in on the conversation: 'Just like his father,' she parried, with a look of mock intolerance.

Prince William was, of course, everybody's baby judging by the thousands and thousands of toys and gifts received both

before and after his birth. The Royal Wedding gifts department, which had been set up at Buckingham Palace early in 1981 to cope with an enormous flood of popular tributes, had to be resurrected for a similar purpose shortly after Diana announced she was expecting, but even their methodical organisation must have been overwhelmed by the continuing deluge of presents – both those sent by post and those given to Diana every time she set foot outside Kensington Palace. The more official gifts – Nancy Reagan's reproduction Chippendale chair, the gold jewellery from the Middle Eastern sheiks, the cases of claret, to be opened on William's 18th birthday in the year 2000, from a French diplomat – were all retained of course, but, as with Prince Harry two years later, the Palace was soon explaining that 'many other gifts are duplicated so lots will have to go to charity.' There was one gift in the other direction: in December 1982, Prince

Charles gave Kit Hill, a 1,000-foot-high beauty spot near Callington, to the people of Cornwall as a leisure site.

Meanwhile, the West Midland Metropolitan Borough Council named a street in Dudley after Prince William, though it was explained that the Queen didn't like this practice, 'until members of the family are old enough to decide for themselves whether they want something to be named after them.' And there was further disapproval for a baby agency which adopted the name 'Prince William Agency' in defiance of the convention that the names of living members of the Royal Family are not used for commercial purposes. Though, as Diana quickly found out, commercial exploitation became an occupational hazard. Shortly after she and Prince Charles moved into Highgrove, one local firm of estate agents began to describe their now fashionable county as 'Royal Gloucestershire' – a rather over-enthusiastic reaction which one of the firm's managers put down to 'negotiators' licence.' The firm who provided the lighting for the Royal Wedding in St Paul's Cathedral featured a picture of the wedding in one of their later advertisements, while a newspaper used a photograph of Charles and Diana on the balcony after the wedding to launch its bingo promotion – the photograph was doctored to show Prince Charles kissing Diana's hand, but holding a bingo card in the other hand!

Taken as isolated examples, these little peccadilloes might be treated as harmless demonstrations of the extent to which Diana has already influenced much of our daily lives. She may not have taken too kindly to it in the early days, however, when almost every move she made became the subject of assessment

and, all to often, criticism. Shortly after Prince William's birth, for instance, she read, no doubt with some satisfaction, of the Family Planning Association's opinion that 'her popularity and the publicity over the royal birth could encourage a lot of others to have their babies early.' But almost immediately afterwards, she was helplessly involved in a loud public discussion on the matter of whooping cough. William was only two months old when a whooping cough scare – caused by an outbreak of the disease among children whose parents had decided against vaccination for fear of possible brain damage – became sufficiently severe for doctors to be publicly begging Diana to have William immunised, both for his own good and as an example to others. And this was followed by a mounting campaign in the press, criticising the fact that William was being

kept out of the public eye. The young Prince's seclusion agitated a public which already doted on him, and there were frequent demands in the ensuing months for more pictures of him. The eagle-eyed passer-by might have spotted him being carried by his nanny near Gatcombe Park in November, or being perambulated round Kensington Gardens in the following months, but it was not enough. Continued secrecy led to the

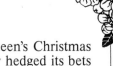

belief that William would feature in the Queen's Christmas television broadcast. One newspaper cleverly hedged its bets and insisted that he *was* included 'in the uncut version' of the recording. It turned out to be a prudent reservation.

Instead, there were two unexpected photo-calls at Kensington Palace just three days before Christmas, when television and still cameramen assembled in Diana's pastel pink and white first-floor study overlooking Kensington Palace Gardens. The event took place at her own suggestion, and she must have felt well rewarded by the success of it all. Her six-month-old son chortled and dribbled away without the ghost of a grumble, sucking his bright yellow teething-rattle and staring, fascinated, at the butterflies which decorated one of the cushions on the pink silk sofa. Diana made him grin by clicking her fingers and chatting to him, while Prince Charles had a crisp white handkerchief at the ready to mop up a sudden delivery of

returned breakfast. 'I expect the baby experts will say we have handled him all wrong', he muttered wryly.

The following day, William was ferried, bobble-hatted, with his parents to Windsor to spend Christmas with the Queen. Official comment on his behaviour in his first six months had been sparse, but already he had earned a reputation for making himself heard. The Queen's press officer's tactful admission back in July that 'he can be heard crying occasionally, but not very often' was amplified by Prince Charles at the christening –

'He gets noisier and angrier by the day'. But at least Prince William was sleeping through the night. By the end of September he was rarely waking up before six in the morning. 'That's a great relief', his mother told a housewife at Tooting shortly before Christmas.

Prince William surprised everyone from the beginning by his enormous appetite: 'He eats endlessly,' his grandfather Lord Spencer told visitors to Althorp five weeks after his grandson was born. The Prince was breast-fed for the first two months of his life, by which time he had doubled his birth weight. By the end of November, he weighed well over sixteen pounds and still, as Diana told Sir Richard Attenborough, 'he never stops eating'. He was fairly well forward physically, having made a few valiant, if unsuccessful, attempts to stand up, though Diana had to admit in November that he was not even sitting up properly. 'I just can't wait for him to walk,' she said during a visit to Cirencester. 'The things they pick up at his age', she added, horrified that at only five months he had already learned to spit.

**B**y this time, new horizons were opening up both for William and in particular for Diana. In the early spring of 1983, she prepared to fly, with her husband and son, half way round the world for a six-week tour of Australia and New Zealand which, for her at least, had already been marred by the endless public gossip surrounding the circumstances in which William was being taken. It was not until four months after the tour was announced that official confirmation was received that William would accompany his parents, and while it ended weeks of speculation and a torrent of advice on the subject, neither it, nor the Palace's assurances that 'there was never any question of leaving him behind' did anything to play down the constant rumour that Princess Diana had fought the Queen long and hard in order to get her way. Several reasons supporting both views were adduced, the hazard of two heirs to the Throne travelling together being cited as a reason for his not going, while the psychological necessity of mother and baby being together as much a possible argued the other way. Very few, if any, commentators suggested probably the most cogent justification for Prince William's presence down-under, though with the prospective election of an Australian Prime Minister committed to the establishment of a republic, the evidence was uncomfortably obvious. In a country where republicanism flourishes so fiercely that even the Queen has stepped up the frequency of her visits there during the last five years, the showing of the young Prince to the Australians as a symbol of the monarchy's continuity was imperative. Had not Edward I done similarly almost exactly seven hundred years before as a stimulus to Welsh sympathy towards the English?

The air of controversy which accompanied the undoubted

excitement of this most eagerly anticipated royal visit since 1954 continued up to the very day on which Diana was first seen by the Australians. The country was still seething with indignation at the circulation of posters showing engagement pictures of Diana which had been so treated that she appeared to be leaning, completely nude, against a lounged-suited Prince

Charles. Charles himself was the centre of a rumoured dispute, in the form of an indirect attack from his old polo friend Sinclair Hill, who was said to be smarting with indignation at not having been chosen to partner the Prince in a polo match due to take place during the tour. Moreover, some opponents of Bob Hawke, the newly elected Australian Prime Minister, and he of the emergent republican views, saw something personally snide in the fact that no official federal gift was to be made to the Prince and Princess – even though apparently, protocol did not make this an essential feature of the visit.

Even Prince William became a focus for criticism. A set of delightful photographs of the young Prince and his parents, taken in Diana's sitting room at Kensington Palace the previous February, were released a few days before the tour began. At first they were received with great alacrity. 'The Commonwealth's heart,' said one Australian newspaper, 'is about to be seized forever by the tiny curling fingers of a nine-month-old baby.'

Sure enough, dressed in a white romper suit with blue smocking, there was Prince William, bigger and better than ever, chewing on a daffodil, trying his hand at a few press-ups on a soft quilted rug, playing with a rather amorphous teddy bear, and a large toy koala. The photographer, Tim Graham, enjoying only his second royal commission, admitted a few problems coaxing his subject into a photogenic frame of mind – 'He did cry a bit' – but the end result was a winner. However, that toy koala spoiled things. The fact, as someone discovered, that it was made out of kangaroo skin horrified animal lovers. So when he was proudly held up by his parents on arrival at Alice Springs, local ears still rang with the strictures of Mrs Maryland Wilson, a member of the Victorian RSPCA, who accused those same royal parents of having 'no concern for wildlife', and voiced her disappointment that Diana had been so insensitive as to allow William to follow the royal example.

As if all that were not enough, Alice Springs copped a

After so many alarums, their arrival seemed not only uncontroversial but thoroughly delightful. To the surprise and rapture of the crowds, their formal welcoming was short on ceremony, and Nanny Barbara Barnes appeared at the top of the aircraft steps, holding Prince William. She brought him down to hand him over to Diana, and everyone was treated to the sight they had all secretly hoped for, before William continued his journey to New South Wales. Diana and Charles had shared a two-bed cabin for the flight, and slept separately from their son, who was accommodated in a cabin with his nanny. Diana was clearly of the opinion that, when you are starting a tour of such enormous dimensions as this one, and with the inevitability of

monsoonal low five days before the arrival, and was at the receiving end of a record 200mm of rainfall in three days. Three people drowned, a hundred were evacuated, trees were felled, bridges swept away and the centre of the town cut off for thirty hours. Worse still, the floods isolated the hotel where Prince Charles and Diana were to stay, and in last-minute arrangements their accommodation was transferred to another hotel, where the presidential suite, including a spa and adjoining sitting room, was made available. It was an irony that, by the time they arrived, the first hotel had dried out, and that the change of plan left its owners high as well as dry, with fifty empty rooms.

jet lag at the end of a long flight, babies were best kept out of earshot if the full benefits of sleep were to be enjoyed. It worked. She seemed as fresh as a daisy when she and Prince Charles arrived, complete with their party of 22 staff, including private secretaries, a lady-in-waiting, press and police officers, and a physician. Prince Charles brought two valets, on the grounds that 'it's a twenty-four-hour-a-day job', in the words of his press secretary, and Kevin Shanley, Diana's celebrated hairdresser, came too. Behind them all was almost a day's flying, which left them with what Prince Charles admitted as 'tertiary jet lag.' Before them lay a gruelling tour of six weeks' duration, with only a smattering of well-timed breaks.

with which she chatted with the obligatory line of dignitaries. No perfunctory handshake and fixed smile from her. It sparked off the reminder that someone had said of the Queen Mother many years ago that she laid foundation stones as if it was the best way of spending an afternoon that she could possibly imagine.

Diana lost no time getting a decent tan. She spent much of her first day relaxing with Prince Charles at the home of Dino Diano, a local businessman, and soaking up the sun was first on her list of priorities. Consequently, everyone commented on her rosy face when she turned up for a press reception late that afternoon, and the story was soon to develop that she was suffering from incipient sunstroke. Despite her long journey, however, she looked and acted brightly enough, though she confessed on that occasion that she felt otherwise. In those circumstances, it seemed an unfair duty which kept her on her feet with a full day of engagements ahead, but the following morning saw her just as bright and breezy, wearing the lightest of bright yellow dresses, and striking everyone by the sheer ease

She certainly bowled over the President of the Northern Territory Council, who dubbed her 'the fairest lady in the land', and welcomed Prince Charles and 'your gracious lady' to Alice. For him, it was the happy realisation of his not-too-optimistic hopes of getting the royal couple to visit the town at all. If nothing else it proved, as he said, the old adages, 'No cheek, no Christmas box,' and 'Faint heart never won fair lady.' With such evident charm, only the most pedantic lip quivered when he addressed Diana as 'my lady' instead of 'Your Royal Highness.'

That all came during a visit to an ambulance station, and it would be unduly sycophantic to deny that Diana was a little out of her depth during this first engagement of the tour. She seemed swamped, and rather nonplussed, by the technicalities of

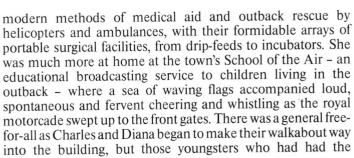

modern methods of medical aid and outback rescue by helicopters and ambulances, with their formidable arrays of portable surgical facilities, from drip-feeds to incubators. She was much more at home at the town's School of the Air – an educational broadcasting service to children living in the outback – where a sea of waving flags accompanied loud, spontaneous and fervent cheering and whistling as the royal motorcade swept up to the front gates. There was a general free-for-all as Charles and Diana began to make their walkabout way into the building, but those youngsters who had had the

imagination to climb onto the roofs of nearby buildings were rewarded with the best overall, if somewhat distant, view of the paragon they had all come to see.

One imaginative idea prompted by this visit was for both Charles and Diana to broadcast informally to the pupils of the school, although what the children would say – both in their own introductory words and in the questions they would be allowed to put to the royal visitors – had been prearranged and vetted. Thus, questions about Buckingham Palace and Prince William's progress were allowed, but enquiries as to whether Charles and Diana slept in a double bed were not! Headmaster Fred Hockley introduced them as 'two very special guests', and over the air from up to 400 miles out, came a tangle of voices, distorted by the irregular air waves, greeting them with 'Good morning, Prince Charles and Princess Diana.' Then came the barrage of questions on matters not too personal, most of them aimed at Diana, and most asking about Prince William. No, Diana explained, he didn't own a bike because 'he's a bit too young.' His favourite toys were his controversial kangaroo-skin koala, a plastic whale that threw out little white balls from its spout, and 'anything that makes a noise.' Diana also confirmed that he had six teeth and, although he was making all the right movements, he couldn't quite crawl yet. There was no doubt that Diana found herself vaguely unnerved by the experience, and more than once she seemed stumped for an answer to what appeared to be quite simple enquiries. Blushing profusely, and clearly put out by a huge contingent of press personnel watching her through a soundproof window, she had to be prompted several times by Prince Charles before she could or would answer certain questions.

She was more settled once she got outside, where she could chat more directly with the children who were lucky enough to see her in the flesh. It was an opportunity that neither she nor her young admirers let slip. It brought home to the Australians, perhaps for the first time, the natural, approachable manner which has made Diana so popular, and Alice Springs will remember this particular occasion as the one which really launched her with the Australian people.

Doubters of the effect of Diana's presence anywhere had their reservations quelled at Ayers Rock, which she visited the next day with Prince Charles. He did not miss the irony of the heavy press contingent descending upon this peaceful scene in what is supposed to be the close season for tourists. Two hundred in number, and transported in eight coaches, the international band of journalists swamped the fifty-strong private tourist representation. The Rock is owned by a trio of Aborigine elders, for whom it has sacred and magical connotations, and they have adopted its caves as places of manhood initiation ceremonies. And although at least one

Aborigine Land Rights flag fluttered noisily in a brisk but pleasant breeze, the official native welcoming party – the owners, their families, and a few settlers from nearby communities – was in no mood for aggressive crusades. They had come to greet Prince Charles and, as they called her, 'the lady.' What would they say to them? 'Just Hello,' was all they promised.

Diana and Charles arrived in the early evening, their eight-car motorcade halting at The Climb – one of the Rock's most accessible ascents, owing partly to the rail built into the rock to facilitate progress. A small cluster of memorial plaques near the bottom immortalised those who omitted to use it and warned those who might still prefer not to. Diana wore a plain, unflattering, loose white dress, which looked as if it had fitted her once, before the much-famed post-natal diets began, but

she was obviously enjoying the prospect of the most spectacular of her engagements, both at home and abroad, to date. Likewise, her meeting with the gnarled elders was probably the most memorable of her many official encounters in the last two years. Afterwards, she was sporting enough to fulfil the hopes of spectators and press alike by taking the obligatory few steps up the lower slopes of the Rock. It proved one of the few symbolic acts of the entire tour; a means of showing willing to identify with the Australians by participating in something peculiarly

and unmistakably Australian. Getting down again, on fairly steep, smooth stone, looked as if it would be more difficult and less dignified – indeed much was made of the fact that in the process she showed a modicum of pristine white petticoat – but she accomplished it all gracefully enough, with a light, and very un-royal skipping movement.

Their guide then took the Prince and Princess to see what every tourist must – sunset on the Rock. The sunset viewing-point was well populated by the time they arrived, and the press

was not long in swelling the ranks, cheering wildly as, at Charles' prompting, Diana turned to pose for photographers against the background of the darkening monolith. There was time for a little royal chat with the other spectators: 'She wanted to know where I came from,' one American woman excitedly told her friends, little suspecting that this is the usual opening gambit in royal conversation. Then both Diana and her husband turned to watch as, in those last minutes of direct light, the Rock changed from puce to rich brown, with the sun playing golden tinges and deep, black shadows among its crevices and outcrops. There was no drama, none of the oohs and aahs associated with firework displays and the like. The imperceptible variations absorbed most onlookers into a whispered silence until twilight came, eventually leaving the Rock – a flat, incongruous backdrop – to its natural, deserted self.

One royal visit to a school is much like any other, but the children and probably the staff too, of Karguru School at Tennant Creek will always claim that there was something special about the visit that Diana made with Prince Charles on their last day in the Northern Territory. The scene was routine enough – school grounds packed with cheering youngsters from

almost a dozen local and outlying schools; a small, proud reception committee headed by the Director of Education; staff busily priming their pupils in behaviour. The presentations were followed by long progresses up the drive to the school entrance, both Charles and Diana chatting earnestly with the children. 'You're lucky,' one boy told Prince Charles. 'Why?' said the Prince. 'Because you're a King.' A sympathetic royal snigger, then the reply; 'Well, not yet.' Meanwhile, the King-to-be's wife was getting to know other children, making one girl's day by accepting her pretty bouquet of white and yellow carnations and small orchids, together with a spoon. 'Is this for Prince William?' she asked. She told another child – an *E.T.* fan – that the film, whose London premiere she had attended three months earlier, had made her laugh – and cry. She chatted amicably with a 14-year-old exile from Stevenage, Hertfordshire, but his friend felt hard done by after his conversation with Diana was cut short when, in his own words, 'she saw some bloke with a camera, and took off.'

'If I were a Princess...' headlined one school display, inviting its children to complete the sentence as an exercise in

imagination. 'I would go to Tasmania,' suggested one. 'I would wear a pretty dress,' said another. 'I would go skating,' stated a third, while a fourth promised, 'I would meet the Prime Minister.' This Princess seemed to want to do none of these, for she was clearly in her element among the children themselves,

and thoroughly enjoying this extension of her original chosen career. One child, wearing a sweat-band over his head, was asked whether it worked. 'Yes,' he replied. 'In that case,' said Diana, referring to the outside temperature of 34°C, 'I think I need one too.' She commended another child on being a Brownie, but added, 'Sewing the badges on is the only bore.' 'I get Mummy to do that,' came the reply. 'Oh, I see!' Diana responded. 'Poor Mummy.' There was much, much more. Eventually, Diana, now holding another bouquet – this time of deep pink and white sweet-peas – saw a display of Scottish reel dancing, and was presented with an Easter egg for Prince William – a reminder that, after nearly three days, she would soon be seeing her son again.

illiam had travelled the 12,000 miles to Australia well, crying only twice in the course of the day-long journey, and waking cheerfully at 6am on the day of the arrival at Alice Springs to join his parents for breakfast. After the welcoming ceremony at Alice he had been taken back onto the aircraft to fly to the country estate at Woomargama in New South Wales, which he and his parents would make their home base for the duration of the Australian tour. William occupied a small suite of rooms overlooking a paved courtyard and a swimming pool, safe and secluded in the 70-year-old homestead situated a mile from the nearest road and three miles from the nearest neighbours. Its proud owners, company director Leonard Darling and his wife Margaret, promised to provide all the necessary nursery furniture – formerly used for their own grandchildren – and convert a changing room beside the swimming pool into a play room if required.

The large crowds awaiting the Prince and Princess on their way to Woomargama that evening made them late getting to the

house, but to Diana's delight, William was wide awake when they arrived – at 9pm in the pouring rain – and she was able to spend an hour with him before he settled down for the night. A day's break – the first of the tour – had unfortunately to be spent indoors owing to continual rain, but the enforced relaxation provided a deserved respite before Diana's first really formal programme of engagements – a two-day visit to Canberra. About a thousand people were at the airport the next day to see her arrive, and the inevitable walkabout thrilled scores of children. There was, as there seems to be at all airports, a strong wind – 'It nearly blew my hat off,' said Diana later – and she was also heard to complain about the cold. But, like her husband, she chatted merrily with them all, and even stooped to take a bunch of flowers from a little boy who crawled under a barrier to hand them to her. It was as good a start to a day's engagements as

anyone could have hoped for, and no-one, at the airport at least, was put out by the fact that the royal couple had already slipped ten minutes behind schedule.

Among a crowd of 3,000 at Canberra's Civic Square was a group of youngsters bearing lettered cards which, when raised, spelled out 'Hello, Princess Diana'. There was a whoop of delight as she came into the crowd's view and, modestly though she took it all, and inclined though she was to take refuge behind Prince Charles, she was clearly much gratified by yet another unmistakably friendly reception. On her walkabout through the crowds she was showered with flowers and gifts. One girl offered six roses from her own garden; another presented a beautifully prepared bouquet of carnations; yet another gave a bunch of large yellow chrysanthemums. Prince Charles received flowers too, and promised to hand these to Diana, along with several letters and pictures.

Diana, of course, was highly in demand, and thoughts of Prince William were rarely far from the surface. According to what she told one mother, he awoke regularly at two in the morning and 'is getting a lot of attention from people.' Another woman held up her young son and told Diana, 'I wish I had a

nanny, like you.' 'I wish I didn't have to leave William with his nanny,' replied Diana. 'I'd rather be doing what you're doing. I'd swap with you any time.' But perhaps the nicest compliment of the morning came from a six-year-old girl who threw her arms around Diana's neck and kissed her, and from the Princess herself who congratulated one lady on her 42nd birthday. 'Life,' said Diana, 'begins at forty, and you've got a two-year start.' The woman was almost in tears of joy afterwards. 'It was a wonderful birthday present,' she said. 'I will never forget it as long as I live.'

The following day brought a reminder that, when Prince Charles is around, Diana prefers to leave the performance of formal duties to him. Visiting a Community Centre outside Canberra, she kept a low profile as Charles unveiled a plaque and declared its library open. She gave her usual demurring smile as he made light of the fact, with a witty speech in which he said, 'I have been elected by a committee of two to do this. We were unable to declare it open in unison – we have not had the time to practise.'

But a grimmer, more trying duty awaited Diana that afternoon. The appalling toll on life, limb and property wrought by recent bush-fires in Victoria and South Australia made the next part of the tour – a visit to a stricken area near Melbourne – one of solemn pilgrimage. After leaving Canberra, Diana had, very tactfully, changed from the bright canteloupe outfit she had worn there into a less formal and very unobtrusive grey and mauve striped dress. It was indeed a harrowing journey as they subsequently drove along roads lined with the blackened remains of forests and woods, the smoked ruins of once decent homes, and the mangled metal of burnt-out motor vehicles. These scenes profoundly affected Prince Charles who, while talking to the victims later, found himself unable even

momentarily to lapse into conversation which was remotely chatty, and hardly managed a smile all afternoon as he expressed his encouragement and concern. The delicacy of the occasion was not lost on Diana, to whom people related reminiscences of lost pets – those stories particularly distressed her – and the slow, somewhat depressing efforts to get back on an even keel. But even amid such mass misfortune, the royal visit engendered great excitement among the children, who clamoured to thrust gifts upon Diana – koalas, teddy bears, toy kangaroos, fruit and flowers – as if the tragedy that had brought her here had never occurred. Eventually, the capacious trunks of two royal cars were

filled with presents. To the observer, this was a symbol of resilience in adversity, just as the tree planted by the royal couple at the end of this sorrowful visit symbolised the regeneration to which everyone was now looking forward.

Diana admitted the following day that, nearly a week after her arrival in Australia, she still felt the residual effects of jet lag, but her problems were nothing to those of some 2,000 people, all victims of other bush fires, whom she and Prince Charles met at

Stirling, near Adelaide, that morning. The size of the crowd was a deceptive measure of the disaster, for as many as 6,000 victims had received invitations to meet the royal couple; most, however, did not want to be reminded of the seven-week-old agony, and the attendance was accordingly much smaller. As before, Diana was well aware of the sensitive nature of her visit, and 'I hope you don't mind the intrusion,' became one of her most frequent pleas as she lost no time meeting the lines of families who had been waiting so long to see her. A frowning Prince Charles again restricted himself to earnest, enquiring conversation, but Diana was busy shaking dozens of hands, doing her best to accept all the flowers and gifts from small children, and talk to them at the same time. One of them, a five-year-old girl, cried just as her moment came. 'It's always the same,' Diana told her mother.

There was, of course, a torrent of questions, anxious and personal, about the losses people suffered both in the fires and in the subsequent floods which, coming too late to quench the

inferno, caused their own extremes of havoc. One woman held out the twisted remains of three metal badges from her family s cars, and photographs of her wrecked home k a graphic statement of the horror of the devastation for Diana to assimilate – and heart-breaking stories of destruction and distress punctuated every few minutes. But Diana's most famous meeting of all that day was with Philip Williams, an 18-year-old volunteer fire-fighter who, standing beside the burnt-out truck in which he had been trapped at the time of the fires, told her of the extensive burns he had suffered, and how during a six-week period in hospital, he had been given skin grafts on all his fingers. He constantly flexed them throught his long conversation with her, in order to keep them supple, and Diana was delighted when he was able to manage a brief hand-shake before she moved on.

Two days later, the mood was well and truly changed again, as Diana became the star of what was then termed Sydney's most brilliant social event of 1983 – a dinner-dance in honour of the royal couple at the city's Sheraton Wentworth Hotel. The exclusivity of the tickets, available mainly to invitees, certainly suggested its brilliance; the shimmer of almost 250 ball-gowns, the chic hair-styles and sparkling jewellery emphasised it; the long list of celebrity names, each paying $75 for the privilege (more if a ticket found its way onto the black market) put it beyond all doubt. The promised presence of the world's most famous married couple seemed to bring half of Sydney to the

immediate vicinity of the hotel to watch the procession of the famous arriving in a blaze of headlights, and to hope for a glimpse of Diana herself. When the time came, the uninvited could have been forgiven for mistaking her arrival for that of the world's most sought-after pop star, so shrill, frantic and prolonged were the shrieks which filled the streets, and so deep did the sound penetrate into the interior of the hotel, where slightly more restrained guests jockeyed respectably for position at the moment of the grand entrance.

The event justified it. Diana's breathtaking impact was achieved not by any grandness of manner – that is not her style – but by the sheer elegance which invariably shines through her endearing brand of slightly embarrassed modesty. Wearing a graceful, mid-blue evening dress shot through with silver slivers, flounced and ruffled, and with a light, generous double skirt, she avoided the temptation of over-dressing; a silver cummerbund and a diamond necklace and earrings providing the only other sparkles. She and Prince Charles were, by tradition, obliged to be the first to take the floor after a

sumptuous meal, and they went straight into a quick-step to the bustling rhythm of 'The More I See You'. Their performance – for in front of five hundred people, that was inevitably what it was – lacked nothing in enthusiasm, though it was noticeably lacking in style. Diana, slightly hesitant, was virtually grabbed by her Prince who whirled her around vigorously, even a little roughly, his jaw contorted to give his features an expression of almost painful effort. But Diana soon began to enjoy the experience, breathless though she seemed at being spun about to the insistent big band beat and the applause from the other guests.

More noise rang in Diana's ears the next day when the sound of 43,000 children's piercing cheers at Newcastle provided an unforgettable experience, and Diana's memories of her short visit with Prince Charles will have been coloured by what she

heard as much as by what she saw. But seeing was important too. 'Don't forget to wave at the end,' urged one of the rehearsal organisers patiently over the loud-speakers in the huge Sports Ground. 'We all want to see you wave to the Prince and Princess, and I'm sure the beautiful Princess Diana would like to see you wave too.' Most of the resounding cheers came during the initial drive in an open car around the outer and inner circuits of the oval – an imaginative idea which left few, if any, of even the tiniest mites without a view of their heroine. There was a loud, supportive cheer for young Alison Watkins, a local school-girl, who confidently and affirmatively delivered a beautifully-spoken address of welcome. Diana leaned intently in her direction as if to study the brave young lady more closely, and Prince Charles made a special point of congratulating her on 'a very fine speech. It can't have been easy on your first occasion in front of so many people.' She must have glowed with pride from that moment on.

A few hours and thirty kilometres further on another welcome awaited Diana at Maitland, where red, white and blue bunting thickly festooned the main street for over a quarter of a mile and crowds stood four deep in places. But this time the inevitable, incessant clamour for Diana began to take a potentially ugly turn. Police were unable to contain a surging flood of people as she and Prince Charles disembarked from their open car to take a hundred-metre walk to the Town Hall. Brought to a high exuberance by patient waiting (the royal couple were over half an hour late) in the blazing sun, the crowds spilled onto the road immediately behind the royal party, and for fifteen quite frightening minutes there was a mêlée of old and young swarming almost mindlessly towards Diana, desperate for the close look at her which seemed the rightful reward for hours of patience. Had the walk been longer, there could have been considerable casualties. On the one hand people became hysterical in their frustrated attempts to get closer; on the other, potential victims - mostly children, but women too - became pathetically distressed and tried frantically, but equally vainly, to extricate themselves from the milling crowd. Police officials fell hopelessly behind and virtually gave up.

Ironically, Diana was not only unaware of this, but was visibly enjoying her walkabout as on no other previous occasion. She even swung off the main route to talk to people who were tucked away in corners, unwittingly encouraging yet more currents of movement in the seething crowd. It seems that even Prince Charles was ignorant of the trouble when he spoke of how much Diana was enjoying 'her crash course in Australian affairs.' But he was delighted to have paid a visit to this pleasantly situated town, and pronounced - as he often did on this tour - on the continuity of monarchy in hoping that Prince William would repeat his parents' visit in years to come. Within an hour of saying so, Prince Charles and his wife were on their way back to Woomargama to see their son, leaving police authorities to take their lesson from the near catastrophe of that hot afternoon.

The two-day visit to 'windy little isle', as Prince Charles called Tasmania, was potentially the most immediately controversial of the tour, bringing him and Diana close, physically and emotionally, to the hot political issue of the effects on conservation of a new dam being built by the Tasmanian Government. On the very day they arrived in Hobart, the Federal Government imposed regulations which it believed would legally prevent the Tasmanian Government from continuing to bulldoze the now famous Wilderness region, and on the day the royal couple left the island its Premier announced that the regulations had no legal effect, and refused to call the development programme off. Prince Charles had already been heralded as a conservationist by the vociferous anti-dam faction, a posse of whose representatives stood guard at Hobart Airport to distribute printed evidence of royal support for their cause to any who would accept. The Prince had indeed already let slip one sympathetic remark to an opponent of the project while he was in Adelaide a few days earlier, and the contention surrounding his visit probably accounted for some unusually surly mannerisms on his part that day. For once, he did not join in

their subsequent approach to Rokeby High School for their first engagement tended to support the impression that this was not going to be a good day, though in events this low-key visit proved pleasant enough. Prince Charles had brightened up considerably and Diana, sporting a tomato red outfit which was almost two years old, delighted the school's five hundred children by her long, chatty conversations with them.

After a private dinner at Government House that evening, Prince Charles and Diana arrived in style at the Wrest Point Hotel to attend a State reception for 450 guests representing a cross-section of Tasmanian society. A dinner-jacket and long

Diana's walkabout, tapping his foot impatiently as she received her usual deluge of gifts and flowers. His services could well have been used elsewhere, since several hundred children, inexplicably lined up beyond the limits of the royal walk, had no chance of meeting or presenting gifts to either of them, and stood in tearful disbelief as the royal car eventually drove off, leaving their earnest affection and innocent loyalty unrequited.

A muted welcome by only a handful of local spectators on

dress affair, this was as glittering an occasion as any they had attended, and Diana herself made a spectacular entrance in a new rich, red, silk dress twinkling with silver spots and heavily flounced at the neck and down the back. More sparkle was provided by her diamond tiara, a thick diamond necklace with a Prince of Wales's feathers pendant, and diamond and pearl earrings. Clearly conscious of the breathtaking impact of her appearance, she smiled broadly and confidently as she followed

Prince Charles to the dais, to the bray of a brass fanfare.

Well may the Tasmanian Premier have called Diana 'your most charming wife' when he welcomed Prince Charles officially. 'In the years ahead,' he continued, 'we are going to grow fond of her.' He assured the Prince that there were 'no doubts about republicanism here; we are 100% loyal to you and to your family' – a remark which was greated by loud cheers. Charles' reply proved to be one of his most entertaining speeches – one in which Diana played a silent, unrehearsed, but amusing part. Speaking of all the 'Good luck' messages during his pre-wedding tour of Australia in 1981, he remarked '...and I was indeed lucky enough to marry her.' Diana, to whom all eyes immediately turned, screwed up her face as if in outraged modesty, and produced a half-mocking, half-threatening glare at the Prince who spun round, too late to catch it as the assembly

erupted with laughter. 'It's amazing what ladies do when your back is turned,' he grinned.

Perhaps only Prince Charles and Princess Diana's whistle-stop tours of Wales – involving visits to up to a dozen communities in a single day – surpassed the village-hopping spree they cheerfully undertook on their second and final day in Tasmania. Leaving Hobart just after nine that morning, they were in Launceston by lunchtime, with hectic stop-go calls at four Midland Highway towns along the way. Diana, wearing a pure white suit with matching veiled hat, was overwhelmed with gifts from children sporting school-made caps bearing 'Welcome' messages. Prince Charles got his share too, including a large and delicious-looking marshmallow Easter rabbit from a 15-year-old school-girl. Most of the flowers that came his way were for Diana, and when he asked one little girl whether he

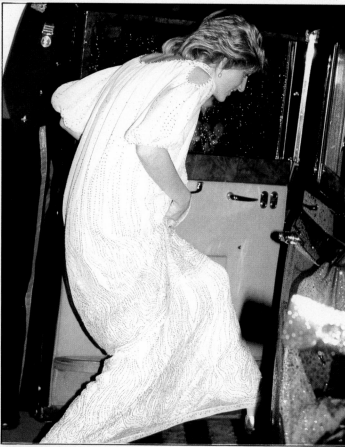

ought to pass them on, she replied, 'No, they're for you.' Diana had to be content with an ingenious gift from two four-year-olds, who gave a pillow packed with pine chips, intended as an addition to Prince William's layette, to make him sleep.

Having reached Launceston, their final engagement of the day was a visit to the Australian Maritime College at Mowbray, where a fifty-minute tour included a demonstration of the maritime survival technique. To the recorded sound of a storm at sea, and the chilling shouts of 'Mayday', eight or nine men 'fell' into the sea, represented by a giant swimming pool, and were picked up by a trio of life-rafts which had been lowered from a simulated ship's side. Not a drop of the chlorinated water reached Diana's bright red shoes, though she gamely stood quite close to the edge of the pool and some of the splashes were enormous. And so the royal couple left the College both dry, and for once, pretty well on schedule. Two hours later they were back at Woomargama with Prince William; there was an evening barbecue, and the young family and their staff could then look forward to their four-day Easter holiday.

In all its 125 years, St Matthew's Church, Albury had never received such august visitors as the Prince and Princess of Wales, who arrived there for morning Communion on a bright and hot

Easter Sunday. Those expecting Diana to sport an Easter bonnet were disappointed; a couple of ribbons dangling from the back of her sea-green straw hat were her only concessions to the festival; for the rest she wore a plain, matching dress with a loose, sleeveless, patterned box jacket. She was not, however, by any means underdressed: all 350 worshippers in the church and the two hundred to whom the service was relayed outside, were attired respectably but without show. Elaborate hats were nowhere to be seen, and some of the men even wore jeans and rolled-up sleeves. As befits a healthy Christian flock, it was an occasion totally without pretension.

The Archdeacon of Albury prefaced his sermon with a reference to the royal couple's having 'come to share with us in our worship' and an assurance 'of our abiding affection and loyalty, and constant prayers, for them and Prince William and for our beloved Queen and all the Royal Family.' The Prince and Princess were the first to take Communion, kneeling together at the sanctuary rail alongside members of their household. After the service, Easter eggs were much in evidence as the royal visitors made their way through thick crowds towards their car; indeed no sooner had they emerged from the church than Diana was swamped with them. 'Is that for me or for William?' she kept

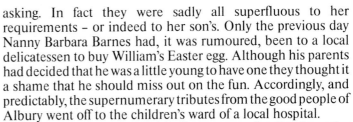

asking. In fact they were sadly all superfluous to her requirements – or indeed to her son's. Only the previous day Nanny Barbara Barnes had, it was rumoured, been to a local delicatessen to buy William's Easter egg. Although his parents had decided that he was a little young to have one they thought it a shame that he should miss out on the fun. Accordingly, and predictably, the supernumerary tributes from the good people of Albury went off to the children's ward of a local hospital.

Prince Charles played his first game of polo since the previous August at Warwick Farm, near Sydney, on the afternoon of that Easter Sunday, though in cool and drizzly conditions which, he sid, 'remind me of the United Kingdom on a summer's day.' For Diana, who was there too, the event had an added attraction; Anne Bolton, her flat mate from bachelor-girl days, and now resident in Australia, was at the ground and, together with her future sister-in-law, Wendy Hill, she and Diana were able to talk about old times together and catch up on their personal gossip. Diana, never one for dressing up on comparatively private and informal occasions like this, was now wearing a simple blue and white striped dress and navy blue blazer.

Prince Charles was playing in defence, for a team chosen by

the President of the New South Wales Polo Club, against a North Coast Team, Tanglewood. Sinclair Hill, the centre – wrongly he insisted – of that ripple of controversy at the outset of the tour, was there to give him advice during the limbering up period before the match, and between each of the six chukkas. 'His father was better rated,' Hill said of him, 'but the Prince is a very much better player. Most people in the polo-playing fraternity would tell you that. It's a great credit to him to come over here and play in full view of the public, for the first time in seven months,' he added admiringly, as he watched him set off onto the field, and Prince Charles himself admitted, 'I found the going a bit hard and I was a bit behind the ball.' As for Diana, her quiet afternoon had shown that she was not as possessive or doting about Prince William as many had been led to believe – at least not sufficiently so as to pass up the opportunity of a reunion with a valued friend nor, as Prince Charles succintly suggested, of 'loyally watching her husband make a fool of himself.'

He had intended to go fishing on Easter Monday, but in the event it rained, so he stayed indoors with his wife and son – indulging, according to Diana, William's newly-discovered passion for Easter eggs. Clearly, Diana's heart had melted and, mindful of her own weakness for sweets and chocolates she had risked William's precious six teeth by introducing him to

chocolate. The following day saw the royal couple at Adelaide at the start of a two-day stay in South Australia, and their first stopping point was the Parks Community Centre. In its indoor sports complex, they saw a display of simulated rock-climbing – something that Diana afterwards vowed she would never go in for; watched a group of Far Eastern refugees playing table-tennis; looked in on youngsters practising handsprings and trampolining – 'I went on one when I was at school; I enjoyed it,' said Diana – and watched a group of ladies going through their fitness-through-dance routines.

There was, of course, time for a short walkabout. Prince Charles spotted a flag being waved by a 77-year-old woman; it was made in 1952 and contained a picture of him at the age of three, with his parents. Diana reserved her comment on the delicate question of her husband's age, but reckoned that Prince William, at almost ten months old, bore a remarkable resemblance to his father at the same age. She also threw in the gratuitous opinion that Charles was 'more handsome then than he is now.' It was solely in order to see Diana that one eight-year-old had travelled over five hundred kilometres to Adelaide that weekend and it proved to be money, time and effort well spent. She was able to present her with a bunch of red and pink roses, and found to her delight that they were Diana's favourite flower.

Later that morning, Charles and Diana's hugely acclaimed entry into the Town Hall for a civic luncheon was marked by the presentation by a four-year-old girl of a bouquet of carnations to Diana, together with a small, fluffy yellow chicken 'for Prince

Charles.' 'I think it must be for Prince William,' corrected the Princess. A disarming grin registered on the toddler's face as she realised that, despite days of rehearsing, there's many a slip. Once inside the main hall, the royal couple heard the South Australian Premier say how pleased everyone was that Prince

Charles had been able so promptly to fulfil his 1981 promise to bring his wife to Adelaide, while the Lord Mayor reminded him that Diana's father had spent some time there in the 1940s. Prince Charles, speaking 'as a proud husband', replied that he could not have hoped for a warmer welcome for Diana. He thanked the people of South Australia for their wedding present of four hundred bottles of its best wine which, he assured them, 'is greatly appreciated by all those we wish to impress when giving receptions,' and for the additional gift of a corkscrew which, he emphasised, would remain after all the wine – much of which had already been drunk – was consumed.

That evening, after a private dinner at Government House, Prince Charles took Diana to the University of Adelaide for an informal disco. Informal at least in intention, because with an escort of six outriders and four staff cars, and a tremulous rendering of the National Anthem played on what seemed to be a rather cheap Bontempi, informality was not readily achieved. In the attempt, the master of ceremonies briefed his teenage audience with an earnestness that bordered on sheer hilarity; 'Don't forget, once they've arrived, I'm not allowed to mention them. So after the Premier and Leader of the Opposition get here, just mill around. All sit down at about one minute to eight. When the Prince and Princess sit down, don't forget – no staring.

Just make it a nice, relaxed evening.' So it was, though despite Diana's much vaunted love of dancing, the royal guests of honour did not foot it very far into the night. With the prospect of much travel the following day, they were back at Government House almost before the last reverberations of the ten o'clock chimes had died away.

Next day, and for the first time on the tour, Prince Charles took over the controls of the plane carrying the royal party as it approached the small farming town of Renmark, an up-and-coming holiday resort in South Australia's riverland. It was the beginning of one of those hectic days when the travelling between engagements seems to be almost as time-consuming as carrying them out, but the obvious sincerity of the welcome – particularly North Renmark Primary School's ten-foot-long sheet plastered with paintings and signatures of its pupils –

proved an encouraging start. Diana's bright scarlet two-piece silk dress with crisp, white cavalier collars won admiring comments from the 1,500-strong crowd, and unrehearsed moments spiced her arrival with charm. A two-year-old boy handed his bouquet of five roses to Diana, then put on a face of such forlorn deprivation that she gave it back to him. And a policewoman snapped a salute so energetically as she opened the car door ready for the drive into the town, that Prince Charles had to duck to avoid her extended elbow. Diana was quick to see the funny side of it; 'You nearly assaulted the Prince of Wales!' she said.

That afternoon, the royal couple were welcomed at Port Pirie with a mayoral speech which, littered with 'Royal Highnesses', recalled that the silver used in the manufacture of Australia's wedding present to them – a set of twenty silver platters – had been produced by the city's major industrial company. Those platters were now matched by the present of a boxed set of silver servers, made by the same craftsmen who had fashioned the platters. Diana also accepted the gift of a small smocked suit for Prince William. Prince Charles assured the Mayor that the

platters were 'greatly appreciated, highly-valued and we use them constantly.' He mused on the coincidence that the maritime approach to the port was via the Spencer Gulf, named in 1802 after Diana's great-great-great-great grandfather. Predictably, he got a large cheer for that revelation.

Rebecca La Forgia went one better than the eight thousand children who applauded so wildly. A 16-year-old student from a local school, she had taken part in the combined schools athletics meeting which Charles and Diana had come to see, and was one of ten pupils to receive a handsome wooden trophy from the Prince on behalf of their respective schools. 'I hope Lady Diana doesn't mind,' she told him within the Princess' earshot, 'but may I give you a kiss on the cheek?' Prince Charles and Diana re-enacted their famous wedding-day balcony scene. He looked at her for instructions; she hitched her shoulders in a resigned shrug of approval. Prince Charles lowered his face. The kiss was given and received in a trice – 'more fun than receiving the trophy,' said Rebecca. 'He's got lovely soft cheeks.' The Prince was obviously bucked by the compliment. Diana giggled. The crowd whooped with delight, everyone enthralled by the moment of unrehearsed fun in this closing moment of a hasty visit. Indeed, almost the whole population rose to the entire,

rare, royal occasion, thousands of housholders decking fences, walls and hedges with patriotic trimmings, and turning out in force to affirm loyalties and satiate curiosities. 'They're gorgeous, both of them,' said one woman. 'I'd like to keep them both for pets.' Several admittedly less colourful examples of enthusiasm were however balanced by the fact that most of the city's employees, given a half holiday from work, spent the afternoon in the pubs, and by the local bookmaker carrying on business as usual. 'Princess Diana?' he queried, trying to look genuinely bemused. 'What race is that in?'

The threat of rain did not deter some four thousand people from greeting Prince Charles and his wife when, after flying direct from South Australia, they landed at Perth for a two-day visit. As if to take up from where Port Pirie had left off, two small children succeeded in making something of a status symbol out of kissing the ever-patient Diana. The following day was a special one for her, marking as it did her first solo duty of the tour. At that time, Fremantle Hospital was one of the few institutions in the Commonwealth that could boast a building named after her – in this case, the Princess of Wales Wing. She now came to visit it, and made the most of the occasion, wearing what everyone acknowledged was the most elegant and vibrant outfit since her arrival in Australia – a stylish, deep pink dress with white spots, and a matching pill-box hat with a pink silk band

tied into a huge rippling bow at the side. Many people were disappointed when, ostensibly for fear of rain, her car sailed well past the originally planned stopping point before Diana alighted, but the more fortunately placed were thrilled to see her at her very best – much more relaxed, taking her time, sparing a quick word and a handshake for the many rather than favouring the few, and giving everyone the chance ultimately to go home and truthfully say they'd seen her. Flowers were almost a foregone conclusion, but Diana's favourite gift was a blue and white toy rabbit, given to her by a local teenager. Long after all the flowers had been loaded into the boot of her official car, the rabbit, on her personal instructions, was placed on the arm-rest next to her seat, and it travelled in her company back to Government House after her visit.

The royal couple joined forces for a trip to Perth's Commonwealth Stadium, where a wash of cheers greeted their arrival and their triumphal open-car tour of the ground. Problems of access proved no deterrent to children who were obviously unable to present flowers to Diana personally; they simply hurled them with remarkably good aim into the car.

When she actually caught one bouquet in mid-air with as neat and effortless a movement as any likely to be seen on the cricket grounds of Australia, she was cheered as if she had just scored a century. At a subsequent civic welcome, Prince Charles recalled his last visit in 1979, when he attended Western Australia's 150th anniversary celebrations, and he took the opportunity personally to thank his audience for their wedding present to him and Diana – a pair of jarrah tubs which 'are now a permanent reminder of Western Australia in our London home.' He hastened to add that he had had the tubs filled with soil and planted with shrubs after 'being worried that our small son was going to climb into them.'

To the left of the dais on which they stood, children held up a hand-painted sign saying; 'Please to talk to us Princess Di', and it was to them that Diana turned as soon as the formalities were over. It marked the start of the longest, best received and most boisterous walkabout she had yet undertaken on the tour, the densely-packed crowd almost beside itself with excitement. For once, it took the form of a procession in which both Prince and Princess walked together in the centre of the roadway, only occasionally darting out towards the crowd to accept some of the dozens of toys and posies held out to them. Nevertheless, Diana received bouquets which eventually filled the arms of four attendant policewomen, while among Prince Charles' gifts were two jars of Vegemite and a kiss from a teenage student. Marriage, it seemed, had not lessened his popularity with the girls.

There was a quiet, expectant buzz in the air at that afternoon's garden party at Government House, and all eyes were fixed on the residence from which Charles and Diana were to emerge and make their way down to the lawns. The Prince looked particularly dapper with a fiery orange marigold in his

buttonhole, while his wife, whose carriage for once compared rather badly with the confident, straight-backed stride of the Premier's wife, wore a delicate powder-blue outfit with deep sailor collars in blue and white. After standing for the National Anthem, they began their long progress through the snaking lines of guests, almost all of whom kept their faces locked in their direction, like daffodils seeking a shifting sun. There was a degree of gentlemanly jostling, parts of the lawn were badly trampled, and one lady fainted in the overpowering heat and excitement of the occasion. And, in a week replete with royal kisses, it seemed appropriate that when, after separately circulating with the guests for nearly an hour and a half, the Prince and Princess came face to face again, Charles should take Diana's hand and, in a public show of gallantry, kiss it. Laughter, applause, and exit.

You had to feel sorry, next day, for the 13,000 schoolchildren waiting for Prince Charles and Princess Diana at the Hands

Memorial Oval at Bunbury. Not simply because of their long and patient wait, but because of the verbal hammering they suffered from Mr John Parker, charged with overseeing general behaviour and obedience to protocol. 'Whistling and calling out,' he informed them over the loud-hailers in one of his more extreme flights of instruction, 'is poor form. Cheering, clapping and the waving of flags is to be encouraged. Do not break ranks. It is imperative that you take all your instructions from me.' It worked, of course, but one had the uneasy feeling that the spontaneity had melted away long before the royal couple arrived. Fortunately, it was a day for individuals as well. A six-year-old girl presented Diana with a bouquet, while the captain of a local high school delivered an articulate address of welcome, assuring the couple that 'all students are united in the wish to see and welcome you both.' During the ensuing performance of gymnastic and musical skills, Diana, chic in a silver-grey two-piece with matching hat and bright red accessories, looked delighted with the efforts of one school band, and tapped her fingers during its jaunty rendering of *Eye Level*. She found the weather bright enough for sun-glasses, her one sneeze turned out not to be the herald of a developing chill, and she only just managed to suppress an irreverent giggle as Prince Charles let out an involuntary swear when a sheet of his prepared speech notes blew away in the wind.

ne agreeable feature of this royal tour was that the big cities did not enjoy all the attention, and that the idea of meeting the people involved small communities as well as large. This was particularly so in the choice of churches for Sunday worship – the grandeur of the city cathedrals being spurned in favour of the intimacy of the small parish church. On their last Sunday in Australia, therefore, Prince Charles and Diana chose St Paul's Church, Holbrook, near Albury as their place of worship, and somehow the town's citizens seemed to cheer longer and with greater sincerity when they arrived looking relaxed after another day's break on the Woomargama estate. The day before, they had been enjoying a swim in its swimming pool, even taking Prince William for a splash, and had gone off in search of kangaroos – vainly it transpired, as they had chosen the heat of the day, rather than day-break or dusk, for their expedition.

As unpretentious as the church itself, Diana wore a modest multi-colour striped silk suit with a deep fuchsia pill-box hat embellished by a matching rosette. Prince Charles followed his own distinctive sartorial lights with a pale yellow tie between his blue shirt and grey suit. The service of Holy Communion was as simple as the surroundings, the plainness of the liturgy relieved by hymns of praise and Easter celebration. But for the patient

crowds the real celebration began when, during the final hymn, the royal couple emerged to speak to a double line of children in the church grounds. This was a prelude to another walkabout and, with the path of habit now well trodden, the usual showers of posies fell into Diana's hands. For Prince William, one young boy offered a boomerang made by his father, who was due to defend his world boomerang-throwing title that afternoon at Albury. 'Made expressly for Prince William,' ran the message carved along the blade, 'and many happy returns.' A little soon, one felt, but better early than late.

Perversely, it seemed, the best was yet to come, and the remaining four days of the Australian tour seemed like an epic tribute to the modern-day goddess Diana. As if reluctant to lose his grip on her, Prince Charles held her hand as they arrived by car in the centre of Brisbane, but the second that Diana stepped from the limousine, it became obvious that he might just as easily have stayed at home. Huge crowds – some estimated them at nearly 100,000 – in alarmingly determined mood gave her a frenzied, riotous welcome, as she began to make her way

along the walkabout route. A few children sneaked beneath the arms of security men and began a craze for converging on her with the most amazing ease. Her Press Secretary declared it 'the biggest crowd that has ever turned out to see them – and that includes their first visit to Wales', but the air of self-congratulation quickly wore off. As police consistently failed to

keep the crowds in order, the crush became a stampede which eventually claimed 150 casualties. Most of them were treated on the spot, though a dozen were taken to hospital.

Sensing danger, Prince Charles advised Diana to quicken her pace and stick to the middle of the pedestrian route. She did so, at one time fairly galloping along to keep ahead of a crowd now in hot pursuit, and avoiding the usual handshakes and kissing routines. 'Had they stopped to talk,' explained a member of her

staff, 'it would have been frightening for little children. The only way to protect the children was to walk down the centre.' There was an orgy of flower-throwing, screaming and fainting as the royal couple moved further and further out of popular reach. 'We seem to have met half the citizens of this great city in one go,' said Prince Charles later, 'and I doubt that there are many left to meet. My wife and I are completely overwhelmed.' The streets around Brisbane's Crest Hotel were jammed that evening, with some people establishing their vantage points four hours before the couple were due there for a State reception. Even inside, Diana could not escape being idolised. Charles shifted uneasily in his seat as singer Simon Gallagher announced before one of his songs that he was singing it to 'the most beautiful woman in the room,' and he looked straight into her eyes as he sang *I'm Really Only Singing This For You*, Prince Charles even paid his own tribute to Diana during that day, after one woman had told him how handsome he was. 'I've a wife who keeps me that way,' he replied.

'I could think of few less interesting places to visit,' said a local commentator of the royal couple's proposed trip the next day to several coastal plantations north of Brisbane, 'with the exception of a tallow factory or a truss manufacturer. Diana, however, must gaze upon nuts and ginger as if they were objects of fascination to rank with the Taj Mahal by moonlight.' As it happened, that was the least of her worries because, after a relatively peaceful visit to a ginger factory, and a gentle ride on a

miniature railway (where she saw her first kangaroo) at a pineapple plantation, the crowds were out in force again. Diana became the focus of hordes of men, women and children screaming her name, and brushing police aside in an effort to reach her, when she visited a nut-processing plant at Maroochydore. Worse was to follow when, on their way back to Brisbane, the royal couple stopped at the Alexandra Headland to take a brief look at the beauty of the Sunshine Coast. But as

soon as they emerged from their car they were swamped by a crowd whose enthusiasm left them with no alternative but to beat a hasty retreat back into it.

Those who were inclined to put all this feverish adulation down to the traditional loyalty of Queenslanders had not anticipated the evidence of the following day's activities in Melbourne, where all the records set only two days earlier in Brisbane were broken. The crowd that turned out to greet Diana and her Prince was, by popular estimates, twice as numerous as in Brisbane, and in places they stood twenty deep behind stout police barriers which on this occasion, happily, were strong enough to prevent a repetition of the earlier chaos. Office workers hung huge flags from the windows of high-rise buildings while, down below in the streets, women actually

broke down in tears as the royal couple passed. Three royalist students from the traditionally republican Melbourne University were at the front of the crowd, dressed in Union Jack waistcoats, black tails and toppers, and singing Diana's favourite hymn, *I Vow To Thee My Country*. They managed to delay Diana sufficiently long to kiss her hand in turn, and present her with red roses. Another group of them thrust bunches of violets into her hands – all compliments of the University's Trinity Royal Society. It was all, as one observer said, enough to make a republican weep. One Melbourne journalist who had been pretty scathing about Diana and had adjudged the tour to be a damp squib, kept a low profile that day, while his colleagues were busy concluding that, had the republican-minded Bob Hawke been taken to the polls after, instead of before the tour, he would not now be Prime Minister.

The almost inexplicable wave of unstoppable affection for Diana was, by coincidence, neatly encapsulated in a piece of theatre staged the following day during the royal couple's visit to the former gold-mining district around Bendigo. As they walked through the Sovereign Hill township, they were approached by a man dressed as a nineteenth-century police trooper, who challenged Prince Charles with the words, 'I have reason to believe that you and your lady answer the description of the wanted couple newly arrived in the colony. In pursuance of my duty, I should arrest you both. However, as I see I am vastly

outnumbered by your loyal supporters, I shall let you off with a warning.' Diana was vastly amused as Charles pushed his equerry forward to deal with the fellow, but she could not have been unaware of her singular effect, not just on the bluff old trooper, but also on the reputedly hard-bitten Australians. She admitted before the tour started that Australia was not the easiest country on which to cut her teeth, yet there was hardly a murmur of serious dissent as she made her devastating way right up to that final fabulous charity ball at Melbourne, where she danced again with Prince Charles, wearing another superb, new,

off-the-shoulder gown, this time in beaded white jersey. As one British columnist appreciatively said on that last day, 'We've got a winner here. And I bet they envy us down under.'

No-one took issue with this categoric statement. Though much of the tour, as the details above demonstrate, was routine, its impact as Diana's first foreign venture made it the most heavily covered tour of modern times, and every particular of its programme, the royal performance, and the popular reaction to it kept news and picture agencies flourishing throughout the world. Diana's formula was unchanged – discretion blended with charm, some popular new lines in fashion, a policy of allowing children the lion's share of her attentions, and taking the lion's share of theirs, and a touching concern for the elderly and the handicapped. Those members of the ordinary public who were fortunate enough to meet her acquired the memories of a lifetime in the few seconds that became their lot, while Prime Minister Hawke's ready agreement with his wife's enthusiastic comments about Diana's magnetic attraction and 'those eyes of hers – they are so beautiful', began to convince wishful-thinking monarchists that he was preparing to lay down his republican arms for ever.

Perhaps it was a little perverse that Australia, with its reputably brisk, no-nonsense impatience with ceremonial and the Mother Country complex, received Diana with hardly a grumble or reservation, whereas the atmosphere in New Zealand, which the royal couple visited immediately afterwards, was at times decidedly hostile. From the very start, the New Zealand police had launched the largest security operation ever for a royal tour, with huge numbers of back-up forces and riot squads at the ready, in an effort so to quell potential demonstrations at the beginning of the two-week visit as to discourage them from gaining momentum as the royal programme continued. 'Our objective,' said one police chief, 'is to protect the royal couple from possible injury or embarrassment.'

It was brave talk, in the teeth of some frightening menaces from many minority groups. Chief among them was the threat from Maori rights groups that 'anything is possible', and that they would not be content, in furtherance of their long campaign for the restoration of their land and fishing rights, with the tame tactics they had relied upon in the past. These included the chopping down of the ceremonial flag-pole at the spot where the Treaty of Waitangi, by which in 1840 the Maoris conceded their sovereignty to Queen Victoria, was concluded. In the event, the

Maori protest turned out to be a much muted one. Barring the presence of heckling groups strategically placed among the welcoming crowds, and a contingent of some two dozen who kept up a barrage of abusive chanting as Prince Charles and Diana were ferried across the Bay of Islands to Waitangi, the worst of their experiences was the much celebrated incident of the bare bottom. On their way into Wellington, the royal visitors were greeted by a Maori who presented his grimacing and contorted features to them as part of the traditional mark of respect – then abruptly turned round, flipped up his skirt, and revealed his backside. Though fetchingly patterned with traditional tattoos, it was otherwise uncovered, and the gesture was later explained as the most outrageous insult in the Maori book. Reports vary as to whether Diana actually saw the incident, but some eye witnesses said she did, and that she looked half shocked and half amused when it happened.

were due in the city, the police discovered that his records showed him to have been a one-time member of the IRA, they took no chances. In Auckland, Diana was confronted by a wall of placards calling for a British withdrawal from Northern Ireland and heard their owners denouncing her husband as 'a bludger' – the New Zealand term for a scrounger. In Wellington, she faced the additional ordeal, not only of watching police dealing with Sinn Fein attempts to disrupt a walkabout, but also of meeting a desperately enthusiastic public to the unpleasant accompaniment of rattling begging bowls held by groups of unemployed youths. She watched with dismay as one

Though the troubles in Northern Ireland seemed at the time to have entered a quiet phase, there was no shortage of IRA sympathisers all over the country. At Christchurch, an Irishman was arrested as a prohibited immigrant; he had entered New Zealand only a few days before on the pretext of an invitation to attend a wedding, but when, shortly before Charles and Diana

policeman engaged in a tug-of-war battle over one particularly offensive protest banner, but sensibly turned her back on those demonstrations that got too hot for her. IRA supporters joined forces with Maori demonstrators at Government House in Auckland, where Diana was attending a garden party, and produced one of the noisiest demonstrations of the tour.

Fortunately, deep in the extensive grounds of the building, she was well out of earshot.

Significantly, there was very little evidence of protest against Diana personally, though her presence afforded a timely opportunity for those who wished to see the end of the monarchy in New Zealand to have their say. Obscene graffiti was sprayed by anti-royalists on a stand at Eden Park, which Charles and Diana visited on their first day in Auckland; ten members of the newly-formed Republican Coalition waved the republican flag in front of them in Wellington; while another forty anti-monarchists maintained a hail of insults in a twenty-minute barracking during a walkabout there. Another noisy, thought not particularly disruptive republican demo awaited them at a State banquet in the city one evening, while at the farewell banquet at Auckland's Sheraton Hotel at the end of the tour, the royal car was assailed by an egg which, filled with red paint, smashed against the windscreen, splattering its contents over

the glass and onto the bonnet beneath. No fewer than two hundred protesters – about a tenth of the total crowd that evening – screamed their hostility, though they were no doubt feeling disappointed that the royal car had got there at all. Its serene, unruffled arrival demonstrated the failure of an early attempt at sabotage, when broken glass was spread all over the

Governor-General had lent the couple, failed to start when rain seeped into its ignition – 'one of the most embarrassing moments of my life,' said its chauffeur. It was almost a quarter of an hour before a substitute Daimler was brought out to take Charles and Diana from the boating centre they had just visited back to Government House. In the meantime, they set off on an impromptu walkabout, during which Diana's yellow outfit became drenched, even under the gaberdine raincoat she was wearing, while the ground under her feet quickly turned to mud and made it a matter of great concentration to stay upright.

road bridge which formed part of the processional route to the hotel. One republican protest gave Diana the chance to see the funny side of things. Early on in the tour she and Prince Charles had gone to St James's Theatre in Auckland to see a performance of the ballet *Coppelia* – an event which was nearly cancelled when the management discovered quick-set cement blocking the lavatories, auditorium seats ripped, and the pervading stench of large quantities of stink-bomb fluid that had been sprinkled near the royal box. Hours of disinfecting and re-perfuming failed to obscure the odour completely, but Diana laughed it off as one of those things. 'Sometimes Prince William smells like that!' she added.

Another of Diana's enemies was the rain, which came down so hard and persistently that it threatened to discourage large crowds and so really tested the strength of popular feeling for her. One of the worst days was at Auckland, when everything seemed to go wrong. The 1976 Rolls Royce Phantom which the

Several other downpours made umbrellas indispensable items of luggage everywhere they went, yet at an ANZAC Day service which Diana attended, she found herself without one when a sudden shower came down strong and hard upon her. Her face, as everyone around her armed themselves with their own umbrellas, was a picture – discomfort, embarrassment, anxiety, and even anger with those who should have provided her with one, were all registered in her features.

But despite all the drawbacks, Diana made her usual inimitable impression with the New Zealanders, showing remarkable poise in the face of all that the weather and the demonstrations could throw her way. As always, the simplest gestures were the most appreciated. At Prince Charles' suggestion, she suddenly crossed from one side to the other of a walkabout route in Wellington, to speak to some blind people. 'I thought it was wonderful of her,' one of them said. 'I know how many times she must have to shake hands. Her handshake was a real handshake – not like a dead fish.' For the majority of the

sighted people, there were not the superlatives to describe her. 'Pretty', 'nice', 'beautiful', said various young girls at Eden Park. 'Luscious, beautiful, every bit a lady,' endorsed a woman admirer at Wainiuomata. For others, it was simply enough to have seen her. One lady sat in the rain for seven hours at Wellington to make sure of her front row place. 'To see her close

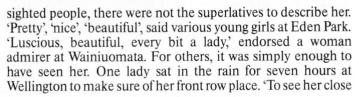

up is worth all the hassle,' she insisted. Younger girls, who only a few years ago would have been disappointed to miss Prince Charles, now conceded that 'it would be nice to meet him, but Diana is more important.' Indeed, Charles got thoroughly used to taking a back seat, and to explaining that some people would simply have to make do with meeting him rather than his wife. 'Hang on, I'll go and fetch her', he once promised; then when his efforts to detach her from other admirers failed, he returned, asking the crowd disarmingly, 'Do you want your money back?' Eventually, he settled for a simple apology. 'I'm sorry, there is only one of her,' became a frequent disclaimer, which he expanded at the farewell banquet. 'Really,' he explained, 'it would have been easier to have two wives, to cover both sides of the road. I could have walked down the middle, directing the operation.'

Much of Diana's popularity derived from her response to the unspoken demands upon her to honour New Zealand's traditions, and nowhere was this more in point than with the

Maoris. Notwithstanding the demonstrations that peppered the tour, the Maori community as a whole is an extremely loyal one and there was universal delight when she graced some of their own special ceremonies. On her first day, she experienced the hongy – that unique Maori greeting in which both hosts and guests press noses together – a pleasant change, someone said, from all those formal handshakes. Diana was not too sure about it at first, and her slight case of nerves was quickly spotted by her welcomers. 'I could tell she was nervous,' said one of them, awarding her not more than five out of ten for her efforts. 'Too hesitant,' said another. 'She needs more practice.' She also seemed a little taken aback during the tribal greeting accorded to her and Prince Charles, in which a stick was thrown at her feet in a ceremonial challenge to the visitors to declare their intentions. She nearly leaped back in fright when the stick came her way – rather too close for comfort, she thought. Her challenger was duly apologetic. 'I thought she would realise it was only a pretence attack,' he said.

There was no pretence about the splendidly traditional journey across the Bay of Islands, towards the end of the tour. So highly did the Maoris esteem Diana that they broke an age-old taboo which forbade them to carry females in their canoes, and she became the first woman to be ferried across the bay by those eighty brawny warriors paddling a colourful ceremonial canoe some 120ft long. It wasn't the most trouble-free of journeys. The canoe had to begin its journey by going backwards to clear the jetty, and it rocked about rather dangerously in a choppy sea in an effort to turn round and face its destination. It was a shallow craft, sitting low in the water, and Diana's attempts to keep dry as she sat on a rubber mat with rushes at her feet were not helped by a leak in the boat which kept the water coming in almost as fast as a pump could expel it. Towards the end of the journey the canoe stuck in the mud and many of the paddlers had to get out to

enable it to reach terra firma. It would have been easier – and more regular – for the warriors to carry her ashore, as tradition dictates, but as no-one could agree about who should be given the honour of doing so, the gesture was foregone.

New Zealand's then Prime Minister, Robert Muldoon, seemed unable to forego the temptation – or so many of his opponents thought – of making political capital out of Diana's popularity in what was generally considered a blatant attempt to revive the fortunes of his ailing Nationalist Party. One observer accused him of being seen at functions which no other leader would have dreamed of attending, of making unforgivable use of the crowds lined up for royal walkabouts by diving into them himself to shake hands, and of using Diana's presence in Christchurch as an excuse to be there himself and give two radio interviews on political issues. 'He turns up like a bad penny,' said one critic. 'Walkabouts are for royal visitors and the public, not for politicians.' But with or without Mr (later Sir Robert) Muldoon, Diana's was the undisputed triumph of the tour. Her superstar charisma thrilled those who had travelled long distances – some as far as three hundred miles – for the chance of a glimpse. Always elegant, demure and friendly, and oozing confidence, style and grace, she pleased the conformist majority of New Zelanders and made their long wait, through the months of postponement, worthwhile.

In the ensuing plaudits from both sides of the world, Diana

was hailed as unbeatable, and regarded as fully blooded, qualified for any job required by her royal position. In the froth of public ecstasy, Prince Charles received less public recognition for his role than he should have done, both for keeping a considerably lower profile than usual, to allow his wife's popularity to blossom and breathe, and for unobtrusively guiding her through the various parts of the tour. To those closely watching, the gentle pull of the elbow, the arm round the waist, the occasional nudge, nod and wink, the frown that indicated concern, the smile that confirmed all was well, showed that the Prince saw his role on the tour as introducing his wife not only to the towns and country areas they visited, but to the way in which royal visits abroad were carried out – protocol, tempo and style.

'I can safely say that Her Royal Highness' decision not to be parted from Prince William struck a warm note among the women of New Zealand,' Mr Muldoon had said on the final day of the tour. Indeed, Prince William's largely unseen presence in

both Australia and New Zealand worked a magnetism all its own. In several of his official speeches, Prince Charles continually emphasised what it meant to him to have Prince William with him. 'I hope,' he had said in Sydney, 'he will grow to regard this country with affection and admiration.' Successive State Premiers took up the theme. In Adelaide, the South

Australian Premier hoped that 'Prince William's presence here will be the first of many visits,' while Tasmania's Premier Gray looked forward 'to meeting Prince William and getting to know him and love him as much as we love you, Sir.' Diana herself was obliged to answer scores of questions about William's welfare during her walkabouts, and in one conversation revealed that, during his first week in Australia he was so unused to the time difference that he began waking up in the middle of the night. Fortunately the weather, disappointingly cold for the Australians, was not dissimilar from the English climate he had just left, and he adapted to it without difficulty. He was also the butt of his father's ready wit. At Hobart, Prince Charles referred to Tasmania's generous wedding present which, he said, 'ensured that our son was born with at least six silver spoons in his mouth. That's why we had to come here – to find out how to get them out.' At a Sydney reception, his jokey revelation that Prince William was being fed at Woomargama on warm milk and minced kangaroo meat – a diet that had been offered to the future King George V during his visit to Australia a century before – backfired. Bombarded with protests from outraged do-gooders, he had to retreat a few days later: 'I was only attempting a joke. I thought Australians had a sense of humour.' Then, as a mischievous after-thought: 'In fact we bring him up on grass and beer.'

Prince William was no less a celebrity in New Zealand. The Maoris called him *Tuakana*, or 'Heir' and made him a kiwi-feather cloak – a small-scale model of one they had already presented to his father. William was billeted at the Governor-General's residence in Auckland, where a top-floor suite had been adapted to include a nursery brightly decorated with animal pictures and mobiles, and, since he had just mastered his first crawl, fitted with a protective swing-gate at the top of the stairs. In his bedroom, which adjoined Nanny Barnes' room, the curtains were lined with black material to keep out sunlight – an unnecessary precaution, it transpired, as the poor weather in New Zealand exceeded even Australia's drab climate. On the

Prince's cot was a quilt appliquéd with pictures of children in colourful overalls and frocks, which a group of New Zealand women stitched to match the one they had sent to London at the time of his birth.

To some of the staff looking after him each day while his parents were out on their royal duties, he tended to look rather grave and serious at times. 'We tried everything to get a smile out of him,' said one, 'but he just looked down at us very seriously as if to remind us of our place.' But he was as different again when he featured in the highlight of his fortnight's stay – the eagerly-awaited photo-call, which eventually took place on St George's Day. Facing manfully up to a posse of forty or fifty cameramen, Prince William set about exploring the secrets beneath the huge floral rug on which he and his parents had established themselves on the lawn of their residence, and showed how well he had, finally, learned to make progress on all fours. Several times his mother and father had to grab him back to the centre of the rug, though not, on one occasion, before he had scooped up a handful of dirt and put it to his mouth. In between giving his

wooden Bizzy Bee toy a great deal of his attention, he managed a few wobbly attempts at standing. It took less than fifteen minutes for all those not yet smitten by his charms to fall victim. Even the New Zealand Government showed its appreciation by providing free disposable nappies, baby foods and toilet requisites in the Air New Zealand plane which took him back home! With him went the pick of over 50,000 gifts from the people his parents met on their journeyings – including a kiwi whose beak opened to the sound of Brahms' lullaby.

When it was time for Prince William to come home, it was to a Britain which offered him some unseasonably cold and rainy weather. Not so his parents, however. 'It has been a fantastic tour,' Diana was reported as saying, 'but I'm absolutely exhausted.' The sentiment was confirmed by her Press

Secretary, who said that 'like the rest of us, she is very tired. It has been a long trip.' She and Prince Charles therefore decided to revive their flagging bodies and souls with a ten-day holiday on Eleuthera, which they hoped would, unlike one they had taken there a year before, remain entirely private. The press respected the royal wish, and the holiday was enjoyed without incident, though many people were disappointed that the date of the homecoming remained a secret, thus depriving everyone of the opportunity to fete Diana after her first, long and successful tour. One of the royal couple's close friends, Sir Harry Secombe, voiced that dismay when he said, 'Princess Diana has become tremendously popular all over the world. A 'welcome home' reception would be a splendid gesture, and she would love it.'

W ithin barely a month of their return to England, Charles and Diana were off again to discharge the last of their 1983 obligations abroad with a 17-day visit to Canada. There was a general feeling at home that, after the phenomenal success of the Australasian trip, the journey to Canada would have little more to offer, but this turned out to be an opinion which failed to take into account the Canadians' well-known taste for celebration and inventiveness, and the almost unquestioning loyalty of Canada's multicultural citizens. In the course of their itinerary, the royal couple were feted by Empire Loyalists, French Acadians, Micmac Indians, and visitors from America, as well as by the descendants of old British Dominion stock and nineteenth-century immigrants from Europe.

Right from the word go, Di-mania became a household word. In Halifax, screaming, frantic women hoisted high their Union Jacks and virtually drowned the welcoming proceedings; at St. John, New Brunswick, both teenagers and older women

were overwhelmed in the heady atmosphere of mass hysteria, and dissolved into tears. As did one young boy in Ottawa, who rushed up to Diana and kissed her. 'I can't believe I just did that,' he blurted through his tears afterwards. Shouts of 'We Want Di' came from every direction, no matter where the royal couple went. Posters showing official portraits of Diana moved from side to side above a sea of heads, along with hand-made banners proclaiming love and loyalty. One in St. John announced, 'We love you. Give our love to little William and the rest of the family.'

More serious consequences of Di-mania attended the opening by Prince Charles of the Police Headquarters building in Ottawa, as scores of people in the crowd of 10,000 keeled over in midsummer temperatures which reached 86°. The Prince himself remarked, on opening the building, that 'its first use will probably be as a first aid post.' He also had a mischievously witty response to one French Acadian who told him that he had been in London for the Royal Wedding. 'Were you really,' replied Prince Charles. 'That was very rash of you. You didn't get over-charged, did you?' Sometimes it seemed as if Diana could not

cope with all the adulation. At a welcoming banquet in Halifax, she received a standing ovation as she entered the room, but was unable to acknowledge it save by an embarrassed lowering of the head. And at one stop during a walkabout in St. John, it seemed as if she was intent on shaking hands with every one of the 40,000 people there. Prince Charles became visibly anxious about her, and after speaking with his entourage, decided to prompt her to speed things up a bit. The pace quickened, though it was probably much against Diana's will. When, at Shearwater, a 91-year-old woman told her, 'You must get tired of meeting so many people and shaking so many hands,' Diana replied, 'Oh no, not at all. I love it.'

The tour was tailor-made for getting the best from the royal visitors. There was a boat trip down the Rideau Canal at Ottawa, and a lobster lunch at Bridgewater, at which Diana refused to wear a bib and tucker because she feared it would not go over her hat without knocking it askew. Prime Minister Trudeau hosted

her and Prince Charles to a barbecue at his country home, and in casual gear they walked around eating from platefuls of smoked salmon and corn cobs. There were children's sing-songs during the many musical performances they heard, though Diana usually looked rather conspicuous as she half-heartedly joined in the singing. And there was that superb Klondike-style entertainment at Fort Edmonton, in which Diana bowled over the invited guests in her high Victorian ensemble of peaches and cream satins and silks, high boots, bustled skirt, whaleboned bodice, parasol and a dainty flowered saucer hat to cover her rather twentieth-century hairstyle. Thousands of balloons went up in her honour at Halifax and at Edmonton, where 65,000 people, assembled at the Commonwealth Stadium for the World University Games, sang 'Happy Birthday To You' – even

State banquet distinguished himself by forgetting to fill Diana's glass with champagne for the royal toast; while, after a dinner in St. John, the New Brunswick Premier forgot to call for the saying of grace until the guests were on their way out. When he did remember, he stopped so suddenly that he bumped into Prince Charles, who was knocked against a door post. On top of all that there were the extremes of weather that caught the royal party napping once or twice. The high summer heat of the Federal Capital was 40° up on the blowy climes of the Maritime Provinces, but you got the impression that Diana preferred the latter. Never one to stand high temperatures easily, she complained of the heat in Ottawa, adding, while talking to two girls wearing swimsuits in the crowd, 'You're wearing the right equipment. I wish I could wear something like that.'

though there were two days to go before her 22nd birthday.

As everyone had long since come to expect, it was a tour for individuals as well as crowds, and incidents both delightful and embarrassing came thick and fast. At Edmonton, the little girl who presented Diana with the official bouquet persisted in walking with her through the main street, determined to tail her through the entire walkabout, until at last someone persuaded her that her services were no longer required. At Halifax, a twelve-year-old boy asked to kiss her hand, and was awestruck immediately afterwards. 'Boy, is she beautiful,' he said. 'I just had to do it.' And Diana herself just had to let a four-year-old blind boy 'see' her by touching her hair, face, shoes and legs in a special private audience, after she had taken a bunch of flowers from him without realising his disability. At Ottawa, a waiter at a

As always, she was swamped with presents, and no article was too trivial to count. Lowest of the low, but as well received as any, was a family set of three coat-hangers someone from a crowd handed her. Scores of others were loaded into her arms for Prince William, and at almost every port of call there were official gifts for him too. A deerskin Indian suit from the Micmacs at Charlo – 'Perfect' she said. 'William will love it'; a model fishing boat from Shelburne; a canoe from St. Andrew's, and a rocking-horse from the inhabitants of Prince Edward Island. There was no indication that the Canadians were put out at not being favoured with the young Prince's presence among them, but there was disappointment. Prince Charles explained that 'we felt that the ship's voyage might not be good for him; life aboard the Royal Yacht would not have suited him', and Diana was quick to show her own feelings. Hardly had she landed at Halifax than she was confessing, 'I miss him very much. I'm sorry we couldn't bring him this time, but we will next time.'

She was missing him even more by the time she got to Ottawa, according to one woman to whom she also revealed, 'He's a beautiful boy and we are both extremely proud of him.'

William's first birthday, which fell at the end of the first week of the tour, while his parents were in Ottawa, gave the Canadians another excuse for celebration. Diana was overwhelmed with presents for him, and special birthday greetings were spread across banners everywhere. Prince Charles had, a few days earlier, regretted that he could not disclose what he and Diana had bought William for his birthday, except to say that 'it's something he won't be able to break,' but very early on the day itself they were up and about, putting through a telephone call to Kensington Palace, where William was busy with piles of other gifts. 'All I could hear were a few squeaks,' said Prince Charles later, explaining that 'he can't talk very well at the moment, of course.'

Somehow, the anniversary prompted the Prince to drop all sorts of hints about increasing the size of his family, and the Canadians felt as privileged to be the receivers of a whole succession of signals to this effect, as Diana was abashed by his continual references to something she clearly found rather

personal and discomforting. In Bridgewater, Charles only just managed to check himself in time when, promising future royal visits to Canada, he said, 'I'm sure that we shall be able to send our son – or perhaps several by then (laughter, applause) – and that's not a hint I can assure you...' At a youth festival in Newfoundland the Prince actually expressed a wish for more children, at which Diana blushed and muttered, 'How embarrassing!' He had done the same thing in public while in Alberta. 'In private,' Alberta's Premier Brian Peckford

commented, 'Diana would have come straight back with a quip. But when there's a crowd, she can't do that and she gets embarrassed.'

At the same time, there was no doubting that as a team, Charles and Diana accomplished everything that was expected of them. Their little jokes at each other's expense, which had been a popular gloss on their official duties in Australia and New Zealand, had the Canadians chuckling just as appreciatively. 'Hasn't she got a lovely view from the back?' said Prince Charles

to a crowd in Ottawa as he turned to see Diana plunging into yet another group of people on the other side of the road. 'It's nearly as old as my husband,' hooted Diana, when somebody showed her a Union Jack that had been made at the time of Queen Victoria's Diamond Jubilee in 1897. But more importantly, Diana had, by the time the Canadian tour ended at the beginning of July, received a great deal of gentle schooling from her husband. He grew accustomed to admitting his own secondary importance as the roadshow progressed, and

contented himself with keeping a watchful and careful eye on Diana, making sure she was not being hopelessly swamped, reassuring her by the occasional squeeze of the hand or a brief word snatched in between the official ceremonies, or guiding her from one place to another with a deftness of hand that was seen only by the most acute observers.

Moreover, it was obvious that Diana had observed and absorbed the skills of her husband when it came to the art of exchanging friendly banter with crowds, without awkward

pauses, personal familiarity or controversial blunders. 'I've matured a lot recently,' she was confident enough to tell Premier Peckford. 'I've learned a lot in the last few months, particularly in the last four. I'm doing my job better now than I was before. I am still finding it very difficult to cope with pressure, but I am learning to cope with it.' Back in Britain there was no doubt about it. When she arrived home for the last time, she found that her absence had done nothing to diminish the interest of her own countrymen in her. As previously, the tour had been followed in the United Kingdom with persistence and close attention, and the newspapers went out of their way to welcome her back and congratulate her on a job well done.

ndeed, the fulsome praise Diana received from the press that July seemed to indicate that its rather over-long period of almost three years spent getting into bad odour with her had come to an end. For there was no doubt that, not only during courtship but since their marriage, the royal couple – Diana in particular – had come in for some very rough treatment at the hands of some sections of Fleet Street whose bread and butter was derived from insinuation, innuendo and intrusion against the new royal recruit. Like most public figures, members of the Royal Family have now learned to live with the fact that those who are accorded a place in the news because of their rank or success remain potential news material twenty-four hours a day, and the intrusive flash of the camera and click of the tape recorder are as much a part of their existence as the very act of breathing.

This, of course, was something which Diana learned with more than a degree of vigour in those late summer weeks of 1980, and only a year later she well appreciated that each aspect of her behaviour would become part of the royal 'image' every bit as much as the well-known mannerisms of any of the established members of her husband's family. If the great and undignified rush for Diana late in 1980 was at all forgivable, it was because, not being royal, she was unprotected from the

convention of respect normally accorded to the Crown, and was thus in a similar position to any other member of the public in whom a potential news story resides. The trouble was that the press' attitude towards Diana then set a precedent for their subsequent treatment of her, so that rumour and scandals have dogged her as closely and as relentlessly as those photographers and journalists did in the four or five months before her engagement.

There is nothing more logical to a journalist who has followed and encouraged a fairy-tale romance with its wonderful, cathartic wedding, than to probe for signs that the bubble has burst. Accordingly, it was not long after her marriage that, having drained all news value out of the engagement and wedding, the newspapers began to get wind of stories which, when published, cast shadows on the contentment which Charles and Diana had made abundantly clear on honeymoon. At first it was all fairly trivial. There was the gentle criticism from the vice-chairman of the Derbyshire Area Health Authority, who took Diana to task for not eating breakfast (an admission which she had made a week or so earlier) and recommended that she should take 'some cereal with a little bran; tea or coffee with milk; and a slice of bread.' More spectacularly, Diana's new portrait – painted by Bryan Organ, ultimately to become one of Prince Harry's godparents – was violently slashed and seriously damaged by a young student while it was on display in the National Portrait Gallery in London. The student, sentenced to six months' imprisonment, was ordered to pay £1,000 compensation towards repair work which, in the event, took about 250 hours of skilled labour to complete. Another untoward incident, this time showing a more doubtful side of the art world, concerned paintings purporting to show Diana in the nude: these were displayed in the Rotherham public house of Mr Brian Williams, but in spite of the furore it caused, the police decided not to bring any charges against him.

But these were small matters compared with the story which burst into the headlines in mid-September, during the long extension to Charles and Diana's honeymoon. All was evidently not well at home, and reports of Diana's inability to

adapt to the royal life-style – even on holiday! – began to appear. She was apparently becoming restless under the pressure of formality at Balmoral, and had wanted to move into smaller premises as soon as the Queen left for London. There were also stories that the Queen had wanted to give Diana a gun-dog for a present, but that Diana had refused it because of her dislike of blood sports. She had also, according to the rumours, refused to accompany the frequent shooting parties at Balmoral, and was reportedly bored and tired by the over-long formal dinner parties there, as well as unhappy about the manner in which she was expected to treat servants. The Palace found itself unable to make any worthwhile comment on matters of such a private nature; it merely denied the story of the move to smaller quarters by explaining that a decision was taken even before the wedding that, when the Queen moved back to London, Charles and Diana would go to live at Craigowan House, so that the Castle could be closed up for the winter and the servants be sent back to London. And it was left at that.

The rumours about Diana not accompanying the royal party on shooting expeditions were contradicted in October by fresh, and more damaging, allegations from the League Against Cruel Sports that she had in fact shot and killed a deer, though none too cleanly, while on a deer-stalking outing the previous week. This led to an immediate outcry, and torrents of public discussion and argument, during which it was also alleged that the Queen was a regular deer-hunter with a practised aim. As far as Diana's

activities were concerned, Buckingham Palace again offered an awkwardly-worded denial whose ambiguity only added fuel to the League's indignation and protest against Diana's alleged support for what it called 'this killing-for-fun brigade which is destroying Britain's wildlife.' These major criticisms and stories, and the adverse publicity they engendered, caused Diana considerable distress which could hardly have been alleviated by the flippant suggestion that she should take a portable stereo cassette player with her on shoots, so that she could be near her husband without being obliged to hear the constant blasts of the guns.

At Sandringham the following January, the theme was expanded. Now, Diana was not only against pheasant-shooting in principle, but was prepared to air her grievances in public, to a speechless Prince Charles. 'You know I didn't want to come here in the first place,' she snapped at him, well within the hearing of scores of milling journalists, as the royals plodded over the

frozen fields in search of game. So that clinched it: the radiant couple of only five months before were now incompatible, and the press who had willed them into their marriage were now looking for signs that it might follow a career similar to that of Princess Caroline of Monaco and her first husband. Already branded as the force behind Charles' recently abandoned participation in horse-racing, Diana was now credited with a will of steel and a determination to get her own way at all costs. Further evidence for the interpretation of events was gleefully retrieved from the sacking of one of Charles' long-serving valets, the dismissal of at least two of Diana's personal detectives, and the noticeable cooling in relationships with some of her husband's most loyal, long-standing and trusted friends.

Out of all proportion to everything except the extent and persistence of public gullibility and obtrusive curiosity, the evolving issues were turned over again and again. The Palace stood tactfully aloof, commenting as infrequently as it could afford, and then mostly with vinegary denials as dismissive as they were scornful. Only once did the Queen herself take action: that was in December 1981 after Diana had spent over a month as the target of photographers who spent hours in the undergrowth around Highgrove for a 'stolen' picture of her at home, or who roamed the nearby town of Tetbury as she did the occasional spot of personal shopping. A meeting of Fleet Street editors took place at Buckingham Palace, where the Queen's press secretary pleaded for the proper observance of Diana's privacy, on behalf of the Queen who was concerned for her more as a daughter-in-law than as a member of the Royal Family. Most editors were in co-operative mood, though one failed to attend and another told the Queen to her face that if Diana cared so highly for her privacy she should send a servant out to buy her wine gums for her.

Because the difficult question of defining legitimate and undesirable coverage was avoided or not properly thrashed out, the meeting failed in the long term. Worse followed two-months later, when the news was leaked that Diana, then four months pregnant, would be going with Prince Charles to spend a ten-day private holiday on the Bahamian island of Eleuthera. Several European *paparazzi* and Fleet Street photographers who had preceded them there spent two days taking pictures of the bikini-

clad Princess, visibly pregnant, sunbathing with her husband and their hosts the Romseys, and the results were transmitted back to London to appear as red-hot exclusives in two of the next day's tabloid newspapers. The publication of the pictures infuriated the Queen, whose press secretary Michael Shea deplored them as being 'in the worst possible taste. It is apparent,' he added, 'that these pictures were taken without the Prince and Princess being aware of this. Such tasteless behaviour is in breach of the normally accepted British press standards in respect of the privacy of individuals.'

The royal protest was not unique: the switchboard at Buckingham Palace was jammed by calls from loyal and outraged subjects; MPs signed motions in the House of Commons, attacking both of the offending newspapers – The *Sun* and the *Daily Star* – and regretting that their editors 'should have fallen so far short of the professional standards of journalism'; while the Press Council started an investigation which eventually brought its erring sons to book for exceeding the bounds of journalistic justification and good taste. Meanwhile, Fleet Street in general disapproved, the *Daily*

*Express* making a particular display of sanctimonious dissociation, as the transgressing editors prepared to throw in the towel. One newspaper executive, however, decried the fuss which everyone was so obviously enjoying, and was disgusted with the two offenders for not making a fight of it. As if to acknowledge his point, they both gave in only with a final touch of defiant mischief. The *Sun* published its apology accompanied by one of the very pictures that had caused the rumpus in the first place, and protested that the photographs 'brought a breath of summer into the lives of millions of our readers back in chilly Britain. Of course it was never our intention to offend. If we have done so, then we are deeply sorry. But we still think that Princess Di looks terrific.'

This transparently tongue-in-cheek assurance was mirrored by The *Sun's* partner-in-crime, of whom it could fairly be said that the lady did protest too much. 'We published out of deep affection,' said the *Daily Star*, wide-eyed with outraged innocence. 'We were pleased to see Diana enjoying herself, and thought our readers would want to share her joy, especially as many of them had telephoned us saying how tired she had looked on television the night before. We felt the British public would want to know that Diana was looking so well and lovely.'

Behind the smoke-screen of words, both papers withdrew their photographers from the island, promised to leave the royal couple in peace, and declared that they would not now be selling the rights to reproduce their pictures to potential customers abroad. The excitement melted away almost as quickly as it had arisen though, as at least one later comment from Diana was to show, forgiveness took a little longer.

Perhaps it was the preoccupation with the Falklands that spring or indeed with the birth of Prince William in June, that allowed the critical clamour generally to die down for a few months. Indeed for a time, and to her delight, Diana found

herself being praised for the speed and apparent ease with which she regained her figure after giving birth, to say nothing of being cited in newspapers and magazines as the example to be followed by newly-confined mothers who despair of ever getting back into shape again. But then even that went sour. A succession of photographs showing Diana to be unusually thin – disturbingly so even to the most sceptical observer – coupled with the story that she had refused this or that dish at official functions on the grounds that 'I am minding my figure', gave credence to a report that she had contracted anorexia nervosa. As we have seen, this modern medical phenomenon had

already struck once in the Spencer family and it was an hereditary complaint. Immediately, Diana's so-called problem assumed the status of a national crisis, with well-meaning advice coming from columnists, doctors, psychiatrists and the like and finding its way into print alongside the latest leak from 'a close friend of Diana's' which revealed the alleged concern of everyone in her circle, from the Queen downwards.

Things were made no easier when, in November, Prince Charles turned up at the Festival of Remembrance without his wife, explaining – according to one source – that she was ill and would not be coming. Five minutes later, the Princess arrived, 'looking grumpy and not at all happy' and, as there was no official explanation for her lateness, a marital tiff was immediately guessed at. It seemed a plausible conclusion to the more impressionable readers of newspapers, and to those avid for fresh scandal, because it came hard on the heels of a revelation that, only a month earlier, Diana had suddenly left Balmoral and flown to London for a shopping spree at Harrods, Harvey Nichols, and – if some are to be believed – almost every other clothes shop in Knightsbridge. The story had run that she was again bored with the weather and the company at Balmoral,

and had left Prince Charles to complete any unfinished business before he went off to Mexico to open a college. In fact, Diana was in London for that meeting with Madame Sadat, but knowledge of this came late, and the rumours were not dispelled. Suddenly her behaviour had become 'increasingly unpredictable' – a phrase much used in the subsequent light of concern over her health.

Since Prince William's birth, Diana had undoubtedly been slimming. Her strenuous efforts to get back into shape had been much applauded, and many young mothers seemed to be copying her example, bursting for any chance information about her diet. But there was an unease at her rather angular, hollow-cheeked appearance, and no matter how vivacious she seemed on any public occasion, the anxiety increased, even

among those not in search of sensation. There was no shortage of diagnoses. She was suffering from post-natal depression, missing her sleep, and had lost interest in food. An unnamed member of her family was quoted as saying, 'I am extremely worried about her. She has become frighteningly thin. But she won't take kindly to advice, however well-meant.' Buckingham Palace was naturally inundated with enquiries about Diana's health, and lost no time in stressing that the Royal Family was 'appalled' by these 'groundless rumours'. 'I would have thought,' said one spokesman, 'that the fact that the Princess of Wales was

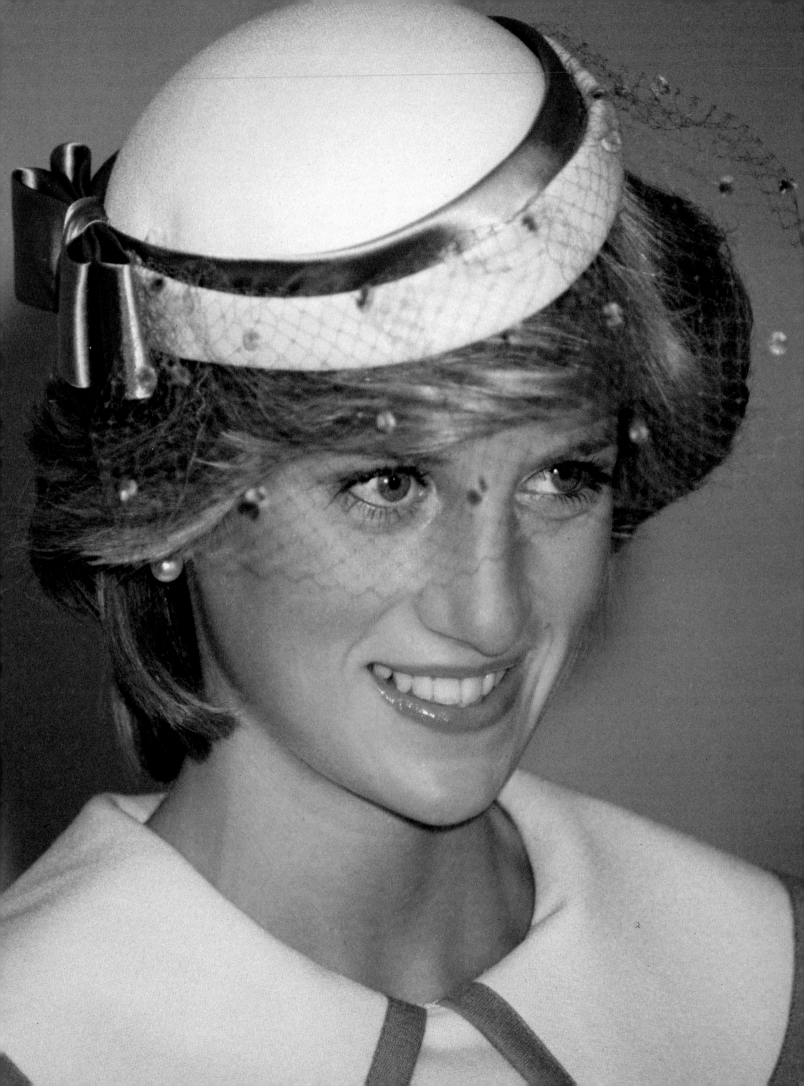

in sparkling form on two public occasions yesterday for millions to see speaks for itself.' Almost desperately, a few days later, he added, 'We ask those responsible for these grossly exaggerated stories to leave her alone, for God's sake.'

Miraculously it happened; the rumours stopped, the gossip-writers and columnists took a more sympathetic line – though without necessarily admitting defeat – and when Nigel Dempster, gossip-columnist for the *Daily Mail* – appeared on television in December to accuse the Princess of being 'a monster, a fiend who is ruling the roost and making Charles desperately unhappy,' Diana soon discovered who her friends really were. Those who only the previous month had asserted that she obviously did 'not have the intellectual capacity to come to terms with what she so blithely took on' now praised her 'inveterate good nature and cheerfulness', talked of her never putting a foot wrong, and commended the way she had charmed and inspired everybody – so much so that every charity was apparently falling over itself to engage her for their major fund-raising events. And when she was twice seen riding a horse at Sandringham the following January – a sure sign that her fear of riding, born of an early fall from a horse, had been overcome – everything was forgiven. She was clearly back in the royal fold, contrite, obedient, conformist.

The truce didn't last long. 'As I get older,' Prince Charles had said in Mexico, 'I find that less privacy becomes available and more and more people seem to be interested in every small and minute aspect of one's life.' As if to illustrate this, the regular army of British journalists followed him and Diana to Liechtenstein in the New Year of 1983 and captured hundreds of

pictures of them as they attempted to enjoy their first ski-ing holiday together. Urged on by the persistence of an even larger contingent of European press, the British photographers were not easily shifted by appeals from the royal entourage, some plain speaking by Prince Charles, and an exhibition of Diana's favourite ploy with unwelcome cameramen – the turned back, the lowered head, and the most thunderous of black, impassive looks. Things improved markedly the following year. Charles and Diana proposed that they should pose for photographs on the first day of their 1984 ski-ing holiday, while the press, having secured their photographs, should undertake to leave the area, allowing them a truly private stay as guests of the Liechtenstein

Royal Family. At first, the British press was divided, two newspapers refusing immediate cooperation. A Swiss magazine, which had hired a helicopter in 1983 to monitor Charles and Diana's movements from the air, threatened their privacy again for 1984, though there was logic in its argument that 'there just cannot be restricted areas in public places.'

When the day came, Charles and Diana duly posed for five minutes in front of eighty photographers who snapped eagerly away while the Prince jokingly offered to fall over for them. Diana – who was so patently less cheerful that one observer

thought that she really could have 'spared the time to look genuinely pleasant' – *did* fall over, quite accidentally, and the photographer who recorded the incident had his film confiscated. Eventually, the couple boarded a ski-lift and sailed away with a final, pointed message – 'Now a very good-bye' – from Prince Charles. The sentiment was formalised by the couple's press officer, who announced that 'the Prince and Princess would expect the remainder of their holiday to be considered private, with no intrusive activity by any member of

the media.' It worked. A few stragglers decided to stay on, but when a German photographer had his camera taken from him by the Prince's detective, even they called it a day and left the slopes to a sprinkling of determined yet eventually unsuccessful freelancers.

Things have been remarkably quiet since then, though Diana of all people knows that she cannot relax while public interest in her continues to show no sign of letting up. She admitted as much during a conversation with a Canadian journalist, which itself turned out to be one of the less savoury incidents of the 1983 visit to Canada. The conversation took place during a press reception given by the royal couple on board *Britannia* – an event frequently staged by senior members of the Royal Family in an effort to maintain a working rapport with

journalists. Contrary to the understanding that such receptions are not coverable occasions, Mrs Diana Bentley who, with her editor husband David, was part owner of the *Halifax Daily News*, was apparently 'bubbling over with so much enthusiasm for Princess Diana' that she reported her off-the-record observations about her 'trials and tribulations at the hands of the wolf-pack-like British tabloid press.' Consequently, the paper's 20,000 readers were treated to descriptions, beneath the banner headline *The Agonies Of A Princess*, of Diana prodding her own chest and saying, 'When they write something horrible I get a horrible feeling right here, and I don't want to go outside.'

Reportedly berating the 'media types' because 'they don't always tell the truth,' Diana allegedly resigned herself to 'five or ten years to get used to it'.

When the story broke, her press secretary, Victor Chapman – also a Canadian – declared himself 'very upset about this.' He described Mrs Bentley's action as 'totally unethical. She has broken all the ground rules set up for these receptions. I am sure the Prince and Princess will be very upset.' He announced that the *Daily News* would not be invited to any future reception for any members of the Royal Family – an embargo imposed with the full agreement of an embarrassed Canadian Government. Mrs Bentley wavered between obstinacy and repentance. Initially justifying her action by reference to her trade ('I am in the news business and it is my duty to report on the royal couple') and accusing Mr Chapman of over-reacting, she offered a tentative olive branch. 'I feel great empathy for the Princess,' she pleaded. 'I would certainly apologise to her if she felt I had been unfair to her.'

ith the Australasian and Canadian tours at an end, everyone seemed to agree that summer 1983 was a good time for Diana to be thinking about her second baby. Sure enough, speculation began to increase through the summer months, after a September visit from Balmoral to London had coincided with the return of her gynaecologist from holiday, and caused immediate and convinced talk that she was expecting again. Buckingham Palace's denial was stated in such carefully chosen words – 'If she is having a baby, it will be announced at the proper time' – that if anything, the speculation increased. By the autumn, the idea was being passed around as if she had some kind of obligation to produce again. Diana was told that a two-year gap between

children was ideal, that to wait longer could increase young Prince Wiliam's sense of isolation, even that she had a duty to ensure the succession to the throne. For her part, she carefully avoided the question in public. She was inwardly staggered when, visiting a sweet factory in Dundee shortly afterwards, she was actually asked whether she was pregnant. 'That's a very personal question,' Diana chided, cleverly answering neither yes nor no, while other workers swore they detected in her all the signs of prospective motherhood. One said that she looked too well not to be pregnant; another that she had 'a special glow'; a third that she was 'definitely blooming'; yet another that she seemed to be acting similarly to a couple of local girls who were themselves expecting. She had already put down one member of the public months before, saying 'I am not a production line, you know,' and when, on a visit to a school for the mentally handicapped late in 1983, one pupil patted her on the tummy and asked how the baby was, Diana merely blushed and said, 'Did I hear right?' Paid royal-watchers declared their certain knowledge not only that Diana *was* pregnant, but that Palace staff had not been told of it, and the tone of orchestrated certainty seemed to give the whole world and his wife justification for weighing in to dispense prediction and advice – from the astrologer Russell Grant, who foresaw that she would have five more children, to the former editor of *Debrett*, who tackled the heady question of possible names for the new infant.

By now the royalty correspondents of the tabloid press were tapping their Palace contacts for confirmation. Almost all were agreed by the middle of September that Prince William would have a nursery companion by the early summer, and on evidence no more convincing than run-of-the-mill throwaway opinions, like the one from an anonymous Balmoral employee, that 'we don't need an official announcement to tell us what is

going on.' In the face of categoric denials from Victor Chapman, coupled with denunciations of the rumours as 'rubbish', only the *Daily Star* trod a wary and considerate path. 'It is not something to make statements about – like a government announcing periodically that we are not at war,' it stated, remaining aloof from a hubbub of clamour which agitated the foreign press as much as the British. The French led by combining rumours old and new in a claim that Diana, though pregnant, was able to conceal the fact because of her anorexia; while an American

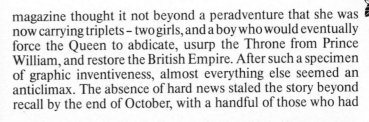

magazine thought it not beyond a peradventure that she was now carrying triplets – two girls, and a boy who would eventually force the Queen to abdicate, usurp the Throne from Prince William, and restore the British Empire. After such a specimen of graphic inventiveness, almost everything else seemed an anticlimax. The absence of hard news staled the story beyond recall by the end of October, with a handful of those who had

confidently predicted a pregnancy the previous month explaining all away by the revelation that Diana was, after all, having difficulty in conceiving and was consequently, according to that faceless legion of unnamed close friends, tense and tearful.

When the Palace announced, at about the same time, that Charles and Diana would be paying a two-week visit to Italy the following October, any remaining hopes of Diana producing in 1984 seemed effectively squashed. This prompted one medical journalist to suggest, early in February, that Diana's dramatic weight loss and the influence of stress were contributory factors which had prevented conception but, that apart, talk of babies was out of fashion while the guesswork was transferred to whether she would meet the Pope or visit Pompeii. So Diana must have felt triumphant when she was able, in mid-February, to announce her expectations after all, and to take everybody by surprise at the same time. The news was received with almost universal delight, nowhere better illustrated than in Coventry where a somewhat shy Princess was to carry out her first subsequent engagement – a visit with Prince Charles to the Jaguar car plant at Allesley. There was much talk about losing shape as the pregnancy progressed, many questions about whether Diana would not like a girl this time, countless enquiries about her health, and some slightly irreverent *double entendres* from the male workforce when Prince Charles complimented them on their production record!

The first baby gifts were received on that day, when a pair of woolly mittens and a toy monkey were tossed through the open window of the royal limousine. The medical profession seemed equally happy with the news, congratulating Diana on perfect timing which would give William a companion at the very juncture when he could enjoy much needed company without the risk of sibling rivalry. The maternity wear business was all smiles again, in the expectation of a boom in the wake of some new Diana fashions. And the Royal Family itself was, to quote Princess Michael of Kent, 'ecstatic'. Of the prospective grandmothers, the Queen was said to be delighted, and to have been in sparkling form at the following day's Investiture at Buckingham Palace, while Mrs Shand Kydd declared, 'I am very excited. They're really happy days when they are safely in the world.' Even Prince Philip, rarely one to be bowled over by news of this nature, admitted to guests at a Windsor Rugby Club dinner, 'We are all very pleased.' As was Diana's sister, Lady Jane Fellowes, at this 'lovely news. It's smashing.'

The announcement of Diana's pregnancy came on the eve of

St Valentine's Day, and gave the press an unexpected bonus to this annual theme which never fails to sell papers. Only the *Morning Star* kept the news well removed from any Valentine connection, offering it a mere, factual five lines on the penultimate page of its six-page edition. The *Socialist Worker* pulled out all its anti-monarchist stops with the headline *Another Royal Brat*, which advertised a discontented, insulting and distasteful article containing the promise that 'this little kid will grow up to be just as big a bastard as all its relatives.' Meanwhile, a Liverpool gynaecologist, Professor Harold Francis, anticipated that, if the royal couple should go on to have

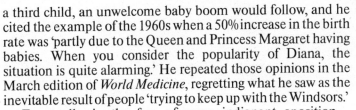

a third child, an unwelcome baby boom would follow, and he cited the example of the 1960s when a 50% increase in the birth rate was 'partly due to the Queen and Princess Margaret having babies. When you consider the popularity of Diana, the situation is quite alarming.' He repeated those opinions in the March edition of *World Medicine*, regretting what he saw as the inevitable result of people 'trying to keep up with the Windsors.'

Eventually, in the face of some indignant oposition – Buckingham Palace described his suggestions as 'presumptuous', while one Member of Parliament said 'It's up to us how many children we want. If Charles and Diana want fifteen, then good luck to them' – Professor Francis backed down. He accepted that 'in Princess Diana's case a slightly larger family is acceptable in order to ensure the succession to the Throne. But,' he warned, 'the optimum number she should have is three.' He was joined by a representative group of West German women who considered that Prince Charles should

now be sterilised, in order 'to take a great physical and mental burden' from his wife. But they at least did not have Diana's support. 'Men don't understand women's determination to have babies,' she said during a visit to Hammersmith Hospital a month later, and a week after that she was saying that although she didn't think she was 'made for the production line, it's all worth it in the end.' That comment followed an admission that morning sickness had again begun to take its toll on her. 'I haven't felt very well since Day One,' she complained as she began to lack some of her usual public fizz. Throughout those early months, it quickly became clear that she was worse affected even than in 1981 by the constant indispositions which took her so much by surprise at the beginning of her first pregnancy.

But she still continued to think positively, hoping, she said about then, 'for a girl this time.' Prince Charles had already expressed the same wish, though his reason – 'so that she can look after me in my old age' – sent the feminists rushing around with protests urgent upon their tongues. It also sent the punters off to the bookmakers, who had opened their ledgers on the choice of names and were then offering shortest odds for Elizabeth, Victoria, Alexandra, George and Richard, while you could get up to 1,000-1 for Tracy, Wayne and Spike. In the battle of the sexes, it was odds-on for a girl, evens for a boy, 25-1 against

twins, 200-1 against triplets. Until early April that is, when a bevy of well-presented gentlemen – 'They weren't exactly wearing coronets or ermine robes, but they seemed to be people who could have a little knowledge from inside,' said a counter clerk – tried to place £700 worth of bets at four different branches of the same bookmakers on the prospect of twins. Wisely – since this occurred at just about the same time as Diana might reasonably have expected to see the results of a scan, and had been reported to have purchased two identical shawls from Harrods – the bookies closed their account on multiple births.

It wasn't until mid-July that Prince Charles put down all those rumours about twins: during a visit to East London, he admitted having wondered whether his wife might produce them, 'but I think not.' So anybody who saw Harrods delivering two cots to Kensington Palace, or Diana buying two sets of baby towels in London, had jumped to the wrong conclusions. Meanwhile Diana, now clearly enjoying her second pregnancy, was busy comparing notes with housewives and expectant mothers all over the country. She counted her blessings during a

June visit to Chester when opening a hospital wing at which infertile women could be treated, told wellwishers at Salisbury that she was doing plenty of swimming and exercises, and confided to workers at a sweet factory in Bridgend that she would eat more of their products if she didn't have to watch her weight. She might have known that these casual comments would soon become excuses for more journalistic inventions, and within the short space of two months she was reckoned to be on a diet of almost anything from royal jelly, honey and wheatgerm oil (to keep her nervous system in order), to fried breakfasts (to satisfy overnight cravings). Soon, the inside stories were becoming more specific than ever. For the price of a newspaper, you could be told that the new baby would be born 'in the early hours of 27th September', or that Prince Charles had arranged for a film to be made of successive X-rays which Diana had undergone, and that, although he knew the sex of his second child as a result, Diana preferred not to know in advance. Looking further ahead, there was mounting speculation on the identity of the lucky man chosen to take the official photographs

of the new baby, and a unique revelation that Diana would be taking both her offspring on a 1985 tour of America – which nobody else knew anything about!

Diana made little concession to the demands of her second pregnancy – certainly no more than with her first. The Royal Family's traditional summer break began, as always, early in August and gave her the excuse to live out the last six weeks of her term without official obligations. Her public engagements had, however, continued almost to the very end of July, and her so-called 'private' visits to Wimbledon, Ascot and polo grounds

throughout the South of England kept her fascinated public abreast of her progress. She and Prince Charles took Prince William to Balmoral as usual, but they were all back in London well before her confinement was due. The fact disappointed the Scots, who had hoped that Diana's Balmoral holiday would run its usual ten-week course, and that her second baby (like the Queen Mother's second child) would be born in Scotland.

So, as with the birth of Prince William, St Mary's Hospital, Paddington was again the focus for the loyal crowd which congregated in the damp September air as soon as Diana's admission to the famous Lindo Wing was announced. True to form, the second child arrived with greater ease and speed than the first – nine hours from that admission, as opposed to the sixteen hours it took for Prince William to be delivered – and

Prince Charles spoke with obvious relief when he told wellwishers that evening, 'The delivery couldn't have been better. It was much quicker than last time.' Nineteen hours later, the baby's names – a refreshing combination of family traditions and popular informality – were published, and three hours after that Diana emerged from hospital dressed in a glowing scarlet coat and bearing the little swaddled bundle that was Henry Charles Albert David – Prince Harry. She looked thoroughly relaxed, overjoyed with her child, a little discomfited at the long obligatory standstill while photographers and film cameramen recorded the scene, and as engaging as ever. It was four years, almost to the day, since that first press picture of her in Charles' company at Balmoral was spread across the nation's daily papers, and the transition seemed remarkable.

**T**hen, back in those early days of 1981, Willie Hamilton had said 'All brides look radiant until the gilt wears off the gingerbread', he reckoned without Diana and her way of doing things. Her radiance has survived both her wedding day and two pregnancies, and she gave ample notice of her determination to combine motherhood and her official duties by the strong-willed programme which got her back into shape very soon after both her confinements, ready for the forthcoming seasons of engagements, and by the end of each subsequent autumn she had emerged like a sparkling butterfly. That rumour that she had cut short her 1982 Balmoral holiday in a fit of pique and boredom, to blow £50,000 or more on a complete new wardrobe, was almost certainly at odds with the truth but, judging by the stylish succession of day clothes and her chic, daring and at times sexy choice of evening wear – all seen for the first time that autumn – the estimate of her expenditure was probably not far out. The range of styles was

enormous – not surprisingly since she is constantly experimenting with new designs and new designers, and has bought clothes from more than two dozen suppliers. Compare that with the Queen's tally of three or four permanent designers, and the Queen Mother's loyal patronage of the House of Hartnell to the exclusion of almost all others.

For all that, Diana does maintain a check-list of distinguishing fashion lines: high ruffled or pie-frill collars pop up from two-piece suits with great regularity, even after four years, while sumptuous ostrich feathers and patterned veiling continue to adorn her petite, velvety hats – a sure hallmark of her favourite milliner John Boyd. Beneath them, her hair has retained its essentially swept-back look, despite the many imperceptible changes in shape and length which, more than anything else, have visibly transformed her from girlhood to the full maturity of a young woman. That transformation seemed complete when, on her first official appearance in public after the birth of Prince Harry, she arrived at Westminster to attend the State Opening of Parliament wearing a completely new hairstyle which took the fashion world by storm. It was classic, sophisticated and stunning in its effect. That original swept-back style had now been taken to its logical, if extreme conclusion, with all her hair brushed away from the forehead towards the back, and collected in a wide chignon pinned in place well clear of the nape of her long, elegant neck. It was, as her hairdresser admitted, 'a very formal style for a very formal occasion', and Diana was quick to modify it afterwards. For the less ceremonial engagements, she retained the styling except for the chignon itself, allowing the hair to fall, not too luxuriantly, to just above the shoulders. The result was a subtle combination of the girlish and the womanly – a reminder perhaps that at only 23, Diana has to strike a balance between looking as mature as her responsibilities demand without losing that youthful, appealing quality which for four years has so entranced her young followers. As her subsequent return to the lines of her former hair-style showed, Diana has merely added new items to her list of options, rather than abandoned old favourites.

Meanwhile, both the generous length of her skirts and the low court shoes she has of necessity favoured have done wonders for the confidence of tall, willowy females everywhere, as well as for the British rag trade and shoe industry. Hats apart, her accessories are minimal. As she does not share what has long been satirised as the great royal fear of pressing the common flesh, she does not insist on wearing gloves on every public or social occasion, and certainly has no time for the long or half-length white gloves which have for decades been the stock-in-trade of her royal elders. Handbags are similarly inconspicuous: apart from the occasional shoulder-bag, a simple clutch bag in leather, for day wear, or in soft or shiny fabric to match her evening gowns, is the most Diana will carry, and as often as not it spends its time tucked away firmly under her left arm. Tights, whether transparent, coloured or patterned, are worn or discarded according to the dictates of comfort, and she does not regard them by any means as a social 'must'.

Jewellery, too, is not essential, so that when she does wear it, an effect is achieved rather than a ritual satisfied. Pearls, once thought to be a dull, middle-aged brand of accessory, are among her favourites, but she has avoided the graduated, three-strand format which seems almost obligatory in royal circles. Diana prefers either a single rope or double or triple twist, or again a choker of from three to seven strands held by a jewelled clasp which can be worn as a centre-piece at the throat, or left less conspicuously at the nape of the neck. She does not wear brooches, for her dresses and coats usually incorporate their own features in buttons, revers or piping, and only on State occasions will she wear dress jewellery – in the form of the cameo portrait of the Queen set in diamonds and mounted on yellow watered-silk ribbon – the Sovereign's personal Order. More spectacularly, for evening occasions, Diana might wear a diamond and emerald choker, or the magnificent diamond and sapphire necklace and earrings set, valued at nearly a million pounds, given to her as a wedding present by the Crown Prince of Saudi-Arabia. Alternatively, she has the choice of a sparkling sunray diamond necklace which the Queen frequently loans her from a collection put together from jewels once owned by the late Queen Mary. Or, more personally, there is the pearl and diamond chain on which she might hang the heart-shaped locket given to her after Prince William's birth, or a solid gold Prince of Wales feathers pendant which was a present from Prince Charles, and matches a gold ring of the same design which is also a replica of one Charles has worn for many years. Diana owns two tiaras – one, from the Spencer vaults, is the highly ornamental affair which she wore to her wedding; the other, a gift from the Queen, is alive with the movement of almost a score of graduated pearl droplets hanging from diamond lovers' knots.

Diana's colourful and original fashion ideas are given full rein when she is off duty, as the occasional holiday photograph, and a multitude of pictures of polo weekends show. Despite the claims of the handbook of that name, she never was a Sloane Ranger, but some of the sartorial trends of that amorphous social group have rubbed off onto her. Hence the quilted jacket – a compromise between the 'horsey' body-warmer and the more formal day jacket – for country events, and the heavy-knitted woollen jumpers and sweaters, with imaginatively designed pictures as well as patterns, for brisk, breezy days on the polo field. Some of these have already become classics, like the famous cardigan illuminated with colourful weather scenes, including rain, sunshine, clouds, lightning and a rainbow, which she wore one August day in 1983. 'She has summed up the day perfectly,' commented the Meteorological Office, observing

wryly that on that very day the summer heat-wave broke up in a series of storms. More popular still was the bright red jumper, closely patterned with white sheep motifs, which she had worn over two years earlier for a photo-call at Balmoral. This time, one – but only one – of the white sheep had been replaced by a black one. Whether she was trying to identify herself as the black sheep of the Royal Family proved an unanswerable question, but the design itself has remained popular ever since.

Nor did she think twice about putting on a pair of thick cord trousers and tucking them into Wellington boots when she and Prince Charles posed for photographs during one of their early spring holidays at Balmoral. But it is the summer polo matches which bring out the best in Diana, and each succeeding year sees her increasingly adventurous. Long, striped, close-fitting slacks, which set off her slim figure perfectly, have given way to more

rakish pedal-pushers, which leave no doubt as to her pretty turn of leg, while a loose blouse or even shirt, sometimes with a cardigan tied casually around her neck in case it should be needed, adds to the overall impression of complete informality. It is on these occasions only that Diana will carry a bag of larger proportions than when on duty. Her favourite is a quilted fabric zip-up bag with a busy floral pattern in patriotic red, white and blue, big enough to contain a pair of sunglasses, a polo programme, a bag of cosmetics and an extra woolly, and still have room left for the sweets that she is said to have such a craving for.

It would be wrong to give the impression that she strives to make herself fashionable, or that she deliberately encourages others to follow her example. She merely knows what she likes, and makes the most of the considerable resources at her disposal for indulging her preferences, while at the same time never

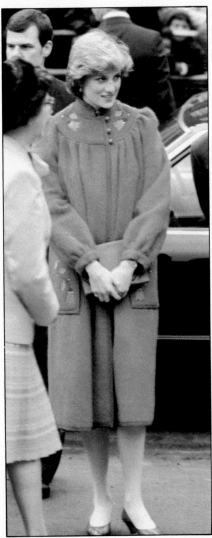

being afraid to try anything once. 'Once' is sometimes the operative word, for like most women in similarly public positions, she has fallen foul of the occasional fashion gaffe. Some of her dresses have proved rather too fussy, in pattern, trimmings or overall design, while others have ventured too far into shapelessness for the public to stomach. The year of her first pregnancy was, predictably, the worst. By October 1982, one Hollywood designer was accusing her of having 'gone off into Queen Victoria's attic' and bemoaning the loss of 'the marvellous progressive girl she once was.' The following January came the news that she had been voted amongst the ten worst-dressed women in the world.

That may have seemed bad at the time, but Diana was already used to the ebb and flow of public criticism. Nine months after that, more than half of a sample of British women voted her Woman of the Year in a poll, while no less a newspaper than the *Sunday Times* revealed in the results of an international fashion survey – 'Money, taste, self-awareness and being seen are the important factors' – that no fewer than seven countries had voted Diana among their top ten world personalities. Three months later, Diana was voted International Best Dressed Woman by twenty New York fashion editors on an interpretation of votes cast by American fashion magazine readers. They called her 'the world's most influential woman of fashion today – in spite of those hats and impending motherhood – a symbol of the young conservative swing.' She was also described as 'not only the year's overwhelming favourite for her personal elegance, but the inspiration for a sweeping trend away from eccentricity and towards dressing up.' This was well-timed praise indeed. At the end of that very month, Diana actually drew wolf-whistles when she arrived at a pop concert in a cream and black tuxedo, complete with black bow tie. 'Diana has set the fashion world reeling – again,' said one expert. 'Just when we'd got used to her feminine frills, she surprised us all by wearing a man's dinner suit to an official engagement. She's proved she's still full of fun.'

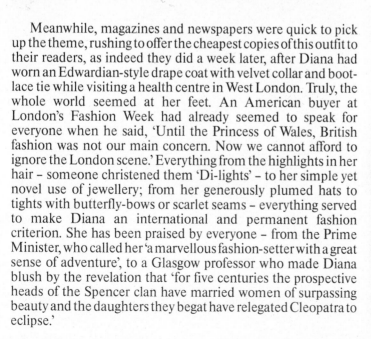

Meanwhile, magazines and newspapers were quick to pick up the theme, rushing to offer the cheapest copies of this outfit to their readers, as indeed they did a week later, after Diana had worn an Edwardian-style drape coat with velvet collar and boot-lace tie while visiting a health centre in West London. Truly, the whole world seemed at her feet. An American buyer at London's Fashion Week had already seemed to speak for everyone when he said, 'Until the Princess of Wales, British fashion was not our main concern. Now we cannot afford to ignore the London scene.' Everything from the highlights in her hair – someone christened them 'Di-lights' – to her simple yet novel use of jewellery; from her generously plumed hats to tights with butterfly-bows or scarlet seams – everything served to make Diana an international and permanent fashion criterion. She has been praised by everyone – from the Prime Minister, who called her 'a marvellous fashion-setter with a great sense of adventure', to a Glasgow professor who made Diana blush by the revelation that 'for five centuries the prospective heads of the Spencer clan have married women of surpassing beauty and the daughters they begat have relegated Cleopatra to eclipse.'

The recent changes in Diana's hairstyle that somehow seemed to mark a new chapter of her life, came in the wake of a change of stylist. Kevin Shanley, who had been Diana's hairdresser since long before her engagement, in the days when it was *she* who visited *him* in his cream-painted salon 'Headlines' in Kensington, was now relieved of his duties in favour of his partner Richard Dalton. Both men maintained a discreet silence about the circumstances of the change, but it is unlikely that Diana was actively dissatisfied with Shanley's four years of hard graft which had worked a succession of subtle transitions in her hairstyle. There does, after all, come a time when a complete change is desired, and the fact that Diana stayed with the same partnership indicates that personal animosity was not a factor here.

It hasn't, by all accounts, always been the case. Diana's early months as the wife of the heir to the Throne were clouded by a succession of personal disputes with various members of her husband's staff – some of them of incredibly long standing.

Foremost among them was his valet for twelve years, Stephen Barry who, three years after the event is still smarting with the memory of the resignation which Prince Charles' marriage prompted and the embarrassed farewell in which Diana took no part. He seemed at the time in no doubt who was behind his departure, and though he attempted to smooth over any unpleasant implications, he wreaked a rather limp revenge by writing a book of memoirs which included some fairly pallid details of the little of Charles and Diana's personal life he was privileged to witness. Two of Diana's personal detectives were also dispensed with amid talk of a conflict of personalities, which quickly prompted the impression that, far from being vulnerable and in need of protection, as most observers had portrayed her, Diana had a will of iron which manifested itself in a determination to shake up her husband's household in much the same way as her stepmother had taken Althorp by the scruff of the neck and transformed it.

Memories of those days have not faded. When, in October 1983, it was announced that Diana's private secretary Oliver Everett was to resign, everyone seemed convinced that she had

given him the cold shoulder. A former diplomat, Everett had been appointed in 1978, at the age of 35, as assistant private secretary to Prince Charles, whose love of polo he shared. After the royal wedding, he transferred to duties which involved running domestic and some financial matters for Diana, but rumours of bitter rows between them began to circulate within eighteen months of the appointment. Buckingham Palace persistently denied this, and refused to comment on his eventual resignation, except to say that Everett had made a career choice to take over as the Queen's deputy librarian in the Royal Archives at Windsor Castle, where he began work in January 1984.

His resignation left Diana without a private secretary, so she now shares Prince Charles'. He is the Hon. Edward Adeane, now in his mid-forties, whose appointment in 1979 protracted a sometimes tenuous family link with the Crown. His great-grandfather, Lord Stamfordham, became private secretary to both Queen Victoria and her grandson George V, while his father Lord (formerly Sir Michael) Adeane was page of honour to George V, equerry and assistant private secretary to George VI, and eventually principal private secretary to the Queen until his retirement in 1972, twelve years before his death. Educated at Eton and Cambridge, a former barrister, a shooting and fishing enthusiast, outwardly and inwardly of a conservative

mould, Edward Adeane seems, in terms of personality and background, far removed from Diana, yet he has been a close friend of Prince Charles since the days before his appointment, and Diana will find it difficult to remove him as she has apparently removed others.

She has, besides, a new equerry in the shape of Lt-Cdr Peter Eberle. He is ten years older than Diana, and has the sort of credentials that make him an ideal candidate for royal service. He is the son of a former NATO naval director, was educated at Dartmouth Naval College and Southampton University, served during his Navy days on *HMS Jupiter* – like Prince Charles – and was on the frigate *Argonaut* in the Falklands conflict, when she

was hit by Argentinian bombs as she covered the British recapture of San Carlos Bay. A tall, straw-haired young man, Eberle was chosen for his post by personal interview, and has that touch of informality which seems to suit Diana, in whose service he has now been for over a year. He works much more closely with her than Adeane, since he is responsible for all the day-to-day organisation of her engagements, preparing detailed programmes for each of her visits to various parts of the country, and answerable directly to her. He has no direct dealings with the press, however – a job that is almost exclusive these days to her genial spokesman, Victor Chapman. Chapman was appointed as an assistant press officer to the Queen on the recommendation of the then Canadian Government, thus extending the Commonwealth connection which the Buckingham Palace press office has enjoyed since the Australian Sir William Heseltine became the Queen's press secretary in the late 1960s. Four times married, Chapman has made himself a popular figure with the huge press contingents which have followed Diana around the world, and has combined a pliable presence (while his Fleet Street adversaries remain responsible) with a tough but rarely aggressive attitude when Diana fears harassment or intrusion of privacy.

Closer still to Diana in their official duties are the four police officers most frequently seen with her. Two of them are more generally associated with Prince Charles' security – Supt John Maclean, reputably the hardest man in the whole of the Royal Protection Squad, whose ability to ski, and firm, decisive action with the press made him the perfect companion on those controversial ski-ing holidays; and the impeccably-dressed Chief Inspector Colin Hayward-Trimming. Then come two personal detectives: 45-year-old Graham Smith, who often finds himself escorting Diana on those endless shopping trips in Knightsbridge or Tetbury, keeping a wary eye on passers-by and long-lens photographers as he carts her shopping bags from one store to the next; and Alan Peters, eight years younger than Smith, a quietly spoken man of such burly, yet athletic build that it can be truthfully said of him that he really does look like a detective. Despite his permanent frown, he is widely believed to get on extremely well with Diana.

In addition to this posse of men, Diana is surrounded and served by members of her own sex. Her three ladies-in-waiting have been with her since before her marriage, and have proved invaluable friends as well as efficient and cheerful assistants. They are all unpaid; they perform their duties as letter-writers on

Diana's behalf and as companions on duty in strict rotation with one another, and maintain a discreet, polite silence about anything that could possibly give rise to an unsolicited revelation in print. For this reason above all else, their names had to appear on a short-list drawn up by the Palace before Diana was able to make her choice. Their trustworthiness emanates from their own royal connections. The eldest of the three is Hazel West, now in her fortieth year, and usually referred to in the Court Circular by her formal married title of Mrs George West. Her husband is a former Lieutenant-Colonel in the Grenadier Guards, and now an extra equerry to the Queen as well as assistant Comptroller in the Lord Chamberlain's office. In this latter post, he helped to make arrangements for Diana's wedding, the clockwork efficiency of which is so often ascribed solely to the Lord Chamberlain himself.

Six years younger than Mrs West is Lavinia Baring; her father, Sir Mark Baring, is chairman of King Edward VII Hospital for Officers in London, where members of the Royal Family, from the Queen downwards, go to be treated for minor ailments. Attractive, slim and smartly dressed, Miss Baring takes pains, despite the need to be at Diana's right hand, to keep herself respectfully distant from her, thus avoiding being included in every picture the photographers take of her employer. By contrast, Anne Beckwith-Smith, Diana's youngest, but principal lady-in-waiting, is probably also the

most instantly recognisable. Never more than a couple of footsteps behind the Princess, her cheerful, slightly plump features seem to accompany Diana everywhere, as she follows up to collect armfuls of flowers and gifts with speed, efficiency and an obvious sharing in the fun of it all. It's a welcome reminder that, in the comparative isolation of her position, Diana needs companions, and it is reassuring to note that the three closest to her in her official life are as loyal and politic as those famous flatmates were in the old days.

Discretion is, of course, the watchword for Diana's relatives as well as for her staff. From the time of her approaching engagement, members of her family have been notoriously difficult to contact, far less willing to speak or be quoted publicly. For all the sneers she suffered, Raine Lady Spencer has revealed nothing of Diana's private life, while her father, now 61, has restricted his comments to the non-controversial, non-intrusive, always appreciative reactions to successive news of Diana's own children – whether expected, newly-born, or growing up. Diana's two sisters have in like manner given nothing away, nor indeed, despite all the temptations, has her mother, Frances Shand Kydd. She in particular sees little need for becoming involved in Diana's life, and has long felt 'maternally redundant', as she puts it. Like Diana, she has in the last four years experienced the pressures of publicity, and is ever

more aware of the need not to let the side down. 'I think I have a responsibility to my family – all of them,' she says pointedly. 'After all, who wants a mother who is an embarrassment?' Preserving her anonymity is all important to her – if at times a little difficult. Once, a customer in her newsagent's shop in Oban saw a picture of Diana in a newspaper. Not realising to whom she was speaking, the customer asked Mrs Shand Kydd, 'Don't you think she's wonderful?' 'It's a bit difficult for me to say,' came the reply. 'Quite right, my dear,' retorted the woman. 'As a shop assistant you shouldn't give opinions. But one thing is for certain: she didn't come out of a home like you and I did.' Mrs Shand Kydd did not let on. 'I never told her,' she said later. 'I never enjoyed anything so much. It was lovely.'

Neither Diana nor her family makes any great public display of their affection for each other, and meetings and gatherings are only accomplished with considerable planning in an effort to maintain the family's right to privacy as much as the separation of Diana's personal life from her official duties. This system has its distinct advantages, particularly when family controversies become public knowledge. Diana may have been dismayed to find her young brother Charles so frequently in the headlines in recent months, during which time he has been making his own

very distinctive forays into young London society. Now over 6ft 2in tall, Charles has his father's build and features as well as his subsidiary title of Viscount Althorp, and when the family moved to Northamptonshire, he completed his primary education at Maidwell Hall, a small boarding school near Althorp itself. He passed a common entrance examination for Eton a year later, became co-editor of the school's journal *The Eton Chronicle*, showed a natural aptitude for the violin and an excellence in both sport and drama. During his last couple of years there, Diana used to visit him whenever she was at Windsor and could afford the time to pop into the school, which was less than a mile away. In the summer of 1982 Charles left Eton with a clutch of three top-grade 'A' levels in English, French and History – he reached S-level standard in English and History – and then spent a year scouring the country for temporary work. Brief spells as a Stock Exchange messenger and a work-hand in a Midlands clothing factory led him to the conclusion that the wealth of the country was unfairly distributed, and that 'we are all too class conscious', though that did not stop him taking Oxbridge entrance exams, which he passed with ease.

He began his further education at Magdalen College, Oxford, and though he found it 'a bit of a anti-climax', he passed his preliminary exams there, and joined the college's rugby team as a flanker. By then his newsworthiness had been proved in several other directions. He had been assaulted during a scuffle in a motorway service area, fined £80 for speeding, banned from the London club Boodles after a contretemps over the alleged non-payment for a bottle of champagne, and criticised for de-bagging a disc jockey at a Notting Hill

restaurant, when out dining with a group of friends. He earned £200 a week as an extra during the making of the film *Another Country*, once caught a shoplifter emerging from Harrods with a pile of cashmere coats during the January sales, and took flying lessons in a Piper Cherokee. A connoisseur of London's night haunts, he has been seen at discos, parties, and even gay clubs in his time, and wearing a whole range of outfits including imitation punk, matinee idol rig, and a particular favourite recently – the Biggles T-shirt with air-ace goggles. It may or may not be the sort of life-style of which Diana approves, and she may feel uncomfortable wondering when her brother will next catapult himself into the gossip columns, but privately there is clearly an affinity and strong affection between the two of them which reflects their closeness in the days of stress and uncertainty at Park House. 'She may be a Princess now,' says Charles, Viscount Althorp, 'but she's still my older sister, and we still enjoy a gossip.'

ut for something like half a decade, there has been another Charles in Diana's life, and in the excitement of all that followed that first, fuzzy photograph of them both at Balmoral in 1980, one aspect of Diana's life has tended to be forgotten. The marriage which was celebrated with such panache in 1981 has been a union of equal partners, yet Prince Charles has been all but ignored, concealed behind the dazzle which has surrounded Diana everywhere. If that has done him a favour, given him a respite from a position of overwhelming celebrity after a lifetime of squinting before cameras and reading sensations about himself in the papers, he has been careful not to say so. Instead he has

Family. Princess Anne may have changed attitudes in this respect briefly in 1973, Princess Michael has certainly done so since, but it is thanks to Diana that royal conduct has been so much less formal and hidebound of late.

That Prince Charles is much more relaxed these days is almost a truism. He once mused that if he got married, 'I wouldn't be able to dance the samba like I did in Rio', but since his marriage, the truth is that his social horizons have broadened. He has been introduced to a new range of friends and relatives – those old school chums of Diana's and their husbands and families. He is now attending more pop concerts than one would ever have thought possible three years ago – and mostly owing to Diana's craze for the pop scene. Even the once

counted himself lucky to have Diana for a wife and has praised her for what he once called 'the wonderful effect she has on everybody.'

He is probably rather too reserved to make a public statement about the effect *she* has had on *him*, but the signs are abundant that new life has been breathed into an existence which, for all its variety and pace, seemed to lack personal fulfilment. The most obvious, and most frequently commented on, are those touching gestures, committed in full public view, which proclaim a combination of relief and gratitude that things have turned out so well – the meaningful meeting of the eyes, the arm placed round the waist or even hip, the hand taken up and kissed with gallantry, the cosy linking of arms, the spontaneous embrace at airport or on polo field. Not many years ago, behaviour like this – a common enough sight, and even considered rather quaint, among young people – would have raised eyebrows if indulged in by any member of the Royal

drab and restricted selection of suits which earned him the criticism of indulging in 'a cult of studied shabbiness' has begun a slow transformation to smarter, double-breasted numbers and more stylish casual clothes. You cannot deny that this is Diana's doing, particularly when it is *her* hairdresser who now cuts his hair into an informal style which does away with those two inescapable alternatives – the slicked-down look or the thick, unruly, ill-combed look. Diana above all has helped him, perhaps without either of them realising it, to achieve what Charles sees as the monarchy's greatest function – 'the human concern which its representatives have for people in what is becoming an increasingly inhuman era.'

The fears, once voiced in furtive whispers, that the intellectual gap between Charles and Diana was too wide to be bridged, have proved – like much of the speculation – wrong, if not exactly groundless. They have clearly given and taken, taught and learned, copied and adapted. For all their differences in upbringing and outlook, there is a chemistry between them, and if some of his remarks in public speeches make her blush, it is less through true embarrassment than for want of the opportunity to react. For when they are together in private, as that Canadian provincial Premier said, 'they are always exchanging one-liners. If he makes a quip, she always comes right back with another one'. More important, Diana is the joint

bearer of the anxieties as well as the joys which her husband found almost impossible to share before; a loyal and sympathetic spirit in a milieu so fraught with the dangers of indiscretion and sudden disaffection, that his own circle of dependable friends had been claustrophobically tight.

Fatherhood is his new dimension. 'A bit of a shock to my system,' he admitted at first, but his new-found status is now a source of rejoicing and indulgence. He is besotted (his own word) with his sons, lavishing upon them an affection which may only be exceeded with the arrival of a daughter. For these mercies and countless others, he has to thank Diana – the girl who, with no doubts at all, accepted him so readily and incontrovertibly on that February evening in 1981, when she said good-bye to the carefree life she could so easily have chosen and eventually taken for granted. For her 22nd birthday, which fell at the end of their tour of Canada, he presented her – in public of course – with a birthday cake which bore the simple words, 'I love you, Darling.' From the way she has made the whole world fall for her, you can't help thinking that he wasn't the only one.

# DIANA'S FASHION DIARY

Dep. Legal B-42093/84

**February 25**    Press Photo call after the official announcement of her engagement to the Prince of Wales.    *Delphinium-blue two-piece suit with long reverse-pleated skirt, and buttonless jacket gathered at the waist under an integral bow. Deep open neck showing a white silk blouse with blue seagull motifs, high neck and with large bow at the lefthand side. Black shoes.*

**March 3**    Attended the première of the film *For Your Eyes Only*, West End, London.    *Full length evening dress in flame-red with glittering gold spot pattern. Low, shaped neckline with thin shoulder straps. Gold and cornelian necklace. Silver accessories.*

**March 9**    Attended a recital of music at Goldsmiths Hall, London.    *Strapless low-cut black taffeta evening dress with full skirt. Matching taffeta shawl with ornate ruffled edges. Silver necklace with small pendant and matching earrings. Black evening bag and matching shoes.*

**March 25**    Visited Sandown Park Races.    *Brown two-piece outfit with midi-length skirt and loose, open jacket over a white blouse with a high frill neck. Matching brown trilby hat, and brown accessories.*

**March 27**    Visited Gloucestershire Police Constabulary Headquarters, Cheltenham.    *Deep-blue two-piece suit with long jacket gathered at the waist and deep white sailor collars meeting under a red ribbon bow at the front. Pearl collar and matching earrings.*

**April**    Official photograph taken at Highgrove House for use in Royal Wedding Souvenir Booklet.    *Bright apple-green silk taffeta evening dress with short puffed sleeves, low, round neck and a full skirt. Heavy earrings of hanging diamonds, and diamond necklace.*

**May 9**    Attended the opening of the Mountbatten exhibition, Broadlands, Romsey, Hampshire.    *Bright green two-piece suit with front-pleated skirt and pleated jacket with line of buttons running down the centre. Sleeves, sash and skirt hem bordered or highlighted with wide bands of blue, green and mauve. White silk blouse with double ruff at the neck. Black shoes and a clutch bag.*

**May 14**    Attended the presentation by the Queen of new colours to the Welsh Guards at Windsor Castle.    *White silk dress with tiny regular L-shaped motifs in grey and maroon, and trimmed and edged with golden-yellow silk. Long full sleeves with buttoned yellow cuffs; panelled yoke and a row of yellow buttons from neck to waist. Matching yellow ribbons at neck. Primrose-coloured hat with up-turned brim and matching ostrich feathers flecked with brown. White shoes.*

**May 22**    Visited General Hospital, Tetbury.

**May 22**    Attended a Thanksgiving service at St Mary's Church, Tetbury.    *Two-piece flame-coloured outfit consisting of a plain skirt and a silk, deep V-necked jacket with a snow storm white pattern. Underneath, a white blouse with frilled, stand-up collar. Black self-patterned bag and matching shoes.*

**May 27**    Attended a Welsh Guards dinner-dance at Merchant Taylors' Hall, London.    *Full-length evening dress in bright red with all-over gold spot pattern and a shaped, frilled neckline held with thin straps. Three row pearl choker, and silver accessories.*

**June 1**    Attended the wedding of Nicholas Soames and Catherine Weatherall at St Margaret's, Westminster.    *Bright red silk dress patterned with tiny white stars and larger stars in blue and green. Matching belt and pie-frill neck and cuffs. Matching red hat with broad silk band and wide flyaway brim ornamented with a huge bow at the back. Red handbag and matching shoes.*

**June 11**    Attended a State Banquet given by King Khalid of Saudi Arabia at Claridges Hotel, London.    *Pale smoke-grey chiffon ball dress with silver spot diamante pattern. Overlaid bodice providing deep flouncing at the neck and waist and see-through sleeves. Pale pink silk bow at the centre of deep V-neck and broad matching sash. Long white gloves. Diamond necklace and earrings. Silver evening bag and shoes.*

**June 13**    Attended the Queen's Birthday Parade, Horseguards Parade.    *Two-piece suit, predominantly sky-blue with small abstract design in white and pink. Loose open jacket with long full sleeves, over a white silk blouse with large frilled collar overlaying the neck of the jacket. Deep-pink waist sash at the top of the skirt. Matching blue-veiled pillbox hat worn over the right temple with a huge white flower at the front. Three row pearl choker. White accessories.*

**June 15**    Attended the Service of the Order of the Garter, St George's Chapel, Windsor Castle.    *Light-green two-piece silk suit with front-pleated skirt and pleated jacket with a line of blue buttons running down the centre. Sleeves, sash and skirt hem bordered or highlighted with wide bands of blue, green and mauve. Wide-brimmed green hat with narrow blue band. Black accessories.*

**June 16**    Attended the first day of Royal Ascot.    *Striped dress in mauve, grey and white with low straight neckline underneath a matching jacket with pleat-frilled collar and cuffs. Matching mauve picture hat with splay-feathered trimming over the brim. White gloves and shoes.*

**June 17**    Attended second day of Royal Ascot.    *Peach-coloured silk suit with fold-over jacket over a white silk blouse with wide flounced overlaying collar. Narrow white tie-belt over the jacket. White hat with pink gardenia on the right side. Choker consisting of three strings of pearls. White accessories.*

**June 18**    Attended the third day of Royal Ascot.    *Red and white candy-striped blouse with large collars, central bow, and full sleeves. Loose, sleeveless academic-style overgarment in tomato red, matching a straight skirt. Red straw hat with white flowers at the back, and matching red handbag and shoes. Choker of three strings of pearls.*

June 19    Attended the last day of Royal Ascot.    *Pale blue and white squared dress with narrow white collars, two parallel rows of blue buttons running from neck to waist, and matching blue-buckled sash. Edwardian-style bonnet in white with veiling tied under the chin. White accessories.*

July 3    Attended the finals of the men's tennis championship at Wimbledon.    *Flower-patterned two-piece outfit in red, white, yellow and pink, on a bright blue background. Jacket with three-quarter length sleeves and a tie-belt at the waist. Underneath, a white silk blouse with V-neck, small collars and tight cuffs. Single row of pearls and white accessories.*

July 15    Attended an exhibition at the Royal Academy of Arts, London.    *Midnight-blue evening dress with regular pattern of silver sequins. Close-fitting bodice with low neck, and slender silver straps.*

July 24    Visited the Army Barracks at Tidworth, Hampshire.    *White silk dress with tiny regular L-shaped motifs in grey and maroon, trimmed and edged with golden-yellow silk. Long full sleeves with buttoned, yellow cuffs; panelled yoke, and a row of yellow buttons from neck to waist. Matching yellow ribbons at the neck. White shoes and clutch bag.*

July 29    Marriage to the Prince of Wales at St Paul's Cathedral, London.    *Ivory-coloured dress in silk taffeta with puff-ball skirt, the shaped bodice of silk taffeta encrusted with sequins and mother of pearl, and with intricately-embroidered lace panels to front and back. Low V-shaped neckline bearing a ruffle of taffeta overlaid with pearl-encrusted lace, and a huge Victorian bow at the centre. Puffed sleeves pointed at the shoulders and gathered at the elbows. Hand embroidered gossamer silk veil, sweeping train of diaphanous silk trimmed with embroidered lace. Soft ivory-coloured silk slipper shoes, top-stitched with an Elizabethan lattice design, with a mother of pearl sequin in each section and a heart-shaped, lace-frilled motif at the tongue. Finely fluted heels hand-painted in gold. Spencer family tiara of entwined heart and flower design, and heavy drop earrings.*

July 29    Departure from Buckingham Palace to begin honeymoon at Broadlands.    *Pale-cantaloupe silk tussore dress with cummerbund sash at the waist and small slit at the hem on the left hand side. Short-sleeved bolero jacket in matching fabric, with frilled white silk organza collars joined by a large bow, and with organza trim on the sleeves. Small straw tricorn hat in matching pink, veiled and trimmed with ostrich feather. Victorian-style choker of six rows of pearls, and small pearl earrings. Pink shoes and matching silk pochette-style handbag.*

August 1    Departure from Romsey via Gibraltar for honeymoon on board the *Royal Yacht Britannia*.    *Long white silk two-piece outfit with elegant flower-spray motifs in red, blue and green, the jacket loose-fitting and self-tying at the midriff. Underneath, a mid-blue vest edged in white. Three string pearl choker. White accessories.*

August 12    Met President and Madame Sadat, Cairo, Egypt.    *Shell-pink silk dress with long sleeves, low V-neck and matching tie belt. Coral-pink necklace. White accessories.*

August 13    Entertained President and Madame Sadat on board the *Royal Yacht Britannia* at Port Said, Egypt.    *Long black taffeta evening gown with horizontal gold and silver stripes on the bodice, and wider bands on the skirt. Low horizontal neckline, and ribbon straps over the shoulder. Informal tie-belt waistband. Small pearl earrings.*

August 19    Photo call for the Press and journalists at the Brig o' Dee, Balmoral.    *Casual two-piece outfit in brown, dull-blue and white dog-tooth pattern. White, collared blouse beneath an open jacket, with brown leather buttons down the centre. White shoes.*

September 4    Attended the Braemar Games, Aberdeenshire.    *Red and black plaid dress-coat with flared skirt and padded full sleeves. Broad, stand-up collar with a row of small black buttons running down to a waistband tied with a knotted black belt. Black tam-o'-shanter hat, and black accessories.*

October 27    Visited towns in North Wales.    *Two-piece suit consisting of a bottle-green dress, slightly flared, beneath a close fitting blood-red jacket. The jacket cut to reveal the dress's frilled cuffs and tie bow at the neck. Matching red hat with flyaway brim and large red bow at the back. Red shoes and handbag.*

October 28    Visited towns in West and mid-Wales.    *Warm blond-brown cashmere coat, loose-fitting and long-lapelled, with a tie belt. Blouse of white silk with frill at the neck. Soft, matching saucer hat with large ostrich feather on right hand side. Brown accessories.*

October 28    Attended a gala concert at Brangwen Hall Swansea.    *Emerald-green taffeta evening dress with deep square neck and short sleeves, beneath a copious black velvet cape. Diamond and emerald choker with matching earrings. Silver evening bag and shoes.*

October 29    Visited towns in South Wales.    *Two-piece suit in aubergine velvet; a generously flared skirt and close-fitting jacket with front button panel enclosed by pale white piping. The heavily-frilled collar of a white silk blouse visible above the neck. Small, matching, aubergine, brimmed hat with cascade of ostrich feather falling on the right hand side. Black shoes and clutch bag.*

October 29    Received the Freedom of the City of Cardiff at City Hall, Cardiff.    *Wedgewood-blue silk chiffon cocktail dress with mustard and white leaf pattern. Ruched bodice and high-frilled neckline. Sapphire and diamond earrings. Blue accessories.*

November 2    Visited the National Film Theatre, South Bank, London, for the opening of the 25th London Film Festival.    *Green-black midi-length velvet dress with large white lace collar overlaid at the yoke. Narrow lace trim to the hem of dress. Matching green satin shoes.*

November 2    Attended the State Opening of Parliament, Palace of Westminster.    *Full-length formal dress in ivory-silk embroidered with occasional large flower-spray design. Deep V-neck and full, sequin-embroidered elbow-length sleeves. Long white gloves. Pearl drop tiara and a three row pearl choker.*

November 4    Attended the opening of the exhibition "Splendours of the Gonzaga", Victoria and Albert Museum, London.    *Light, filmy, off-the-shoulder evening dress of silk chiffon. Predominantly white with soft, swirling designs in pink and blue, with sequined diagonals across the whole garment. The neckline generously frilled and topped by pale blue bows matching the broad waistband. Choker consisting of six rows of pearls, and silver accessories.*

November 5    Attended a luncheon given by the Lord Mayor of London, Guildhall, London.    *Thick, flame-red coat woven in Welsh wool, striped stitch-effect with vertical lines of blue and yellow. Heavy fringing at collar, cuffs and hem. Underneath, a waistcoat in similar material, over a blue blouse frilled at the neck and cuffs. Small mid-blue wool hat, veiled and feathered. Matching shoes and handbag.*

November 7    Attended the Royal British Legion Festival of Remembrance, Royal Albert Hall, London.    *Simple, black silk dress with subtle grey spots. Round, medium-level neckline, and spray of poppies on left hand side. Simple string of pearls, and black accessories.*

November 8    Attended the Remembrance Day Service, Cenotaph, Whitehall.    *Black coat-dress with a white silk lace-edged yoke bearing a black bow at the centre. Black feathered hat, and black accessories.*

November 12    Visited York and Chesterfield.    *Silk dress patterned with regular abstract designs in black, red and white. White frilled collars and cuffs, and a black bow at the centre of the neck. Tall-crowned black hat with black gloves, shoes and handbag.*

November 18    Switched on the Christmas lights, Regent Street, London.    *Black satin two-piece suit over a white blouse with cravat-style neck. Piping on the back collar of the suit, brought forward as loose tassels in the front. Silver shoes and black watered-silk clutch bag.*

November 19    Planted three cherry trees in The Copse, Hyde Park, London.    *Red and black plaid dress-coat with flared skirt and padded, full sleeves. Broad stand-up collar with row of small black buttons running down to a waistband tied with a knotted black belt. Ruffle of a white silk blouse visible at the neck. Brown shoes.*

November 23    Opened the new Post Office, Northampton.    *Bottle-green two-piece suit with a jacket heavily embroidered on the front seams with flower patterns in red, pink, white and cream. Pale pink blouse with large frilled collar overlaying the jacket. Loose, turban-style hat in matching green with large feather feature. Bottle-green accessories. Three rows of pearls worn as a choker.*

November 30    Visited the Royal Opera House Covent Garden to see a performance of Romeo and Juliet.    *Long black evening dress with warm, hip-length jacket in white fur. Single row of pearls. Black accessories.*

December 10    Attended a Christmas Carol Service, Gloucester Cathedral.    *Grey tailored cossack-style coat with high stand-up collars. Matching astrakhan hat with bow at the side, complemented by a large matching muff. Black knee-length boots.*

December 21    Attended a Christmas Celebration at Guildford Cathedral.    *Bright-red wool coat over a matching red skirt, and blouse of matching colour with small green and white butterfly design. Matching red hat with upturned brim and full-face veiling. Red shoes, black gloves and clutch bag.*

December 25    Attended the Christmas Morning Service at St George's Chapel, Windsor.    *Below-the-knee coat in turquoise wool, with leaf-green embroidered panels and pockets, and pink, plum and gold flower designs on the yoke and pockets. Small matching turquoise pillbox hat. Aquamarine handbag and shoes. Black gloves.*

1982

January 23    Visited the January Fair at the Dick Sheppard School, Tulse Hill, London.    *Outfit as worn at St George's Chapel Windsor (above) but without hat or gloves.*

February 2    Attended the British Film Institute Dinner, 11 Downing Street, London.    *Deep-sapphire evening dress, lavishly trimmed with white lace fichu and corresponding lace ruffles at the cuffs. Low-cut plunging neckline. Diamond drop earrings with sapphire centres. Pearl necklace with sapphire centre. Silver clutch bag and shoes.*

February 11    Visited the studios of Independent Television, London.    *Loose shift dress with three-quarter length sleeves, over long, full sleeved, ruff-necked, white blouse. Wide, generous, white collar, overlaying the yoke of the dress, with a dark bow and falling ribbons at the centre of the neck. Soft slipper shoes, with large bows.*

February 16    Left London for ten-day holiday in the Bahamas.    *Pale-cream shift dress beneath a warm white wool jacket. White shoes.*

February 27    Returned to London from the Bahamas.    *High-waisted maternity smock in blue and white gingham, with open neck showing the frill of a white blouse underneath. White woollen jacket, and white shoes.*

February 28     Attended a reception to mark the centenary of the Royal College of Music, St James's Palace.

February 28     Attended a service of Thanksgiving for the College, Westminster Abbey.          *Fuchsia-pink coat with wide apron-style panels at the yoke, a stand-up ruff at the neckline, and wide piping around the collar falling loose to the front with pom-poms. Matching hat with bow on the left underside of the wide brim. Black accessories.*

March 4     Attended a Gala Concert, Barbican Centre, London.          *Full-length silk burgundy dress in Jacobean style with deep square neckline bordered by a small cream frill, and white lace flounced beneath the three-quarter length flounced dress sleeves. Sun-ray diamond necklace, and diamond and pearl drop earrings. Silver evening bag and shoes.*

March 8     Attended the Charity Première of *The Little Foxes* at the Victoria Palace Theatre, London.          *Full-length champagne-coloured evening gown embroidered with sprays of sequins against a faintly squared background. Low-cut neckline complemented with ornate diamond necklace. Sleeves puffed and gathered. Silver evening bag and shoes.*

March 14     Attended a concert of music at the Royal Albert Hall.          *Tomato-red evening gown, maternity-style, with flashes of gold sequins crossing in diagonal formation. Narrow white trim at the low neck and cuffs. Single row of pearls. Voluminous black cape over the top for outdoor use.*

March 18     Visited the Cheltenham Horse Racing Festival on Gold Cup Day.          *Black maternity dress with white polka dots, ruffled at neck and sleeves, beneath a large loose mohair coat in red, with large collars laid over the shoulders. Matching red saucer hat with wide brim, and a large rosette at the back. Brown shoulder bag and shoes.*

March 22     Visited projects assisted by the Prince's Trust at Huddersfield and Newcastle upon Tyne.          *Black maternity dress with white polka dots, frilled at the collar and cuffs. Deep-pink coat in mohair with enormous fringed collars covering the shoulders and much of the bodice. Black clutch bag and shoes.*

March 30     Visited Roundhay Park, Leeds.

March 30     Opened St Gemma's Hospice, Leeds.          *Baize-green wool coat with large black Victorian Gothic motifs forming a continuous design from the front of the bodice to around the neck. Black trim on the cuffs and stand-up collars. Matching green hat, high-crowned, with a broad green silk band, and a bow and falling feathers on the right hand side. Black accessories.*

April 2     Attended the opening of the Chinese Community Centre, Liverpool.          *Fuchsia-pink coat with wide apron-style panels at the yoke, stand-up ruffles at the neckline, and wide piping around the collar, falling loose to the front with pom-poms. Matching hat with bow on the left underside of a wide brim. Black accessories.*

April 3     Attended the Grand National, Aintree.          *China-blue maternity dress with double ruffle down the bodice and an additional ruffle at the neck. A generous burgundy-red mohair coat with large collars laid over the shoulders. Matching red-felt saucer hat with wide brim and a rosette at the rear.*

April 7     Opened the new Sony Television Factory, Bridgend.          *Pastel-blue maternity dress patterned with white polka dots, and with long, frilled sleeves. Warm, pink, woollen military-style coat, toggled on the left hand side, and with tall stand-up collars. Three row pearl choker worn clasp to front. Small, pink pillbox hat with large satin rosette at the back. Pink clutch bag and matching shoes.*

April 20     Arrived in St Mary's, Scilly Isles.          *Simple green summer dress, sailor-style with white collars. White shoes.*

April 20     Toured St Mary's during an evening walkabout.          *White polka dot blue maternity dress with stand-up frills on the cuffs and flatter frills around the neckline. Single row of pearls. Black slipper shoes with bows.*

April 21     Visited the island of Tresco.          *Black dress with white polka dots, over a pink blouse with ribbons at the neck. A long black wool coat. Black shoes.*

April 22     Attended lunch for staff and tenants of the Duchy of Cornwall, St Mary's, Isle of Scilly.          *Flowing, self-patterned maternity dress in mid-blue, with open neck bordered by ruffles and revealing a pink blouse with tie neck beneath. Black handbag and black shoes.*

May 18     Opened the Albany Trust Community Centre, Deptford, London.          *White polka dot blue maternity dress with stand-up frills on the cuffs, and flatter frills below the neckline. Three row pearl choker. Black accessories.*

June 12     Attended the Trooping the Colour, Horseguards Parade.          *Emerald-green coat-dress, maternity-style, with half-length gathered sleeves, a gathered yoke line and V-neck wing collars. Small edged saucer hat with veiling and bow at the side. Three row pearl choker.*

June 17     Attended Royal Ascot followed by polo on Smith's Lawn, Windsor.          *Long pale-pink maternity dress with round neck and long sleeves. The matching pink hat which was worn for Ascot was removed for the visit to Smith's Lawn, when the Princess wore a warm white wool cardigan. White accessories.*

June 22     Left St Mary's Hospital, Paddington after the birth of Prince William.          *Long green maternity dress with small white polka dots and white collars. Pink shoes.*

July 26     Attended the service of Thanksgiving and Reconciliation after the Falklands conflict, St Paul's Cathedral, London.     *Royal blue dress patterned with small black dots, buttoned to the left side of the neck and gathered at the waist by a broad tasselled black belt. The hem ornamented with large black Paisley motifs between patterned bands. Black straw veiled hat with small burst of matching feathers. Black accessories.*

August 4     Christening of Prince William, Buckingham Palace.     *Salmon-pink short-sleeved dress with close flower design in white and blue. Bodice gathered by matching belt tied in large bow at the side. Wide-brimmed straw hat in matching pink with silk band and bow. String of pearls bearing a heart-shaped pendant in the middle.*

September 3     Attended the wedding of Carolyn Pride, Chelsea Old Church, London.     *Raspberry pink, loose fitting silk dress with high neck, dropped waist, elbow length sleeves, and large white sailor collars. White straw platter hat with navy trim and matching petal bow beneath the brim. Three strand pearl choker, white quilted clutch bag and white shoes.*

September 4     Attended the Braemar Gathering, Aberdeenshire.     *Dull green and gold plaid effect squared dress, with stark white Peter Pan-style collars and cuffs. Perky Glengarry bonnet in bottle green velvet, with emerald trim and black ribbons. Black shoes and handbag.*

September 19     Attended the funeral of Princess Grace of Monaco, Monte Carlo.     *Black dress and coat with mandarin collar, broken only by a silver necklace with a heart-shaped locket. Wide-brimmed Spanish style straw hat with fully enveloping veil. Matching accessories.*

October 12     Paid an informal visit to London to accompany Prince Charles on his way to Portsmouth.     *White silk-satin Puritan blouse with lace trim and large black bow at the neck. Long wool cardigan and moire skirt.*

October 26     Attended a concert given by Mstislav Rostropovitch at the Barbican Centre, London.     *Emerald green silk taffeta full length evening dress, with square neck, short puffed sleeves and a matching silk waist band. Diamond and emerald choker and matching earrings; silver evening bag and shoes.*

October 29     Attended a performance by the Welsh National Opera, New Theatre, Cardiff.     *Pale blue-grey silk chiffon evening dress with sequin spots. Deep V-neck, and the bodice overlaid with a fine flounce to include see-through sleeves. Pale pink bow at décolletage, and matching broad sash. Heart-shaped pendant on a silver chain, and matching silver accessories.*

November 2     Opened a new extension to the Royal School for the Blind, Leatherhead, Surrey.     *Rich, deep-green velvet coat with close-fitting bodice buttoned down the centre, and voluminous skirt. Visible frills of the collar and cuffs of a white silk blouse. Small bowler-style hat in matching green velvet with a silk band and large bow at the back. Brown accessories.*

November 3     Attended the State Opening of Parliament, Palace of Westminster.     *Full length white chiffon dress beneath a pure white mink jacket. Spencer tiara and diamond splay necklace with pearl drop earrings.*

November 3     Attended a celebration tea in aid of the Pre-School Playgroup Association, Hyde Park Hotel, London.     *Mid-blue cocktail dress covered with a leaf design in gold and white. Full see-through sleeves gathered and frilled at three-quarter length; frills at the neckline above a ruched yoke. Matching clutch bag and court shoes.*

November 9     Attended a charity dinner and fashion show in aid of Birthright, Guildhall, London.     *Slender crepe-de-chine ankle-length silk dress with one shoulder neckline. Overall pattern of blue and white hoops on a rich mid-blue background. Double frill at the neck: at the dropped waistline a blue sash tied posy-effect at the side. Pearl drop earrings and three row pearl choker. Silver evening bag and shoes.*

November 10     Attended the opening of the Victorian Heyday Exhibition, Portsmouth.

November 10     Inspected the *Mary Rose*, Southsea.     *Grey wool coat-dress with slightly flared skirt, the bodice relieved by five pairs of black buttons down the centre and black collar and cuffs. Cherry red leather boots.*

November 10     Attended a dinner aboard *HMS Victory*, Portsmouth.     *Full length silk cerise dress in Jacobean style with deep square neckline bordered by a small cream frill and white lace flounced beneath the three-quarter length dress sleeves. Single row of pearls. Silver evening bag and shoes.*

November 13     Attended the Festival of Remembrance, Royal Albert Hall.     *Black long sleeved dress with stand-up collars. A spray of triple poppies on the right hand side. Single string of pearls. Black accessories.*

November 14     Attended the Service of Remembrance, Cenotaph, Whitehall, London.

November 14     Attended the Service of Remembrance at Wellington Barracks.     *Black coat and dress, with single poppy and fern on the right hand side, over a white frilled neck silk blouse. Choker pearl necklace. Black straw veiled hat with small burst of matching feathers. Black matching shoes and clutch bag.*

November 16     Attended the welcoming ceremonies for Queen Beatrix of the Netherlands, Westminster Pier.  ·     *Bright cyclamen pink suit with a long sleeved jacket gathered at the yoke, buttoned down the centre, and with luxurious integral ruffle at the neck. Waistband of broad matching ribbon with long tails. Wide brimmed hat in two-tone pink. Black accessories.*

November 18      Attended a State Banquet given by Queen Beatrix of the Netherlands at Hampton Court Palace.      *Pure white silk chiffon evening dress, low necked and with fine, flounced elbow length sleeves. Pearl drop tiara and earrings, with four stranded pearl choker. Queen's Family Order and the Sash of the Order of the House of Orange.*

November 22      Visited Cirencester Playgroup, Forum Youth Centre, Cirencester.      *Deep red and black plaid dress-coat with generously flared skirt and puffed sleeves at the shoulders. The high neck swathing of a white silk blouse just visible at the throat.*

November 23      Visited Capital Radio, Euston Road, London.      *Plain beige-blond suit with loose jacket edged deep brown above the lapels, over a blouse of white and beige with black pinstripes, tied scarf-style at the neck. Brown clutch bag and shoes.*

November 25      Visited Merioneth district of Gwynedd.      *Maxi-length beige-brown wool coat with large squares marked out in thin black lines, five pairs of black buttons up the bodice and black collars. Matching light brown beret generously proportioned and with mid-brown trim. Knee-length brown boots; black accessories.*

November 26      Visited the Wrexham area of Clwyd.      *Thick, flame red coat woven in Welsh wool, striped stitch-effect with lines of blue and yellow. Heavy fringing at collar, cuffs and hem. Underneath, a silk blouse with ornate cavalier-style collars edged with lace. Small mid-blue wool hat veiled and feathered. Matching shoes and handbag.*

November 30      Visited the Hearsay Community Centre, Catford.      *Suit in pine-green wool, wide shouldered and with tight lapels. Heavy stitch-type edging on all panels and seams in mid-green relief. Brown leather shoulder bag and shoes.*

December 2      Visited the Great Ormond Street Hospital for Sick Children, London.      *Bright pink two-piece suit with military-style jacket over a white silk blouse with a frilled neck. Black patent leather clutch bag and black shoes.*

December 2      Attended the première of *Gandhi*, Odeon Theatre, Leicester Square.      *Light, filmy, off-the-shoulder evening dress of silk chiffon. Predominantly white with swirling design of soft pinks and blues all diagonally sequined. The neck-line generously frilled and topped by pale blue bows matching the broad waistband. Prince of Wales' feathers pendant on a gold chain, and silver accessories.*

December 3      Visited DHSS office, Fleming House, London.      *Warm blond-brown cashmere coat, loose-fitting and long-lapelled, with a tie belt. Blouse of white silk with frill and jabot. Black clutch bag and shoes.*

December 6      Visited the Millan Asian Community Project Playgroup, Wandsworth.      *Burgundy woollen coat-dress with expansive yoke accommodating the dense gathering of the sleeves at the shoulders. Matching tie belt separating the bodice from a full skirt of generous folds.*

December 7      Visited Handsworth Cultural Centre, Birmingham.

December 7      Visited Belgrave Lodge, Coventry.      *Deep aubergine below-the-knee dress buttoned down the bodice front, over a white silk blouse with plain cuffs and a heavily frilled neckline. Small hat matching the dress, with a large ostrich feather at the side. Black shoes and clutch bag.*

December 7      Attended the Philharmonic Orchestra's Gala Concert at the Royal Festival Hall.      *Rich, deep sapphire velvet evening gown with expansive décolletage overlaid with intricate lace fichu. Saudi-Arabian sapphire pendant and matching earrings. Silver evening bag.*

December 8      Visited the Royal Marsden Hospital, Fulham Road, London.      *Silk suit of large formal motifs in turquoise, red, white and black, the skirt of mid-calf length, and bolero style jacket. A turquoise silk blouse visible at the midriff, cuffs and as a large tied square outside the jacket at the neck. Black accessories.*

December 8      Attended a charity gala performance, Royal Opera House, Covent Garden.      *Red and silver diamante-studded chiffon ball gown with spaghetti straps beneath a full length black cape. Diamond necklace and earrings, and silver accessories.*

December 9      Visited the Charlie Chaplin Adventure Playground, Lambeth.      *Scarlet wool coat with black trimmed cuffs, and a deep V-neck accentuated by wide black lapels. Underneath, a plain white blouse with a pearl-surrounded jet cameo at the throat. Black clutch bag and shoes.*

December 9      Attended the première of *E.T.*, Empire Theatre, Leicester Square.      *Sumptuous full length strapless evening gown of red, purple and black taffeta, patterned with broad alternating horizontal stripes. Tube top with stand-up frill. Emerald and diamond choker, and matching earrings; silver evening bag and high heeled shoes.*

December 15      Opened the Neo-natal Intensive Care Unit, University College Hospital, London.      *Plain shiny blue-black coat with mandarin collars and radiating gathers at the shoulders. Small, close fitting grey hat with all round veiling and a matching burst of ostrich plumes at the side.*

December 20      Attended the Birkenhead Training Centre.

December 20      Attended a Christmas celebration, Liverpool Cathedral.      *Grey wool coat-dress with slightly flared skirt, the bodice relieved by five pairs of black buttons down the centre and black collar and cuffs. Black Tam-o'-shanter edged with a scarlet band bearing a small matching bow at the side. Black accessories.*

December 22       Photo-call with Prince Charles and Prince William at Kensington Palace.       *Red dress with wide, deep sailor collars and short sleeves, all edged with a double white trim. Underneath, a white silk blouse frilled at the neck and cuffs.*

December 25       Attended Morning Service at St George's Chapel, Windsor.       *Bright cyclamen pink suit, its long sleeves gathered at the yoke, buttoned down the centre and with luxurious integral ruffle at the neck. Waistband of broad matching ribbon with long tails. Wide-brimmed hat of two-tone pink. Black accessories.*

1983

January 17       Attended a reception in connection with "Britain Salutes New York", Royal Academy of Arts.       *Silk suit of large formal motifs in turquoise, red, white and black, consisting of a mid-calf length skirt and bolero-style jacket. Underneath, a turquoise silk blouse visible at the midriff, cuffs and as a large square over the neck of the jacket. Black accessories.*

January 30       Attended a Great Gala at the Royal Albert Hall.       *Shocking pink coat-dress with a bodice buttoned military-style over a white silk blouse with frilled neck. Sapphire and diamond earrings, and dark blue accessories.*

February 2       Visited the Parchmore Methodist Church Youth and Community Centre, Thornton Heath, Surrey.       *Aquamarine two-piece suit comprising midi-length dress and a long jacket belted at the waist, with long sleeves puffed at the shoulders and a military-style front with large black buttons. Black accessories.*

February 3       Attended the Mountbatten Concert, Royal Albert Hall.       *Classical off-the-shoulder evening gown in shimmering lilac silk taffeta, with a large intregal bow at the centre of the neckline. Single row pearl necklace and silver evening bag and shoes.*

February 4       Opened a new Intensive Care Unit, Royal Hospital for Sick Children, Bristol.       *Pine-green wool suit with wide shoulders and lapels drawn tight to the neck. Seams and panels stitched in highlighting mid-green. Small off-centre pillbox hat in matching green with ostrich feather burst at the back. Matching clutch bag and shoes.*

February 7       Attended a reception in connection with the Yorkshire Appeal for Cancer Relief, Garrowby, Yorkshire.       *Olive-green velvet dress with large white lace collars covering the shoulders, and lace hem. Single row of pearls and pearl drop earrings.*

February 8       Visited the International Spring Fair, National Exhibition Centre, Birmingham.       *Deep blue velvet two-piece suit with midi-length skirt, long full sleeves, a broad waistband and panelled bodice, all over a white silk blouse frilled at the neck and cuffs. Matching veiled velvet hat with a silver-grey ostrich feather at the back. Sapphire and diamond earrings. Brown leather clutch bag and shoes.*

February 16       Visited Nightingale House for the Elderly, Clapham, London.       *Two-piece suit in aubergine velvet; a generously flared skirt and close fitting jacket with front button panel enclosed by faint white piping. The heavily frilled collar of a white silk blouse visible above the neck. Small matching aubergine brimmed hat with cascade of ostrich feather falling on the right hand side. Black shoes and clutch bag.*

February 17       Visited the Royal Hospital for Sick Children, Glasgow.

February 17       Visited the Homesteading Scheme, Easterhouse, Glasgow.       *Long, military-style, unbelted coat in bright delphinium with bold black buttons, black-edged false pockets, and black mandarin collars. Small saucer hat with brim, large satin bow at the back, and veiling over half face. Black clutch bag and shoes.*

February 18       Attended the Ice Show, Wembley.       *Plain, shiny, blue-black coat with mandarin collars and radiating gathers at the shoulders. Black clutch bag and shoes.*

February 22       Visited the factory of Glaxo Pharmaceuticals, Ware, Hertfordshire.       *Long white laboratory smock over normal day clothes, and a trilby-style white hat.*

February 25       Opened Brookfields School for the Mentally Handicapped, Tilehurst, Reading.       *Royal blue coat-dress with broad tie belt and black edging to mandarin collars and front button-up panel. Small, rimmed saucer hat in matching blue, with high veiling. Diamond and sapphire earrings. Black shoes with bows, and black clutch bag.*

March 2       Opened a new shopping centre, Aylesbury, Buckinghamshire.       *Rich deep green velvet coat with close fitting bodice buttoned down the centre and generously flared skirt. Small bowler-style hat in matching green velvet with a silk band and a large bow at the back. Brown accessories.*

March 4       Visited Prince of Wales Trust Organisations in Glasgow and Edinburgh.       *Grey wool coat-dress with slightly flared skirt, the bodice relieved by five pairs of black buttons down the centre and black collar and cuffs. Black Tam-o'-Shanter edged with a scarlet band and with a small matching bow at the side. Black accessories.*

March 9       Attended the presentation of a charter to the new borough of West Devon, Tavistock.

March 9       Visited under-five playgroups at Bovey Tracey and Tavistock.

**March 9**      Visited Duchy of Cornwall Farms on Dartmoor.      *Maxi-length beige-brown wool coat with large squares marked out in thin black lines, five pairs of black buttons up the bodice, and black collars. Low trilby-style velvet hat in deep brown with matching band and small bow beneath the back of the brim. Brown suede handbag and matching shoes.*

**March 13**      Attended the Baptism of Alexandra Knatchbull, the daughter of Lord and Lady Romsey, at Romsey Abbey. *Shocking pink coat-dress with the bodice buttoned military-style and with stand-up collars over a white silk frilled blouse. Matching pink hat with a silk hatband and a full-face veil.*

**March 17**      Attended the exhibition "Better Made in Britain", Kensington Exhibition Centre, London.      *Silk suit of large formal motifs in turquoise, red, white and black, the skirt of mid-calf length and a bolero-style jacket. Underneath, a turquoise silk blouse visible at the midriff, cuffs and as a large square falling over the top of the jacket at the neck. Black accessories.*

**March 18**      Left Heathrow Airport for Australia.      *Deep blue velvet coat-dress with midi-length skirt, long full sleeves and a panelled bodice. Brown shoes.*

**March 20**      Arrived at Alice Springs Airport at the beginning on the tour of Australia.      *Simple silk aquamarine dress with button-up short sleeves and wide collars with pointed and scalloped edges. White handbag and shoes.*

**March 21**      Toured St John Ambulance regional centre, Alice Springs.

**March 21**      Visited Alice Springs School of the Air.

**March 21**      Attended open air buffet luncheon, Telegraph Station.      *Bright yellow silk frock with white abstract motifs. High necked, with wing collars and a pin tucked front. White waistband and matching clutch bag and shoes.*

**March 21**      Visited Ayers Rock.      *Light white cotton dress buttoned from neck to hem, with half-length sleeves and a narrow belt on a broad sash. White shoulder bag and soft beige slipper-shoes.*

**March 22**      Toured Karguru School, Tennant Creek.

**March 22**      Lunched at the Eldorado restaurant, Tennant Creek.      *Loose cotton mint-green skirt below a hip-length, pure white blouse, tunic-style with short sleeves and pin tucked panels framing the bodice. White accessories.*

**March 24**      Arrived at Canberra to be welcomed at the Civic Square.

**March 24**      Visited Parliament House site and information centre.

**March 24**      Lunched at the Premier's residence.      *High-necked two-piece silk chiffon outfit in turquoise; the jacket buttoned down the centre, pin tucked at the sides and belted with a bow at the front, the skirt ample and of mid-calf length. Small matching saucer hat with cable trim and light veiling. White low-heeled shoes and matching clutch bag. Three strand pearl choker.*

**March 24**      Attended a State Dinner given by the Governor-General, Government House.      *Gold coloured silk taffeta evening dress, the bodice patterned with rays of diagonal stripes, low-waisted, with deep V-neck and sleeves puffed at the shoulders. Spencer tiara, sapphire pendant on a silver chain, and matching sapphire and diamond earrings. Queen's Family Order worn on dress.*

**March 25**      Visited Woden Special School, Deakin.

**March 25**      Toured Erindale Community Centre, Waniassa.

**March 25**      Attended garden party at Senate Gardens, Canberra.

**March 25**      Visited Australian War Memorial, Canberra.      *Cantaloupe-pink suit and hat worn as going away outfit after the Royal Wedding, except that the sleeves of the jacket had been lengthened and finished with white cuffs.*

**March 25**      Visited bush fire areas, Cockatoo, Victoria.      *Long lightweight frock of multi-coloured stripes with a narrow tie belt and flounced neck and shoulders. Elbow length sleeves. White accessories.*

**March 26**      Visited bush fire victims and rescue workers at Stirling, near Adelaide.      *Simple, pale blue, belted dress relieved by white flyaway collars, and white cuffs on full-length leg-of-mutton sleeves, and a pink bow at the bodice. White accessories.*

**March 28**      Arrived at Sydney to be welcomed at the Opera House.

**March 28**      Watched children's programme of music and dancing.

**March 28**      Attended a buffet luncheon at Parliament House.      *Salmon-pink, short-sleeved dress with close flower design in white and blue. Bodice gathered by matching belt tied in large bow at the side. Wide-brimmed straw hat in pink, with matching band and bow. Single row of pearls, white shoes and clutch bag.*

March 28    Attended a charity ball at the Wentworth Hotel.    *Blue and silver silk chiffon evening dress, heavily flounced from shoulders to hem, and with a broad silver-coloured cummerbund-style belt. Silver shoes and evening bag. Pearl drop earrings, diamond sunray necklace.*

March 29    Attended a school children's outdoor gathering, Newcastle.

March 29    Attended a reception at the City Hall, Newcastle.

March 29    Attended a State reception at the Town Hall, Maitland.    *Pale pink pinstriped silk chiffon dress with full skirt, beneath a short-sleeved crossover jacket with a broad buttoned waistband. Small matching veiled hat with plaited trimming and large silk bow at the back. White shoes and clutch bag.*

March 30    Visited Rokeby High School, Tasmania.

March 30    Crossed Hobart Bay from Bellerive to Waterman's Dock.

March 30    Attended a luncheon at Government House, Hobart.    *Red and white candy-striped blouse with large collars, central bow and full sleeves. Loose sleeveless academic-style over-garment in tomato red, matching straight skirt. Red straw hat with white flowers at the back, and matching red handbag and shoes.*

March 30    Attended a State reception at the Wrest Point Hotel, Hobart.    *Scarlet evening gown with subdued silver spot pattern. Wide neckline overlaid with matching flounce. Spencer tiara with diamond flower and pearl drop earrings, and diamond pendant showing the Prince of Wales' feathers. Queen's Family Order worn on the dress.*

March 31    Whistle-stop tour of Tasmania, calling at Kempton, Oatlands, Ross and Campbell Town.

March 31    Attended buffet luncheon, Albert Hall, Launceston.

March 31    Planted tree in the Civic Square, Launceston.

March 31    Visited the Australian Maritime College, Mowbray.    *Off-white wool suit with long jacket over a white blouse with mandarin collars. Small white saucer hat with a cluster of flowers in white and gold, and veiling over half the face. Bright red shoes and clutch bag.*

April 3    Attended Divine service at St Matthew's Church, Albury.    *Blue-green silk dress beneath an off-white square quilted full-sleeved jacket with miniscule flower patterns in blue, green and red. Blue-green straw hat with band of watered silk, rounded off by a bow and hanging ribbons at the back.*

April 3    Watched Prince Charles playing polo at Warwick Farm, near Richmond.    *Low-waisted dress of blue and white stripes –horizontal on the bodice, vertical on the skirt, with white crossover collars. Navy blazer and matching shoes.*

April 5    Toured the Parks Community Centre, Adelaide.

April 5    Attended a State reception, Adelaide Town Hall.    *Two-piece suit in light brown, beige and white vertical stripes, the jacket buttoned down the front with wide, shallow pockets, over a luxuriantly-frilled cream silk blouse. Straw-coloured hat with wide brim and a broad white band. Beige accessories.*

April 5    Attended a disco dance, University of Adelaide.    *Plain black silk dress beneath a white silk long top with black leaf motifs. Casual tie belt at waist. Black and white peep-toe shoes.*

April 6    Attended a civic reception, Renmark Community Hotel.

April 6    Visited the Jane Eliza Landing and cruised down the River Murray.

April 6    Attended Combined Schools Sports Day, Port Pirie.

April 6    Arrived at Perth Airport.    *Bright red suit with low-waisted, long-sleeved top surmounted by deep, wide, white collars with scalloped and pointed edges. White straw hat with wide brim and scarlet trim. Matching red accessories and a three strand pearl choker.*

April 7    Visited the Princess of Wales Wing, Fremantle Hospital.

April 7    Attended children's display, Bentley Hockey Stadium.

April 7    Attended a civic welcome, Council House, Perth.    *Fuchsia-pink dress with small white spots. Apron-style skirt, with bodice tied at top. Matching pink hat of swirling silk brought into a large posy feature at the side. White shoes and clutch bag.*

April 7    Attended garden party at Government House, Perth.    *Pale-blue suit consisting of a shift dress beneath a light tunic with three-quarter length sleeves and wide sailor collars. Top, hem and collars highlighted by white bands. Matching blue hat, with light veiling on the brim. Single row of pearls.*

April 8      Attended a gathering of school children, Hands Oval, Bunbury.

April 8      Attended a civic reception, Council Gardens, Bunbury.      *Silver-grey silk skirt with small white butterfly pattern; matching loose jacket over a blouse of white with sailor collars tied at the base. Maroon waistband. Silver-grey straw hat with up-turned brim and a veil bow at the back.*

April 10     Attended Divine service, St Paul's Church, Holbrook.      *Two-piece suit of yellow, maroon, blue and white stripes, horizontal on an accordion-pleated skirt, vertical on a long, straight jacket frilled and bowed at the neck. Tiny crown-top hat of crushed raspberry, with tumbling, frilled rosette on the left side.*

April 11     Arrived at Brisbane for a walkabout and civic welcome at the City Hall.      *Silk, gentian-violet dress with co-ordinating daisy patterns in white, dividing diagonally across the front. Small, plain white hat with a burst of ostrich feather at the back. White accessories. Single row of pearls.*

April 11     Attended a State reception at the Crest International Hotel, Brisbane.      *Slimline silk taffeta evening dress in shocking-pink, with spaghetti shoulder straps topped by large bows. Spencer tiara, sapphire and diamond pendant earrings, and silver accessories. Queen's Family Order worn on the dress.*

April 12     Visited Yandina Ginger Factory.

April 12     Toured C S R Macadamia Nut Plant.

April 12     Attended a luncheon given by Maroochy Shire Council.

April 12     Toured Sunshine Plantation.

April 12     Visited Buderim and Alexandra Headland.      *Bright yellow silk frock with white abstract motifs. High-necked with wing collars and a pin tucked front. White waist band and matching clutch bag and shoes. Wide-brimmed picture hat in white, with matching plaited band between brim and crown, and large flower to the right side.*

April 14     Arrived at Melbourne.

April 14     Visited Paisley Housing Estate, Altona.

April 14     Attended welcoming ceremony, Bourke Street Mall, Melbourne.

April 14     Attended a State luncheon, Government House.      *Red polka-dot white dress beneath a close-fitting scarlet jacket edged in white. Wide-brimmed white hat trimmed with red. Matching red shoes and clutch bag, and a three row pearl choker.*

April 14     Attended Variety Concert, Melbourne Concert Hall.      *Long, rose pink silk evening dress, patterned with cream-gold hoops, with expansive pink and cream flounces at the neck, on the sleeves, and round the waist. A large cream silk bow at the waistline. A single row of pearls, and pearl drop earrings, with gold evening bag and shoes.*

April 15     Visited Ballarat.

April 15     Toured reconstructed Township, Sovereign Hill Historical Park.

April 15     Attended a Buffet luncheon, New York Theatre.

April 15     Visited Bendigo.      *Two-piece suit consisting of a dress and quilted jacket of off-white fabric, closely patterned with tiny flowers in blue, red and green, the jacket edged and buttoned in blue. White silk blouse just visible beneath. Small, mid-blue, brimless saucer hat with plaited edges and high veiling. White accessories.*

April 16     Returned to Melbourne to stay at Government House.      *White silk dress with tiny regular L-shaped motifs in grey and maroon, and trimmed and edged with gold and yellow silk. Long, full sleeves with buttoned yellow cuffs; yoke-style collar and a row of yellow buttons from neck to waist. Matching yellow ribbons at neck. White accessories.*

April 16     Attended a dinner dance at the Melbourne Hilton Hotel.      *Slim, close-fitting evening gown in pale cream and silver with subtle random zigzag patterns, the one shoulder neckline revealing a bare left arm. Pearl drop earrings with pearl and diamond clasps, and silver evening bag and shoes.*

April 17     Left Melbourne for New Zealand.      *Slender, red silk dress, patterned with small white stars and larger stars of blue and green. Chin-high ruffed collar and full sleeves frilled at the cuffs. Brilliant blue slouch-style hat with matching ostrich feather feature on left side. Red court shoes and clutch bag.*

April 17     Arrived at Auckland.      *Cream wool coat-dress with tan trimming at collars and tan buttons on the bodice. Tan-trimmed cream pillbox hat with brown bows on either side. Black shoes and clutch bag.*

**April 18**      Attended a gathering of children and Maori communities at Eden Park Stadium, Auckland.      *Deep, apple green dress with tiny white spots, except for a diagonal white pin-striped panel across the bodice. Spotted waist band embellished with pin-striped bow. Small white bowler style hat with generous ostrich feather ornament at the back. White accessories.*

**April 18**      Attended a performance of Coppelia, St James's Theatre Auckland.      *Classical, off-the-shoulder evening gown in shimmering lilac, with a large intergral bow at the centre of the neckline. Gold and diamond pendant, showing Prince of Wales's feathers, and small pearl drop earrings. Silver evening bag and shoes.*

**April 19**      Visited Milford School, Auckland.

**April 19**      Attended the opening of the Waterwise Boating Centre, North Shore, Auckland.      *Drop-waisted woollen coat-dress in pastel yellow, frilled at the neck and cuffs. Matching yellow straw hat trimmed with white and sporting a sunflower at the back. Black and navy accessories.*

**April 19**      Visited fire fighting headquarters, Manukau.      *Loose-fitting silk two-piece suit in navy blue with white abstract designs, over a simple white pin tucked shirt with wing collars. Large white hat with white flower and plaited stem band, over a wide translucent brim. Navy accessories, sapphire and diamond earrings.*

**April 20**      Arrived at Wellington, to be welcomed at the Town Hall, for a walk-about in the city centre.      *Blue-green suit with long, tailored jacket bearing a row of large black buttons, military-style, from waist to neck. Underneath, a white silk blouse with a close-frilled neck just visible. Small-edged saucer hat in matching blue-green fabric, with large, fussy rosette. Black accessories.*

**April 20**      Attended a State banquet at Parliament House, Wellington.      *Pale blue-grey silk chiffon evening dress with sequin spots. Deep V-neck, the bodice overlaid on a fine flounce to include see-through sleeves. Pale pink bow at décolletage with matching broad sash. Silver accessories, with the Spencer tiara, crystal drop earrings and a single row of pearls.*

**April 21**      Visited Wainuiomata.      *Two-piece suit consisting of an off-white dress beneath a quilted jacket of off-white fabric, closely patterned with tiny flowers in blue, red and green, the jacket edged and buttoned in blue. Silk white blouse with stand-up collar. Pale blue pill-box hat with large satin bow at the back white handbag and low-heeled shoes.*

**April 21**      Attended a Government Ball at Wellington.      *Gold-coloured silk taffeta evening dress, the bodice patterned with raised diagonal stripes, low-waisted, with deep V-neck and sleeves puffed at the shoulders. Queen's Family Order worn on dress. Heart-shaped necklace, silver evening bag.*

**April 22**      Visited Upper Hutt City.

**April 22**      Planted trees in Queen Elizabeth Park, Masterton.

**April 22**      Visited Kowhai Park, Wanganui.

**April 22**      Visited Prince Edward at Wanganui Collegiate School.      *Royal blue coat dress with broad tie belt, black edging to mandarin collars and front button-up panel. Small, rimmed saucer hat in matching blue, with high veiling. Black clutch bag and low heeled shoes.*

**April 23**      Photographic session with Prince Charles and Prince William in the grounds of Government House, Auckland.      *Casual emerald-green dress with snowstorm pattern, buttoned down the front of the bodice and the left side of the skirt. Large detachable white collar with scalloped points.*

**April 24**      Attended tribal welcoming ceremonies at the Poho-o-Rawiri Meeting House, Gisborne.      *Two-piece silk suit in turquoise, the long, full sleeved jacket having a tucked bodice and close-frilled cuffs. Small matching saucer hat with plaited edge and flower and veiling gathered at the back. White accessories.*

**April 25**      Attended ANZAC Day Remembrance Ceremony, War Memorial, Auckland.      *Soft grey coat dress with broad tie belt and white edging to mandarin collars and military-style front panel. Matching pillbox hat with white trim and white ostrich feather burst on right side. White clutch bag and court shoes.*

**April 25**      Attended a garden party at Government House, Auckland.      *Plain black silk dress beneath a white silk long top patterned with black leaf motifs, and a wide black silk waistband. High-crowned hat in white straw with complementary wide black silk band. Three row pearl choker.*

**April 26**      Attended the opening of the Tauranga Community Centre.      *Off-white wool suit with long jacket topped by stand-up collars, and plain skirt. Small white saucer hat with cluster of white flowers and half veil. Cherry-red clutch bag and shoes.*

**April 26**      Attended a civic reception at Auckland Art Gallery.      *Cocktail dress of ivory silk with tucked bodice, full sleeves gathered at the elbow and an expansive lace-trimmed flounce at the yoke. Single row of pearls. Red clutch bag and day shoes.*

**April 27**      Visited Otago Boys High School, and unveiled a plaque.

**April 27**      Welcomed at the Octagon, Otago.      *Long, military-style, unbelted coat in bright delphinium with bold black buttons, black edged false pockets and black mandarin collars. Small matching saucer hat with plaited band and a large silk bow at the back.*

April 28    Visited Christchurch for walkabout.

April 28    Watched a flying display at the RNZAF Base, Wigram.    *Warm blond-brown cashmere coat, loose-fitting and long-lapelled, with a tie belt. Blouse of white silk with frill at the neck. Black clutch bag and shoes.*

April 29    Travelled across the Bay of Islands in a Maori canoe.

April 29    Attended Maori festival at Waitangi.    *Sunshine-yellow dress with mandarin collars beneath a matching quilted jacket buttoned diagonally to the left of the neck. Matching saucer hat with white and yellow plaited edging and a yellow veil. White accessories.*

April 29    Attended a State banquet at Auckland.    *Light cream silk evening gown with fluted bodice, frilled at the neck and with lace-trimmed flounced sleeves. Pearl drop tiara and earrings, and a five row pearl bracelet. Silver lozenge-patterned evening bag and matching shoes. Queen's Family Order worn on the dress.*

April 30    Departure from Auckland for Eleuthera.    *Single narrow-belted dress in emerald-green silk-chiffon. Plain neckline and long sleeves ruffled at the cuffs. Three row pearl choker. White handbag and shoes.*

May 11    Arrived back at Heathrow Airport from Eleuthera.    *Butter coloured dress with half length frilled sleeves and frilled collar; low waisted bodice buttoned down the front. White shoes.*

May 13    Opened an adventure playground for the handicapped, Seven Springs, Cheltenham.

May 13    Visited Paradise House, a young people's training college, Painswick, Gloucestershire.    *Bold patterned black silk dress with large petal motifs in red, white and pale blue, the waist tied with a wide black band. Large lace-edged white silk collar and matching lace frills at cuffs. Small pearl earrings. Black accessories.*

May 17    Attended the opening of the exhibition "Renaissance at Sutton Place", Guildford, Surrey.    *Full length sleeveless silk taffeta evening gown with deep V-neck and heavily ruffled shoulders. Close-fitting waist. Black lace diamond-studded collar.*

May 18    Opened the New Tyne Bridge, and opened a new food factory near Newcastle.    *Deep blue velvet two-piece suit with midi-length skirt, long full sleeves, a broad waistband and panelled bodice, over a white silk blouse frilled at neck and cuffs. Matching veiled velvet hat with silver-grey ostrich feather at the back. Sapphire and diamond earrings. Brown leather clutch bag and shoes.*

May 19    Attended the presentation by the Queen of new standards to the Household Cavalry, Horseguards Parade.    *Off-white wool suit with long jacket and plain skirt, over a cream blouse generously flounced at the neck, with frilled cuffs. Small white saucer hat with cluster of white feathers and half veil. Three row pearl choker. Cherry red clutch bag and shoes.*

May 20    Opened a new housing scheme for the elderly, Cranmer House, Canterbury.

May 20    Visited Canterbury Cathedral.    *Cream wool coat-dress with tan trimming at collars and tan buttons on the bodice. Tan-trimmed cream pillbox hat with brown bows either side. Brown shoes and bag.*

May 23    Attended a concert given by the Royal College of Music, Royal Albert Hall.    *Light, filmy, off-the-shoulder evening dress of silk chiffon. Predominantly white with soft swirling designs in soft pinks and blues, with sequinned diagonals. The neckline generously frilled and topped by pale blue bows matching the broad waistband. Single string pearl necklace, with pearl drop earrings. Silver accessories.*

May 24    Attended a charity luncheon, Dorchester Hotel.    *Silk gentian-violet dress with co-ordinating daisy patterns dividing diagonally across the front of the bodice. Two rows of pearls forming a choker with the sapphire clasp as a centrepiece. Diamond and sapphire earrings. White accessories.*

May 24    Attended the Live Music Now dinner, Apsley House, London.    *Gold coloured silk taffeta evening dress; the bodice patterned with raised diagonal stripes, low waisted, with deep V-neck and sleeves puffed at the shoulders. Pearl drop earrings and gold necklace with heart-shaped pendant. Matching accessories.*

May 25    Attended a polo match at Windsor Great Park.    *Rust-coloured, 'pedal-pusher' cropped trousers with shallow turn-ups and a drawstring waistbelt. Cream silk blouse with embossed flower print, and frilled Victorian neckline, with a bright red sweater thrown casually over the shoulders. Large, quilted shoulder-bag with a blue, rectangular centre surrounded by white, and patterned with red designs. Red shoes.*

May 27    Visited Duchy of Cornwall properties, including the town of St Columb Major, Cornwall.    *Silk turquoise coat-dress with high neck, buttoned military-style to the right hand side with large black buttons. Slim fitting with slightly puffed, gathered, tight sleeves. White silk blouse with frilled collar and cuffs visible. Black accessories.*

May 29    Attended a polo match at Windsor Great Park.    *Fitted, quilted jacket in pink, blue and white with mandarin collars, over a white blouse with button-over neckline. A straight, pleated white skirt with belt. Coral-coloured shoulder-bag with long, narrow strap, and matching coral shoes. Pearl stud earrings.*

June 1      Opened the Royal Preston Hospital, Lancashire.

June 1      Opened the factory of Joseph Arnold and Co. Ltd., Accrington.      *White silk dress with large scarlet polka-dots. Matching scarlet jacket with deep and wide lapels trimmed in white, and full sleeves to elbow length. Straw hat in co-ordinating white with red trim.*

June 4      Attended a charity dinner dance, Broadlands, Hampshire.      *Slim, figure-hugging evening gown in pale cream and silver, with subtle random zig-zag pattern, the fabric gathered over the right shoulder, leaving the other shoulder bare. Pearl drop earrings; diamond bracelet and silver evening bag and shoes.*

June 6      Attended the première of the film *Octopussy* at the Odeon Theatre, Leicester Square.      *Slim, close fitting evening gown in pale cream and silver with subtle random zig-zag pattern, the fabric gathered over the right shoulder in a one-shoulder neckline style. Pearl drop earrings; diamond bracelet and silver evening bag and shoes.*

June 10      Took the Salute at the Founder's Day Parade, Royal Hospital, Chelsea.      *Pale blue outfit comprising a dress beneath a loose jacket, buttoned in the centre, with sailor collars and sleeves falling to below the elbow. Top, hem and collar picked out by white bands. White flower at the back. Sprig of deep green oak leaves on the jacket. Three row pearl choker. White accessories.*

June 11      Attended the Queen's Birthday Parade, Horseguards Parade, London.      *Cream silk dress with white cloud design, long-sleeved with elliptical neckline. Matching wide-brimmed hat with grey silk band. Single string pearl necklace. Soft grey leather handbag and white shoes.*

June 12      Attended a polo match at Windsor Great Park.      *Warm, bright red sweater with all-over design of large, white sheep, though with one sheep knitted in black. Underneath, a white blouse with collars overlapping the top of the sweater and cuffs visible at the wrists. White slacks and red shoes. White, padded clutch bag with small rose-spray designs.*

June 14      Left London for Canada.      *Silk aquamarine dress with buttoned short sleeves and wide collars with pointed and scalloped edges. Blue-green straw hat with band of watered silk, rounded off by a bow and hanging ribbons at the back. White, padded clutch bag with small rose-spray designs in green and red.*

June 14      Arrived at Halifax, Nova Scotia, to be welcomed at the Garrison Grounds.      *White silk dress squared with red lines, with matching red broad belt and cravat. Matching red Robin Hood-style hat with a satin bow, red clutch bag and matching court shoes.*

June 14      Watched the Beat the Retreat from the *Royal Yacht Britannia*, Halifax.      *Deep-blue silk cocktail dress.*

June 15      Visited the ship repair unit, Halifax dockyard.

June 15      Viewed St George's Church restoration programme.

June 15      Planted a tree during a walkabout in Halifax Commons.

June 15      Attended a buffet luncheon at Government House.      *Cream wool coat-dress with tan trimming at collars and tan buttons on the bodice. Tan-trimmed cream pillbox hat with brown bows either side. Brown shoes and bag.*

June 15      Attended dinner given by Premier Trudeau in Halifax.      *Light cream silk evening gown with fluted bodice, frilled at the neck and with lace-trimmed flounced, sleeves. Pearl drop tiara earrings, and five row pearl bracelet. Silver evening bag and matching shoes. Queen's Family Order worn on the dress.*

June 16      Visited Loyalist Buildings, Shelburne.

June 16      Attended a buffet luncheon, Bridgewater.

June 16      Visited cultural exhibition, Lunenberg.      *Bright red Spanish-style 'zoot suit' – a long, wool, gaberdine double-breasted jacket topped by the tie neck of a black spotted white blouse; and a straight skirt. Tall, black, flamenco-style hat and black bag and shoes.*

June 17      Welcomed at City Hall, Saint John, New Brunswick.

June 17      Attended a wreath-laying ceremony at the Loyalists' cemetery.

June 17      Visited Rothesay Collegiate School.      *Pastel-yellow wool coat dress with drop waist and frills at neck and cuffs. Matching yellow straw hat trimmed with white and sporting a sunflower at the back. Black and navy accessories.*

June 17      Attended a provincial dinner, Saint John.      *Blue and silver silk chiffon evening dress heavily flounced from shoulders to hem, and with a broad silver-coloured cummerbund style belt. Silver shoes and evening bag. Spencer diamond tiara and diamond and pearl earrings. Queen's Family Order worn on the dress.*

June 18      Visited Rotary Memorial Park, Dalhousie.

June 18      Attended a picnic luncheon and entertainment, Sugar Loaf Park.

June 18      Visited Campbellton.      *Loose fitting silk two-piece suit in navy blue with white abstract designs, over simple white pin-tucked shirt with wing collars. Large white hat with white flower and plaited stem band over a wide translucent brim. Navy accessories, sapphire and diamond earrings.*

June 19      Attended a service at All Saints' Church, St. Andrew's.

June 19      Attended Lt-Governor's reception.      *Off-white wool suit with long jacket and plain skirt, over a cream blouse generously flounced at the neck, with frilled cuffs. Small white saucer hat with cluster of white flowers and half veil. Cherry-red clutch bag and shoes.*

June 20      Arrived at Ottawa to be welcomed on Parliament Hill.      *Blue, gold and white vertically striped dress with horizontally-striped bodice, cuffs, waistband and hem. Small white bowler-style hat with ostrich plume at the back. Necklace with gold heart-shaped pendant, and white accessories.*

June 20      Attended an official dinner at Rideau Hall.      *Slimline silk taffeta evening dress in shocking-pink, with spaghetti shoulder straps concealed by large bows. Pearl drop diamond tiara, diamond and pearl earrings, diamond and gold necklace with Prince of Wales feathers pendant. Queen's Family Order worn on the dress.*

June 21      Visited Ottawa Police Headquarters.

June 21      Attended Kiwanis Club luncheon at the Château Laurier.      *Cream silk suit with white cloud motifs and a narrow grey belt. Matching soft leather handbag. Grey hat with matching silk band. A single string of pearls. White shoes.*

June 21      Attended a barbecue at Kingsmere Farm.      *Plain pastel-blue dress with wide white collars meeting beneath a broad, ribboned, pink bow. White cuffs with small blue buttons. White accessories.*

June 22      Travelled by boat on the Rideau Canal.

June 22      Attended the inauguration of the Ottawa Police Headquarters.

June 22      Left Ottawa for St. John's, Newfoundland.

June 22      Attended reception and tree-planting ceremony at Government House.      *Pale-pink pin-striped silk chiffon dress with full skirt, beneath a short-sleeved crossover jacket with a broad, buttoned waistband. Small matching veiled hat with plaited trimming and large silk bow at the back. White shoes and clutch bag. Single string pearl necklace.*

June 23      Attended youth festival, King George V Memorial Field, St. John's.

June 23      Watched youth displays, St. John's Memorial Stadium.

June 23      Visited Janeway Child Health Centre.      *Red polka-dot white dress beneath a close-fitting scarlet jacket edged in white. Wide-brimmed white hat trimmed with red. Matching red shoes and clutch bag.*

June 23      Attended Provincial Premier's dinner, Newfoundland Hotel.      *Gold-coloured silk taffeta evening dress, the bodice patterned with raised diagonal stripes, low-waisted, with deep V-neck and sleeves puffed at the shoulders. Pearl drop diamond tiara with diamond and pearl drop earrings, and a gold necklace with a heart-shaped pendant. Silver evening bag. Queen's Family Order worn on the dress.*

June 24      Attended the opening of St. John's anniversary celebrations at Canada Games Park.

June 24      Toured Cape Spear National Park.

June 24      Attended Mayoral buffet luncheon, City Hall.      *Two-piece suit in emerald-green, with long double-breasted jacket and reverse-pleated skirt. Plain white silk blouse with stand-up collars. Small, jaunty, green hat with matching ostrich feather at the side. White accessories.*

June 25      Welcomed at Town Hall, Harbour Grace.

June 25      Watched musical entertainment, St Francis Field.

June 25      Attended buffet luncheon, at St Francis School.      *Long, military-style, unbelted coat in bright delphinium with bold black buttons, black-edged false pockets and black mandarin collars over a black and white spotted silk neck scarf. Tall, wide-brimmed hat and black bag and shoes.*

June 27     Arrived at Charlottetown, Prince Edward Island, to be welcomed at Province House.

June 27     Visited City Hall, Charlottetown.

June 27     Toured Ravenwood House Agricultural Research Centre, and planted a tree.     *Wedgewood-blue pleated dress with straight, drop-waist bodice. Wide, white, sailor-boy collar with ornamental lace effect edges, joined by a central bow of blue ribbon. Small matching pillbox hat, veiled and with a side bow. White clutch bag and court shoes.*

June 27     Attended evening musical display at Montague.     *Deep pink, generously skirted suit with a double-breasted high-necked jacket with mandarin collars over a white blouse. Black accessories.*

June 28     Arrived at the Yacht Club Wharf, Summerside.

June 28     Welcomed at the Memorial Park, Summerside.

June 28     Visited senior citizens' home, Summerset Manor.

June 28     Attended a garden reception given by the Lt-Governor, Charlottetown.     *White silk dress with tiny, regular, L-shaped motifs in grey and maroon, and trimmed and edged with golden-yellow silk. Long full sleeves with buttoned yellow cuffs; yoke-style collar and a row of yellow buttons from neck to waist. Matching yellow ribbons at neck. Small primrose-coloured hat with upturned brim and matching ostrich feathers flecked with brown. White shoes.*

June 28     Watched racing at Charlottetown Driving Park.     *White, shallow-pleated dress beneath a quilted, close fitting jacket of white, pink and blue stripes, with a line of buttons in matching fabric. Pale pink clutch bag and shoes.*

June 29     Arrived at Edmonton, Alberta, to be welcomed at the Legislature Building, City Hall.

June 29     Walkabout in Sir Winston Churchill Square.     *Bright red suit with low-waisted, long-sleeved top, surmounted by deep wide white collars with scalloped and pointed edges. White straw hat with wide brim and scarlet trim. Matching red accessories, and a single row pearl necklace.*

June 29     Attended Fancy Dress barbecue at Fort Edmonton Park.     *Mid-Victorian-style bustled dress in cream silk with faint pink trimmings and delicate lace collar, cravat and cuffs. The skirt generously gathered at the sides, the bodice close-fitting and buttoned down the centre. Small cream platter hat trimed with silk bows, lace and small pink flowers. Cream boots.*

June 30     Toured cultural exhibition, Convention Centre, Edmonton.

June 30     Visited Athletes' Village for luncheon.

June 30     Attended a degree-conferring ceremony, Universiade Auditorium.     *Silk gentian-violet dress with co-ordinating daisy patterns in white, dividing diagonally across the front. Small plain white hat with a burst of ostrich feather at the back. White accessories.*

June 30     Attended provincial dinner Government House.     *Tomato-red evening dress in silk taffeta with narrow shoulder straps and integral see-through over-bodice patterned with large flowers. Spencer tiara, with pearl drop diamond earrings. Silver shoes and evening bag. Queen's Family Order worn on the dress.*

July 1     Attended the opening of the World University Games, Commonwealth Stadium, Edmonton.

July 1     Left Canada for London.     *Midnight-blue dress with fuchsia-pink bubble designs. High, close collar above a buttoned bodice. Crushed raspberry jacket with triangular double-breasted panels and long sleeves. Midnight-blue straw hat, trimmed with matching ostrich feather. Dark blue accessories.*

July 6     Attended a dinner in aid of the Help Poland Fund, Hatfield House, Hertfordshire.     *Off-the-shoulder evening gown in lilac silk taffeta, with a large integral bow at the centre of the neckline. Gold and diamond pendant bearing the Prince of Wales' feathers. Small pearl drop earrings. Silver evening bag and shoes.*

July 6     Visited the Elmhurst Ballet School, Camberley, Surrey.     *Blue, gold and white vertically striped dress with horizontally striped bodice, cuffs, waistband and hem. Necklace with gold heart-shaped pendant, and white accessories.*

July 6     Attended a polo match at Windsor Great Park.     *Long, white, silk two-piece outfit with delicate flower-spray motifs in red, blue and green, the jacket loose-fitting and self-tying at the midriff. Underneath, a mid-blue vest edged in white. Gold necklace with a large, flat gold disc pendant. Blue shoes.*

July 7     Visited St Mary's Hospital to see Lady Sarah McCorquodale after the birth of her baby.     *Cool, two-piece polka-dot outfit, the sleeveless tunic top held down by a narrow belt. White, padded bag with rose-spray designs. White peep-toe shoes with small bows on the front.*

July 8        Opened the new Fisher-Price toy factory, Peterlee, County Durham.        *Cream silk dress with design of white clouds overall, long sleeves with elliptical neckline. Matching wide brimmed hat with grey silk band. Single string pearl necklace. Soft grey leather handbag and white shoes.*

July 12        Opened Spencer House, St Andrew's Hospital, Northampton.

July 12        Visited Lord and Lady Spencer, Althorp, Northampton.        *Grey silk suit with small white butterfly pattern. Long white collars broadening round the neck and tied in front. Deep full sleeves brought to tight cuffs. Matching grey round hat with up-turned brim and veiled at the back. White clutch bag and shoes.*

July 12        Attended a polo match at Windsor Great Park.        *Light blue and white shift dress with low neckline and shoulder straps, candy-striped horizontally across the bodice and vertically down the skirt, with a frill around the waist. White, padded bag with rose-spray designs in green and red. White shoes.*

July 13        Attended the Queen's garden party, Buckingham Palace.        *Plain peach silk dress beneath a loose, silk, off-white and peach jacket. The jacket vertically striped, with three-quarter length sleeves, and tied with a matching ribbon belt at the waist. Large-brimmed off-white hat with, at the base of the crown, matching plaited band relieved by a large white flower-burst to the right. Single strand pearl necklace. White accessories.*

July 15        Visited craft producers at Brongest, Dyfed.        *Loose, cotton, mint-green skirt below a hip-length, pure white blouse, tunic-style with short sleeves and pin-tucked panels framing the bodice. Single row of pearls and matching pearl earrings. White clutch bag and matching shoes.*

July 20        Attended a rock gala concert, Dominion Theatre, London.        *Turquoise silk two-piece suit, with shallow-pleated skirt, and loose-fitting top gathered at the drop-waist level. A loose bow in front below a deep, white sailor-boy collar. Gold hoop earrings; white fabric clutch bag with small rose-spray designs, and matching white shoes.*

July 21        Attended a Variety Club luncheon, Guildhall, London.        *Fuchsia-pink dress with small white polka-dot pattern. Apron-style skirt below a wide matching belt, with bodice buttoned at the back tied at the top. Matching pink hat, the rim swathed in silk meeting in a huge rosette at the back. White accessories.*

July 22        Attended the opening of the King's Lynn Festival, Norfolk.        *Sea-green silk cocktail dress with iridescent pattern of small stylised butterflies. Elbow-length sleeves and mandarin collars, edged with cream, and the dress tied by a wide cream ribbon fastened on the left. Single pearl earrings.*

July 24        Attended a polo match at Windsor Great Park.        *White summer dress, patterned with blue and red discs, and highlighted by crisp, white cuffs at elbows, white collars forming a shallow neck, and a white knotted belt. Thin, gold necklace with a large, flat, gold disc pendant. Gold clasp earrings. White shoes.*

July 26        Opened the new Grimsby General Hospital, Humberside.        *Pale cantaloupe silk tussore dress, with cummerbund sash at the waist and small slit at the hem on the left hand side. Short-sleeved bolero jacket in matching fabric, with frilled white silk organza collars joined by a large bow, and organza trim on the sleeves. Small straw tricorn hat in matching pink, veiled and trimmed with ostrich feather. Small pearl earrings; pink shoes and matching pink silk handbag.*

July 27        Attended the Queen's garden party at Buckingham Palace.        *Front-buttoned dress striped in mauve, grey and white, with loose, pleat-frilled collar and cuffs, under a matching jacket. Mauve picture-hat with splay-feathered trimming over the brim. Sapphire and diamond earrings. Grey shoes.*

July 29        Attended a polo match at Cowdray Park, West Sussex.        *White silk blouse with sailor-boy collars, tucked into figure-hugging, blue and white pin-striped slacks worn with a white belt. Low, white, peep-toe shoes with bows and block heels. Large, quilted bag in blue with white surrounds and small, red motifs.*

August 3        Attended the opening of New Spinal Injuries Centre, Stoke Mandeville Hospital, Aylesbury, Buckinghamshire.        *Cream silk suit with white cloud motifs, a narrow grey belt and matching soft leather handbag. Grey hat with matching silk band. White shoes and a three row pearl choker.*

August 4        Visited Clarence House on the occasion of the 83rd birthday of Queen Elizabeth the Queen Mother.        *Two-piece seersucker suit, close-striped vertically in black, grey and pink, the tight fitting jacket buttoned at the bottom, with sleeves raised at the shoulders, and sharp lapels over a cream silk blouse. Grey accessories.*

August 9        Attended a polo match a Cirencester Park, Gloucestershire.        *Black and white leaf-patterned silk top tucked into a long white pencil skirt. Black belt.*

August 15        Travelled from London to Aberdeen to begin summer holidays at Balmoral.        *Red and black plaid dress-coat with flared skirt and padded full sleeves. Broad stand-up collar with row of small black buttons running down to a waistband tied with a knotted black belt.*

September 3	Attended the Braemar Games, Aberdeenshire.	*Deep emerald green velvet suit with generously flared skirt and close fitting jacket accentuated at the waistline by a cummerbund-style belt. Bowler hat in matching green velvet with a silk band and a large bow at the back. Brown accessories.*

September 7	Visited the Keiller Marmalade and Sweet Factory, Dundee.	*Dull green and gold plaid-effect squared dress with stark white Peter Pan-style collars and cuffs. Black shoes and matching handbag.*

September 10	Visited the Youth Employment Scheme Centre, Coatbridge, Glasgow.	*Dark grey wool dress over a white silk blouse, its collars and bow brought over the neckline of the dress. Black accessories.*

September 21	Visited a centre for mentally handicapped children and adults, Westoning, Bedfordshire.	*Two-piece wool suit in emerald green, with long double-breasted jacket and reverse-pleated skirt. Plain white silk blouse with stand-up collars. Choker consisting of three rows of pearls. White accessories.*

September 21	Attended an All Stars rock concert in aid of the Prince's Trust, Royal Albert Hall.	*Two-piece outfit in silver satin consisting of a smooth satin skirt and a quilted ripple-effect jacket. Beneath the jacket, a white blouse with a bow at the neck. Matching shoes and handbag.*

October 2	Visited the Princess Louise Scottish Hospital, Bishopton, Renfrew.	*Thick flame-red coat woven in Welsh wool, striped stitch-effect with vertical lines of blue and yellow. Heavy fringing at collar, cuffs and hem. Small mid-blue wool hat veiled and feathered. Matching shoes and handbag.*

October 2	Attended the Royal Scottish Variety Performance, Kings Theatre, Glasgow.	*Long rose-pink silk evening dress, patterned with cream-gold hoops with expansive pale cream flounces at the neck, on the sleeves and round the waist, and a large cream silk bow at the waistline. Single row of pearls and pearl drop earrings. Gold evening bag and shoes.*

October 6	Attended the Barry Manilow Concert, Royal Festival Hall, London.	*Slimline silk taffeta evening dress in shocking pink, with spaghetti shoulder straps concealed by large bows. Single string pearl necklace, and pearl drop earrings.*

October 24	Travelled from Aberdeen to London at the end of a summer holiday at Balmoral.	*Slim-cut, double-breasted, herringbone coat in mauve-grey, with black velvet collars. Worn over a cream blouse with stiff wing-collars and a soft, informal tie-bow at the centre. Gold clasp earrings.*

October 24	Attended a performance of *Hay Fever*, Queen's Theatre, London.	*Full-length evening gown in mid-blue silk, with a straight, low-cut neckline supported by a matching ribbon halter, and with a ribbon belt at the waist. Five-string pearl and diamond bracelet; medium-length pearl drop earrings. Silver evening bag and matching shoes. A deep blue velvet cape was worn for the arrival.*

October 25	Attended the wedding of Anne Bolton and Noel Hill, City of London.	*Two-piece seersucker suit, close-striped vertically in black, grey and pink, the tight-fitting jacket buttoned at the bottom, with sleeves raised at the shoulders, and sharp lapels over a cream silk blouse. Broad-brimmed dove-grey hat; mid-grey shoes and deep grey clutch bag.*

October 26	Received a copy of *Stories for a Prince*, Café Royal, Regent Street, London.	*Silk dress with busy abstract flower pattern in black, red, white and blue, and with a black ribbon bow centrally placed over an expansive white Jacobean fichu, intricately edged with delicate lacework. Matching lace cuffs. Red accessories.*

October 27	Opened the West Indian Parents' Family Centre, Brixton, London.	*Bright red Spanish-style tailored suit, with a long, wool, gaberdine, double-breasted jacket topped by the tie neck of a black-spotted white blouse. Slim-cut straight skirt. Black clutch bag and matching shoes.*

November 1	Opened a new block, London Chest Hospital, Bethnal Green.	*Emerald-green two-piece suit; the long, tailored jacket having a deep V-neck over a white silk blouse topped with a posy-bow; the skirt of straight cut and inverse-pleated. A green tricorn hat, with a matching ostrich plume; black shoes and matching handbag.*

November 2	Attended the unveiling by the Queen of the statue of Earl Mountbatten, Foreign Office Green, London.	*Electric blue two-piece suit consisting of a front-pleated skirt over a straight hip-length jacket with an adorned round neck. Matching blue high-necked blouse. Small, veiled, blue hat with cerise crown and large cerise bow at the back, complemented by a cerise and blue false kerchief on the left hand side of the jacket. Sapphire and diamond earrings. Black suede clutch bag, and matching leather shoes.*

November 2	Presented prizes to winners of a project sponsored by the Pre-School Playgroups Association, Kensington Palace.	*Navy blue dress with large, rich pink bubble designs, and a high close collar above a buttoned bodice. Matching deep pink jacket with triangular double-breasted panels and long sleeves, over a white blouse with a pie-frill collar. Dark blue shoes.*

November 7	Attended a concert given by Placido Domingo, Royal Festival Hall, London.	*Edwardian-style velvet evening jacket over a tube-top taffeta dress, horizontally striped in red, purple and black. Emerald and diamond choker necklace, with long-drop emerald and diamond earrings. Silver evening clutch bag, and matching shoes.*

November 9	Attended the dedication of the Falkland Islands Campaign Memorial, Guards' Chapel, London.	*Moss-green velvet suit, with a generously flared skirt and close-fitting jacket accentuated at the waistline by a cummerbund-style belt. A cluster of three poppies worn on the right hand side of the coat; the small frill of a white blouse giving relief at the neck. Matching green hat with a swathed ribbon finished by a bow at the back. Clutch bag and shoes in red leather, to match the poppies.*

November 9        Attended the tenth anniversary dinner of Independent Local Radio, Mansion House, London.        *Ankle-length, scarlet evening dress in duchess silk, with shoe-string straps beneath a boat-necked filmy chemise top embroidered with a floral pattern and finely dusted with sequins. Long-stemmed diamond and pearl drop earrings. Silver clutch bag and matching shoes.*

November 12        Attended the Festival of Remembrance, Royal Albert Hall, London.        *Black, velvet, sashed coat-dress with a spray of three poppies held by a jewelled clasp on the right side, and with a silk bow at the top of the buttoned bodice. Underneath, a white, high-necked blouse with frilled cuffs. Black clutch bag and red and black shoes.*

November 13        Attended the Remembrance Day ceremony, Cenotaph, Whitehall, London.        *Black, V-necked coat with a cluster of three poppies held by a jewelled clasp on the right lapel. Beneath, a black blouse with integral bow at the neck. Broad-brimmed tall-crowned black hat. Pearl stud earrings. Black accessories.*

November 17        Visited the British Deaf Association Headquarters, Carlisle, Cumbria.        *Blue two-piece suit consisting of a front-pleated skirt over a straight hip-length jacket with an adorned round neck. Matching blue high-necked blouse. Small, veiled, blue hat with cerise crown and large cerise bow at the back, complemented by a cerise and blue false kerchief on the left hand side of the jacket. Diamond horse-shoe earrings. Black suede clutch bag and matching leather shoes.*

November 18        Visited Maytrees Home for the Blind, Bristol.        *Tailored, woollen coat of mid-red, with black collars, lapels and cuffs. Underneath, a white blouse with wing collars and black silk ribbon-bow. Tiny red pillbox hat with black piping, veiling and a large black tassel. Shiny black leather clutch bag; black stockings and matching shoes.*

November 21        Visited Atlantic College, St Donat's, Wales.

November 21        Visited Cardiff Community dance project, South Wales.        *Long, military-style, unbelted coat in bright delphinium, with bold black buttons, black-edged false pockets and black mandarin collars over a black and white spotted silk neck-scarf. Tall, wide-brimmed hat and black bag and shoes, all complemented by the unusual addition of short, black gloves. Jewelled stud earrings.*

November 29        Attended a National Rubella Council reception, Lancaster House, London.        *Silk suit of large formal motifs in turquoise, red, white and black, and consisting of a mid-calf-length skirt and bolero-style jacket. Turquoise silk blouse showing at the mid-riff, at the cuffs, and as a large tied square outside the jacket at the neck. Black accessories.*

November 29        Attended the Red Dragon Ball, Grosvenor House Hotel, London.        *Sea-green, matt silk organza ballgown, with occasional random diamante studding, featuring a drop-waisted, close-fitting sheath bodice worn off the right shoulder, but with a huge compensating bow at the left shoulder; and deep, soft inverse-pleated skirt. Single-strand choker of diamonds with pearl drop pendant. Matching pearl single-drop earrings. Silver evening bag and matching shoes.*

December 2        Opened the Wantage Adult Training Centre, Oxfordshire.        *Deep blue, velvet, two-piece coat-dress with midi-length skirt, long full sleeves, a broad waistband and panelled bodice, all over a white silk blouse with a bow overlapping the top of the dress. Matching velvet hat with a front veil and a silver-grey ostrich feather at the back. Sapphire and diamond earrings. Brown leather clutch bag and matching shoes.*

December 6        Opened the Park Lane Fair, Park Lane Hotel, Piccadilly, London.        *Short, tailored, herringbone jacket with long sleeves and unbuttoned neckline to reveal a cream-coloured silk blouse. Slim, knee-length skirt over tinted stockings. Black shoes and handbag.*

December 7        Visited the Queen Elizabeth II Silver Jubilee Activity Centre, Burseldon, Hampshire.        *Grey, tailored coat with piped sleeves, heavy braid down the centre and on the cuffs, and deep, stand-up Astrakhan collars. Matching Astrakhan cossack-style hat, with a small bow to the right, and a huge matching muff. Three-string pearl choker and small pearl-drop earrings. Black, knee-length boots.*

December 14        Photocall at Kensington Palace with Prince Charles and Prince William.        *Oatmeal, woollen two-piece suit, with a fully pleated skirt and a hip-length long-sleeved top with a casual, loose, cowl neckline. Rust-coloured leather belt and matching calf-length boots. Gold clasp earrings.*

December 19        Visited the victims of the IRA bombing of Harrods, Westminster Hospital and St Thomas's Hospital, London.        *Dark oatmeal two-piece wool suit consisting of a midi-length skirt supported by a soft chestnut-brown leather belt, and a long, narrow lapel jacket over a cream silk blouse with concealed buttons and a gold-rimmed cameo centre pin. Brown leather shoulder bag and matching shoes.*

December 20        Opened a new Extra Care Centre, Abbeyfield Downing House, Withington, Manchester.        *Honey-coloured, tailored coat-dress with wide-pleated skirt and medium V-neck bodice with chocolate velvet collars. Underneath, a striped blouse in white, pale blue and beige, with a high neck-swathe and cravat. Brown suede clutch bag and brown leather shoes.*

December 20        Attended the Malcolm Sargent Cancer Fund Carol Concert, Free Trade Hall, Manchester.        *Deep brown-black midi-length velvet dress with close-fitting, full-length, lace-frilled sleeves and buttoned bodice, with an expansive lace fichu at the neck. Single pearl earrings surrounded by small diamonds. Black clutch bag and matching shoes.*

December 25    Attended Morning Service at St George's Chapel, Windsor Castle.    *Off-white suit, the jacket having a stand-up collar extended on the right side to provide a flounce falling to the waist, and complemented on the left by an ox-blood coloured false kerchief. Matching shallow saucer hat, with brim skirting the forehead, and leaving the crown on the left to form an independent feature with an alternative facet in ox-blood red.*

1984

January 1    Attended Morning Service at Sandringham Church.    *Velvet coat-dress in moss green, with three-quarter length flared skirt, and the bodice with full-length, close-fitting sleeves, and short V-neck with stand-up collars. Underneath, a cream silk blouse with a central ruffle. Bowler hat in matching green velvet and generously beribboned. Neutral-coloured muff with embroidered design.*

January 8    Arrived at Zurich Airport to begin a skiing holiday in the Alps.    *Rainbow-striped sweater beneath a hip-length mohair jacket, horizontally patterned in shades of blue and grey, and with a huge overlaid collar. Grey woollen trousers tucked into red calf-length leather boots, with turn-down tops.*

January 9    Photocall on the ski slopes of Hoch Eck, Malbun, Liechtenstein.    *Close-fitting, deep cardinal-red ski-suit. White wool snow hat with broad navy blue turn-up; navy ski-gloves.*

January 24    Attended a Grocers' Company reception, Grocers' Hall, London.    *Deepish blue silk chiffon cocktail dress with mustard and white leaf pattern. Ruched bodice separated from the skirt by a broad blue belt, and high, frilled neck. Diamond and sapphire stud earrings. Matching blue clutch bag and blue shoes with black heels.*

February 8    Attended the funeral of the Duke of Beaufort, Badminton, Gloucestershire.    *Black mourning coat and matching trilby hat. Small diamond and pearl stud earrings. Black handbag and shoes.*

February 8    Attended a reception given by the 2nd King Edward VII's Own Goorkhas, Ritz Hotel, London.    *Long-sleeved fitted dress in blue-black velvet, with small formal grey spot pattern. Plain, rounded neckline. Pearl choker necklace. Black and red symmetrically-striped patent leather shoes.*

February 11    Left Heathrow Airport for Oslo, and arrived at Fonebu Airport.    *Bright cobalt-blue woollen suit consisting of a three-quarter length jacket with inverse-pleated sleeves and a tailored skirt just visible beneath. Blue and white candy-striped blouse evidenced by frilled cuffs and wide wing collars over large cravat bow falling outside the jacket. Matching blue tights. Envelope-style suede handbag. Diamond and sapphire stud earrings.*

February 11    Attended the London City Ballet's performance of *Carmen*, Konserthaus, Oslo.    *Navy-blue velvet cape, removed to reveal an ankle-length scarlet evening dress in duchess silk with shoe-string straps, the bodice overlaid by a boat-necked filmy chemise top embroidered with a floral pattern and finely dusted with sequins. Triple twist pearl necklace and antique pearl and diamond drop earrings.*

February 12    Planted a tree in the grounds of the British Embassy in Oslo.    *Moss-green velvet coat-dress, with generously flared three-quarter length skirt, overlaid by a bodice with full-length sleeves and a short V-neck with stand-up collars. Underneath, a cream silk blouse with a central ruffle. Gold earrings. Light beige clutch bag, and calf-length boots.*

February 15    Visited Jaguar Cars Limited, Allesley, Coventry.    *Lilac wool coat buttoned to the neck, and with thick, stand-up collars. Small satin saucer hat with stand-up brim and a spray of feathers at the back. Black shoes and clutch bag.*

February 21    Visited the Royal Marsden Hospital, Sutton, Surrey.    *Aubergine velour coat-dress of generous cut and with ornamental scroll piping at the waist and on turned-up cuffs. Silk white blouse just visible beneath, with mandarin collars and central tie-bow. Matching aubergine tricorn hat with double ostrich feather across the right side. Black clutch bag and matching shoes.*

February 22    Visited the British Red Cross Society's national headquarters, Grosvenor Crescent, London.    *Royal blue two-piece suit consisting of a tunic-style jacket, long-sleeved and high-collared, over a pale-spotted white blouse with a cravat flourish, and an inverse-pleated skirt of below-the-knee length. Matching accessories.*

February 29    Visited St Mary's Hospice, Selly Park, Birmingham.    *Tailored woollen coat of mid-red, with black collars, lapels and cuffs over a black silk blouse. Tiny red pillbox hat with black piping, veiling and a large black tassel. Shiny black leather clutch bag; black stockings and black shoes.*

February 29    Attended a concert given by Genesis, National Exhibition Centre, Birmingham.    *Off-white tuxedo-style jacket over a matching blouse with formal wing collar and black bow tie. Black trousers. Small gold clasp earrings. Black, leather clutch bag and matching shoes.*

March 2    Arrived at Aberdeen Airport for a weekend at Balmoral.    *Heavy, blue and black, hip-length, wool jacket over a warm, full, beige skirt. Multi-coloured floral-patterned headscarf. Small, thin-strapped red shoulder purse. Knee-length leather boots.*

March 6    Attended a Jewish Welfare Board dinner, Guildhall, London.    *Full-length crinoline-style chiffon evening dress in flame-red, with small, regular, gold spot pattern. Low-contoured neckline held by thin shoulder straps. Gold and diamond necklace; diamond and sapphire drop earrings arranged in triangular groups to match the clasp. Silver evening bag and shoes.*

March 7    Visited the Lisson Grove Health Centre, London.    *Slim-cut double-breasted herringbone coat in mauve-grey, with black velvet collars. Worn over a white shirt with stiff wing collars, and a narrow cravat exposed round the neck and tied loosely in front. Shadow-black stockings, and black clutch bag and shoes.*

March 9    Visited the Sue Ryder Home, Leckhampton Court, Cheltenham.    *Lilac wool coat buttoned to the neck, and with thick, stand-up collars. Small satin saucer hat with stand-up brim and a spray of feathers at the back. Black shoes and clutch bag.*

March 15    Visited Sheffield.    *Loose, royal blue, military-style coat falling to just above the knees and with full-length inverse-pleated sleeves and deep vertical-cut side pockets. Worn over a matching below-the-knee skirt, and a bright blue and white striped blouse with generous collar and wide, full cravat-style bow. Narrow-brimmed blue saucer hat with matching plait trim and off-the-temple veiling. Matching blue bag and shoes.*

March 22    Visited T W Kempton Limited, Leicester.

March 22    Visited Charnwood Mencap Society, Loughborough.    *Bright cobalt-blue woollen suit consisting of a three-quarter length jacket with inverse-pleated sleeves and a tailored skirt just visible beneath. Blue and white candy-striped blouse evidenced by frilled cuffs and wide wing collars over a large cravat bow falling outside the jacket. Small-rimmed matching blue saucer hat, with plaited trimming and a veil bow at the back. Blue fabric clutch bag, and matching blue tights and shoes.*

March 23    Opened the Royal National Orthopaedic Hospital's new spinal injuries unit, Stanmore, Middlesex. *Aubergine-coloured velour coat-dress, full-skirted but with tight sleeves, over a white blouse with wide Jacobean collars, and intricate ornamental lace fringing. Small aubergine tricorn hat with double ostrich feather across the right side. Matching bag. Silver-grey shoes.*

March 27    Opened the new rehearsal studios for the Welsh National Opera, Cardiff.    *Military-style coat in royal blue with full-length inverse-pleated sleeves and deep, vertical-cut side pockets. Underneath, a bright blue and white striped blouse with generous collar and wide, full cravat-style bow, and a royal blue skirt worn below the knee. Narrow-brimmed blue saucer hat with matching plaited trim and high veiling. Matching clutch bag and shoes.*

March 29    Visited the Metropolitan Police Training Centre, Hendon, London.    *Spanish-style, soft, grey coat with faint herringbone pattern and black velvet collar. White blouse with a black cravat and a black bolero felt hat. Back-seamed stockings with ankle-level butterfly bows. Black shoes and clutch bag.*

April 3    Visited the Workface Centre, Glastonbury.    *Mid-blue woollen coat with high, thick collars, puffed sleeves and large covered buttons. Matching blue velvet hat with small raised brim and a spray of blue floating feathers at the back. Black clutch bag and black shoes.*

April 5    Visited the Royal Doulton Tableware Factory, Burslem, Stoke-on-Trent.    *Tailored woollen coat of mid-red, with black collars, lapels and cuffs. Underneath a black shirt-blouse with loose black silk ribbon bow. Small red pillbox hat with black piping, veiling and a large black tassel. Shiny black leather clutch bag; black stockings and matching shoes.*

April 10    Met the Amir of Bahrain at the beginning of his State Visit, Windsor Castle.    *Artist-style silk smock of busy abstract floral design in pink, white and blue, and a fully-pleated knee-length matching skirt. A large, blue, draped bow centred at the top of the smock between white, square-scalloped collars with gauze borders. Deep blue clutch bag, and matching stockings and shoes.*

April 11    Visited British Airways, Heathrow Airport, London.    *Tailored coat in mauve-grey herringbone, with velvet collar. Underneath, a white silk blouse with a fussy cravat bow at the centre of a high neck. Black clutch bag; black stockings and matching shoes.*

April 16    Attended a rehearsal of the National Children's Orchestra, Wellington College, Berkshire.    *Navy blue shoulder-pleated coat, gathered across the back, with deep V-neck showing a blue-black dress, leaf-patterned in white, its high, heavily-frilled neck centred by a matching rose ornament and frill-cuffed long sleeves. Navy clutch bag and matching shoes.*

April 22    Attended Easter Day Morning Service, Windsor.    *Loose silk smock of close abstract floral design in pink, white and blue, with a fully-pleated knee-length skirt in matching fabric. The smock overlaid by white, square-scalloped collars with gauze borders, and set off by a central bow in blue ribbon. Large-brimmed white boater, trimmed at the front with a large flower. Deep blue clutch bag and matching shoes.*

April 29    Attended a polo match, Windsor Great Park.    *Long-sleeved, hip-length wool sweater, with wide pink and white horizontal stripes, worn over a white, open-necked shirt and loose, white calf-length trousers. White slip-on shoes.*

May 8    Accepted an honorary fellowship of the Royal College of Physicians and Surgeons of Glasgow.    *Casual, loose-fitting silk smock with a busy, abstract floral design in pink, white and blue, worn over a fully-pleated knee-length matching skirt. A large, blue, draped bow centred at the the top of the smock between white, square-scalloped collars with see-through borders. Deep blue clutch bag and matching shoes.*

May 14    Attended the Royal Society of Arts' banquet, Piccadilly, London.    *Ankle-length champagne-coloured evening gown with a soft, square-trellis pattern supporting sprays of silver sequins. Deep, round neck and dramatic double-draped sleeves gathered below the elbow into a tight, buttoned cuff. Spencer tiara, diamond necklace with gold diamond and sapphire Prince of Wales' feathers pendant, and small pearl-drop earrings. The Queen's personal Order worn on the left side. Plain silver clutch bag and matching shoes.*

**May 20**      Attended a fund-raising concert, Royal Opera House, Covent Garden, London.      *Two-piece, loose-fitting, cream chiffon evening gown, with long bodice and skirt, both heavily sequinned with a waterfall pattern. Elbow-length sleeves split and regathered at the shoulders, and low, rounded neckline symmetrically complemented by a single row of pearls. Medium-drop pearl earrings. Silver clutch bag and shoes. Black velvet cape for arrival.*

**May 21**      Visited the Chelsea Flower Show, Royal Hospital, Chelsea.      *Blue-black woollen midi-length coat with low V-neck and three-quarter length sleeves, exposing the high collar and ruffled sleeves of a black blouse with random white spots. Sapphire and diamond clasp earrings. Shocking pink, thin-strapped shoulder bag and matching shoes with wide pink bows.*

**May 21**      Attended a concert given by the Bach Choir and English Chamber Orchestra, Royal Festival Hall, London. *Loose-fitting dress in emerald green lurex, with matching overlay and loose neck-tie over shoulders and full, loose sleeves tightly gathered into cuffs at the wrists. Twelve-inch slit at left side of dress. Long-drop emerald and diamond earrings. Black leather clutch bag and matching shoes.*

**May 23**      Visited The Albany, Deptford, London.      *Artist-style silk smock of busy abstract floral design in pink, white and blue, worn over a fully pleated knee-length skirt of matching fabric. A large, blue, draped bow centred at the top of the smock between white, square-scalloped collars with gauze borders. Deep blue clutch bag and matching stockings and shoes.*

**May 24**      Attended a polo match, Windsor Great Park.      *Blue and white striped two-piece, loose-fitting outfit, consisting of a below-the-knee length skirt of vertical stripes, and a long, horizontally-striped bodice overlaid with a white sailor collar, and with sleeves gathered at the elbow. Tiny gold drop earrings. Large white mohair cardigan and matching white peep-toe shoes.*

**May 29**      Attended the opening by Prince Charles of the Street Farm Workshops, Doughton, Tetbury.      *Loose-fitting deep blue wool coat over a red and white candy-striped skirt. Underneath, a white silk blouse with mandarin collars, partly concealed by a wide, red ribbon informally knotted at the centre of the neck. Small pearl stud earrings. Red half-moon clutch bag, and red and white line-patterned shoes.*

**May 30**      Visited Chester and Warrington.      *Loose, navy blue coat with deep, V-neck exposing a white silk blouse with wing collars and false tie. Matching navy skirt, with abstract design in white. White saucer hat with navy trim and underside, shallow veiling and a deep upturned brim on the left side. Navy clutch bag and shoes.*

**June 6**      Opened Callard and Bowser's new factory, Waterton, South Glamorgan.      *Bright red, loose-fitting coat with long, narrow lapels over a red and white striped maternity dress, and white blouse with frilled top and red ribbon tie. White straw hat, edged with red, and with double red band on the base of the crown. Envelope-style leather clutch bag in matching red; and red shoes with white line designs.*

**June 7**      Attended a polo match, Windsor.      *Raspberry-pink silk dress, sleeves loosely gathered at the elbow, and overlaid with wide, white, sailor-style collars joined by a long ribbon drop at the front. Loose, white mohair cardigan with sleeves rolled to elbow length. Bright pink shoes.*

**June 8**      Attended a rock gala, Royal Albert Hall, London.      *Bright green sequinned evening dress, loose-fitting and long-sleeved with integral high-neck underbodice and overlaid yoke. Plain silver clutch bag and matching shoes.*

**June 11**      Attended the film premiere of *Indiana Jones and the Temple of Doom*, Empire Theatre, Leicester Square, London.      *Electric blue, satin evening dress with softly-draped top and low sash effect gathered into a huge bow to the left hand side. Full, billowing skirt. Triple rope twist pearl necklace. Silver, lozenged-patterned clutch bag, and silver shoes.*

**June 12**      Photocall at Kensington Palace for Prince William's second birthday.      *Raspberry-pink silk dress, let out for maternity wear, with loose sleeves gathered at the elbow, and overlaid with wide, white, sailor-style collars joined by a long ribbon falling to waist-length at the front. Matching pink shoes.*

**June 16**      Attended the Queen's Birthday Parade, Horseguards Parade, London.      *Lavender blue two-piece suit; a front-pleated skirt, and a loose, hip-length jacket with three-quarter length cuffless sleeves, and shoulders overlaid with a white deep-yoked collar decorated with blue scrolling. Small, matching blue pillbox hat with white trim, half-face veiling, and a bow on the right side. Triple twist pearl necklace. Long, white clutch handbag and white shoes.*

**June 20**      Attended Royal Ascot, and a polo match at Windsor Great Park.      *Deep salmon-pink, self-spot, two-piece silk suit, wide-pleated in the skirt; the jacket loose with deeply cuffed sleeves, wing collars and a large matching neck-tie with long, falling ribbons. Light, full-brimmed straw hat in matching pink with off-white upper brim and band. White clutch bag with scalloped flap, and white shoes.*

**June 27**      Visited Salisbury and Odstock.      *Lavender blue two-piece suit, consisting of a front-pleated skirt, and a loose, hip-length jacket. Sleeves worn to three-quarter length and without cuffs, and a deep-yoked collar overlay in contrasting white, decorated with lavender blue scrolling. Small, matching blue pillbox hat with white trim, half-face veiling and a bow on the right hand side. Long white clutch handbag, and white shoes.*

**June 28**      Attended a polo match, Cirencester.      *Bright blue below-the-knee culottes, with a voluminous, soft pink woollen sweater over a white wing-collar blouse. Matching blue shoes.*

**July 1**      Attended a polo match, Cirencester.      *Raspberry-pink silk dress, drop-waisted, and with loose sleeves gathered at the elbow, the neck-line highlighted by a wide white sailor-style collar culminating in a long, falling ribbon. White shoes with small pink bows. White quilted clutch bag with tiny posy designs in blue, red and green.*

July 4        Attended the Wimbledon Lawn Tennis Championships.        *Raspberry-pink silk dress, let out for maternity wear, with loose sleeves gathered at the elbow, and overlaid with wide, white, sailor-style collars joined by a long ribbon drop at the front. Matching pink shoes.*

July 5        Attended a concert given by Neil Diamond, National Exhibition Centre, Birmingham.        *Loose-fitting dress in emerald green lurex, with matching overlay and loose neck-tie over the shoulders, and full, loose sleeves tightly gathered into cuffs at the wrists. Twelve-inch vertical slit from the left side hem of the dress. Silver-grey clutch bag and matching shoes.*

July 18        Attended the wedding of Laura Greig and James Lonsdale, Holy Trinity Church, Knightsbridge.        *Deep, salmon-pink two-piece suit in self-spot silk, with wide-pleated skirt. A loose jacket, deeply cuffed at the sleeves, and with wing collars matched by a large neck-tie with long, falling ribbons. Light, full-brimmed straw hat in matching pink, with off-white upper brim and band. White clutch bag with scalloped flap, and white shoes.*

July 24        Opened the Harris Birthright Research Unit for Fetal Medicine, King's College Hospital, London.        *Lavender blue two-piece suit; a front-pleated skirt, and a loose, hip-length jacket with three-quarter length cuffless sleeves, and shoulders overlaid with a white, deep-yoked collar decorated with lavender blue scrolling. Small, matching blue pillbox hat with white trim, half-face veiling, and a bow on the right side. Long white clutch handbag and white shoes.*

July 26        Attended a performance of the Royal Tournament, Earl's Court, London.        *Ice-blue satin evening dress with softly draped top, and low sash effect gathered into a huge bow to the left hand side. Full, billowing skirt. Small diamond and pearl single necklace. Silver, lozenge-patterned clutch bag and matching shoes.*

July 29        Attended a polo match, Windsor Great Park.        *Raspberry-pink silk dress, let out for maternity wear, with loose sleeves gathered at the elbow, and wide, white, sailor-style collars overlaying the neckline, and falling as ribbons to hip-length at the front. Matching pink shoes.*

August 1        Private shopping expedition in Knightsbridge.        *Light blue and white striped summer two-piece outfit with half-length gathered sleeves, and white, sailor-style, detachable ribbon collar. Blue and white spotted canvas shoulder bag, and flat white shoes.*

September 16        Left St Mary's Hospital Paddington, after the birth of Prince Harry.        *Long, slimline, scarlet wool coat with deep V-neck and panelled yoke, and gathered below the shoulders. Underneath, a red and white candy-striped blouse with white collars and a knotted scarlet ribbon. Matching red low-heeled shoes.*

October 11        Official photographs to celebrate the birth of Prince Harry.        *Luxuriant dress in pure white silk, with puffed three-quarter length sleeves gathered at the shoulders, silk-covered buttons and stiff mandarin collars. Sapphire and dimond clasp earrings.*

November 6        Attended the State Opening of Parliament, Westminster.        *Light cream silk evening gown with fluted bodice, frilled at the neck and with lace-trimmed flounced sleeves. Diamond Spencer tiara, pearl-drop earrings, a five-row pearl bracelet, and the Queen's personal Order worn on the dress. Plain silver gussetted clutch bag, and silver shoes.*

November 8        Visited Dr Barnardo's International Treatment Project, Newham, London.        *Tailored Edwardian-style coat in grey herringbone with black velvet collars and cuffs, worn over a white, collared shirt with a wide bow-tie. Small pearl earrings. Black leather clutch bag and black shoes.*

November 10        Attended the Festival of Remembrance, Royal Albert Hall, London.        *Black velour dress-coat with silk ribbon belt, over a white blouse with high frilled collar. A cluster of three poppies pinned to the right hand side of the coat's bodice. Pearl drop earrings. Black shadow stockings, black shoes and black clutch bag.*

November 11        Attended the Service of Remembrance, Cenotaph, Whitehall.        *Close-fitting black wool coat with deep V-neck revealing a black silk blouse with central cravat. A sprig of three poppies upon the right hand side lapel. Tall-crowned black hat with wide brim. Black clutch bag and matching shoes.*

November 13        Visited the National Deaf, Blind and Rubella Association Family Centre, Ealing, London.        *Military-style coat-dress in lightweight wool, with turnback sleeves, and mandarin collars over a white blouse with a large, central bow falling outside the dress. Black clutch bag and black shoes.*

November 15        Launched P&O's new cruise-liner *Royal Princess*, Southampton.        *Scarlet wool two-piece suit consisting of a hip-length jacket with white buttons, and a below-the-knee length skirt with a slight flare. Worn over a black blouse with long sleeves and plain cuffs and a wide tie-bow falling outside the jacket. Matching scarlet beret with black trim and black satin sailors' twin tails at the back. Small semi-precious stone drop earrings. Black clutch bag and gloves, black shadow tights with scarlet seams and black and red shoes.*

November 20        Attended the Royal Variety Performance, Victoria Palace Theatre, London.        *Silk chiffon evening dress with lightly elasticated off-the-shoulder neckline, predominantly white with soft swirling designs in pink and blue, and with sequined diagonals across the whole. Broad, pale blue waistband and matching silk ribbon bow at the centre of the neckline. Gold and diamond necklace with Prince of Wales' feathers pendant. Silver clutch bag and matching shoes.*